THE POETICS OF

EROS IN ANCIENT GREECE

# THE POETICS OF
# EROS IN ANCIENT GREECE

*CLAUDE CALAME*

*Translated by Janet Lloyd*

PRINCETON UNIVERSITY PRESS

PRINCETON, NEW JERSEY

Originally published as *I Greci el l'eros: Simboli, pratiche e luoghi*
Copyright © 1992 Gius. Laterza & Figli Spa, Roma-Bari
English translation copyright © 1999 by Princeton University Press
Published by Princeton University Press, 41 William Street, Princeton, New Jersey 08540
In the United Kingdom: Princeton University Press, Chichester, West Sussex
All Rights Reserved

*Library of Congress Cataloging-in-Publication Data*

Calame, Claude.
[Greci e l'eros. English]
The poetics of eros in Ancient Greece / Claude Calame ; translated
by Janet Lloyd.
p.    cm.
Includes bibliographical references and index.
ISBN 0-691-04341-8 (cloth : alk. paper)
1. Erotic poetry, Greek — History and criticism.   2. Literature and
society — Greece.   3. Sex in literature.   I. Lloyd, Janet.
II. Title.
PA3111.C35   1999   881'.01093538 — dc21   98-37129   CIP

This book has been composed in Sabon

The paper used in this publication meets the minimum requirements
of ANSI/NISO Z39.48-1992 (R 1997) (*Permanence of Paper*)

http://pup.princeton.edu

Printed in the United States of America

10   9   8   7   6   5   4   3   2   1

"Have you not yet noticed that pleasure, which is certainly the sole motive for union between the two sexes, is nevertheless not enough to form a bond between them?"

Father Choderlos de Laclos, *Les Liaisons dangeureuses*, Paris, 1782 (Letter CXXXI, from the Marquise de Merteuil to the Vicomte de Valmont)


Ἡμῖν βασιχεὺς καὶ ἄρχων καὶ ἁρμοστὴς ὁ Ἔρως.

So we see Love chosen as king, chief magistrate, and harmonizer.

Plutarch, *Amatorius*, 763e, quoting Hesiod, Plato, and Solon

# CONTENTS

*LIST OF ILLUSTRATIONS*   xi

*FOREWORD*   xiii

*PREFACE*   xvii

*NOTE ON TRANSLATIONS*   xix

*LIST OF ABBREVIATIONS*   xxi

TRAGIC PRELUDE
The Yoke of Eros   3

*PART ONE:* THE TOPICS OF EROS   11

CHAPTER I
The Eros of the Melic Poets   13

   *1. The Actions of Bittersweet Eros   14*
   *2. Physiologies of Erotic Desire   19*
   *3. Strategies of Love   23*
   *4. A Variety of Passions   29*
   *5. Metaphors for the Assuaging of Desire   33*
   *6. The Erotic Charms of Poetry   36*

CHAPTER II
The Eros of Epic Poetry   39

   *1. Scenes of Mutual Love   39*
   *2. Scenes of Seduction   43*
   *3. Beguiling Words   46*

*PART TWO:* THE SYMBOLIC PRACTICES OF EROS   49

CHAPTER III
The Pragmatic Effects of Love Poetry   51

   *1. The Erotic Functions of Melic Poetry   52*
   *2. The Loves of Alexandrian Writers   56*

CHAPTER IV
The Pragmatics of Erotic Iconography   65

   *1. Figurative Representations of Love   65*
   *2. The Functions of Erotic Images   72*

*PART THREE:* EROS IN SOCIAL INSTITUTIONS  89

CHAPTER V
Eros in the Masculine: The *polis*  91
  *1. The Propaedeutic Practices of the Symposium*  93
  *2. Erotic Practices of the Palaestra*  101

CHAPTER VI
Eros in the Feminine: The *Oikos*  110
  *1. An Intermediate Status: The* Hetaira *at the Banquet*  111
  *2. The Transition to Maturity: The Young Wife*  116

CHAPTER VII
Dionysiac Challenges to Love  130
  *1. The Institution of Comedy*  133
  *2. The Institution of Tragedy*  141

*PART FOUR:* THE SPACES OF EROS  151

CHAPTER VIII
The Meadows and Gardens of Legend  153
  *1. Eroticized Meadows*  154
  *2. The Orchards and Gardens of Aphrodite*  157
  *3. Flowers, Fruits, and Cereals*  160

CHAPTER IX
The Meadows and Gardens of the Poets  165
  *1. The Metaphorical Spaces of Love*  165
  *2. The Ideal Domains of the Gods*  167
  *3. Religious Gardens*  170

*PART FIVE:* THE METAPHYSICS OF EROS  175

CHAPTER X
Eros as Demiurge and Philosopher  177
  *1. Eros as a Cosmogonic Principle*  178
  *2. Erotic Forms of the Initiation to Beauty*  181
  *3. Love as a Metaphysician*  186

CHAPTER XI
Mystic Eros  192
  *1. Eros in the Orphic Theogonies*  193
  *2. The Mystic Aspects of Eros*  195

ELEGIAC CODA
Eros the Educator 198

*BIBLIOGRAPHY* 201

*NAME INDEX* 207

*SUBJECT INDEX* 211

# ILLUSTRATIONS

Pl. I.     Attic black-figure cylix, around 540 B.C. Berlin,
           Staatliche Museen 1798.                                  73
Pl. II.    Attic black-figure amphora, sixth century B.C.
           London, British Museum W 39.                            74
Pl. III.   Attic black-figure amphora, around 540 B.C. The Art
           Museum, Princeton University, L. 1990.60.               75
Pl. IV.    Attic black-figure amphora, around 540 B.C. The Art
           Museum, Princeton University, L. 1990.60.               76
Pl. V.     Attic red-figure cylix, around 500 B.C. Berlin,
           Staatliche Museen 2279.                                 77
Pl. VI.    Attic red-figure cylix, around 500 B.C. Berlin,
           Staatliche Museen 1964.4.                               78
Pl. VII.   Attic red-figure cylix, around 510 B.C. Paris, Musée
           du Louvre G 13.                                         79
Pl. VIII.  Black-figure white alabaster, early fifth century B.C.
           Berlin F 2032 (copied by F. Lissarrague).               80
Pl. IX.    Attic red-figure column crater, around 485 B.C. Rome,
           Villa Giulia 1054.                                      81
Pl X.      Attic red-figure column crater, around 485 B.C. Rome,
           Villa Giulia 1054.                                      82

## PHOTOGRAPHIC CREDITS

Pl. I, V, and VI: Staatliche Museen, Berlin (phot. Jutta Tietz-
    Glagow).
Pl. II:    British Museum, London.
Pl III:    The Art Museum, Princeton University, Princeton,
           New Jersey.
Pl. VII:   Musée du Louvre, Paris.
Pl. IX and X: Museo Nazionale di Villa Giulia, Rome.

# FOREWORD

*Froma I. Zeitlin*

IN RECENT YEARS, one of the most fruitful areas of inquiry into the life, thought, and culture of ancient Greece has been the study of that elusive figure-concept called Eros and the specific nature and extent of erotic experience. The Greeks themselves divinized carnal desire in the figure of Eros, attesting to the enduring power of this most essential of human instincts. For them, Eros, as configured in literature and art, in myth as in cult, in drama as in philosophy, is claimed to be universal, holding sway over all of nature, and to have irresistible appeal, even to the gods themselves. In most versions, he is the child of the goddess Aphrodite; in others, he arises with the first stirrings of creation; while in the famous, but idiosyncratic, myth attributed to Socrates in Plato's Symposium, he is the child of Poros (Resources) and Penia (Poverty), by nature neither mortal nor immortal but always oscillating between a condition of plenitude (life) and loss (death). From the archaic period through the classical and Hellenistic ages and down to the end of antiquity, the Greeks never ceased their explorations into the physiology and psychology of desire. Recording endless and varying encounters with the power of Eros through storytelling, dramatic enactments, personal lyrics, visual imagery, and theoretical speculation, they also transmitted to the Western imagination the powerful idea that their version of a universal Eros was indeed universal.

In our contemporary climate of research, however, where mystery has yielded to demystification, universals have given way to historical specificities, and the claims of nature are ascribed rather to notions of cultural constructs, social institutions, and discursive practices that change and diversify over time, the investigation of Eros has taken a different turn. We look now to Eros as a historically and culturally conditioned set of rules, ideas, images, fantasies, norms, and practices. The emphasis falls on difference rather than on perceived affinities or continuity of influence. The Greeks are not "us," they are "other"; and Eros, above all, can serve as the ultimate proof of the conviction that every culture determines its own variety of meanings for "nature," its own shifting representations of the human body, its own perceptions of sex and gender, and above all, its own historical psychology and social expectations.

In this enterprise, Claude Calame's expertise is indisputable. In his two-volume study of choruses of girls in archaic Greece (*Les choeurs*

*de jeunes filles en Grèce archaïque*), published a little more than twenty
years ago (1977) and now available in English translation (1997), Calame produced a pioneering work in myth, cult, poetics, and social practices, which for the first time demonstrated the significance of feminine
initiations into adulthood and revealed the fundamental significance of
Eros in the acculturation of the young. This work became indispensable
reading. He continued to take the lead in the field, both in a volume he
edited in Italian, *L'Amore in Grecia* (1983, 4th ed. 1988), which further
defined the parameters of inquiry, and even more, in numerous essays of
his own which pertain in whole or in part to questions of ancient Greek
sexual attitudes and concepts.

While a great deal of work has been produced on these topics in
recent years, including the last two volumes of Foucault's investigation
of the "history of sexuality," Calame's contribution to the subject of
Eros in this small but authoritative book represents the sum of his
thinking over a number of years. The voice is distinctive and it is magis-
terial. It bears the hallmarks of his unusual combination of skills that
joins philological acumen with an anthropological point of view. The
erudition is prodigious, in full control of primary sources, secondary
literature, and theoretical issues. Yet in its selection and organization of
a vast amount of disparate material into a lucid but complex whole, the
book is easily accessible to any reader, both the specialist and non-
specialist, at whatever level of guidance and information is desired.

Calame begins rightly with a semantic study of Eros as well as its
mythic and cultural framework before setting out to look more historically at the differences between archaic and classical Greece, with
strong attention to differences of modes of expression and their respective social venues. Calame persuasively argues that Eros is first of all
rooted in the literary and pictorial genres, which give a variety of expression to concepts of Eros, which in his view are the "inventions" of
poets and painters that left an enduring mark on future developments.
Eros, as he puts it, is both a divine figure and a physiology of desire,
with certain symptoms and certain modes of action which operate in a
network of social relations. Poetry (and its performance on dictated occasions) was itself an institution in its own right and played a major
role in Greek civic life. Thus, starting from poetry and iconography and
their symbolic values, Calame marks his intention to specify a history of
Eros that is dependent on its institutional roles—in ritual celebrations,
in educational practices of an initiatory type, in a variety of social settings, in the Dionysiac theater of tragedy and comedy, as well as in real
and imagined topographies of space (e.g., meadows, mountains, and gardens)—to conclude finally with an attestation of the central significance of
the power of Eros in cosmology, philosophy, and mystic speculations.

The heart and center of the work is quite properly the institutional role of Eros — how Eros actually "works" in the society of the aristocratic and later democratic polis, divided between homoerotic and heterosexual relations. In the world of men, Eros functions particularly in its pederastic manifestations in the two social contexts in which men and boys interact: the symposium, or private banquet, on the one hand, and the palaestra or gymnasium, on the other. Both contexts are viewed in their educational aspects for integrating future citizens into the polis (and its public space, the agora) and for regulating modes of behavior and proper erotic etiquette. Calame acutely distinguishes between male companionship and its pedagogical emphasis on politics, masculine civic and social qualities, ethical maxims concerning fidelity, justice, or wealth and its female counterpart (known to us mainly through Sappho), where the aim is not to establish enduring bonds of companionship (or *philotês*) as the basis for a future political group but rather to lead the adolescent girl to the *philotês* of conjugal relations and to her domestic and ritual roles in the city.

Thus, in the world of women, Calame takes up the household or *oikos* as the obvious venue for addressing the erotic roles of women as girls, brides, and adult wives, with the exception of the *hetaira* (or female companion), who is present at male banquets and who participates in the proceedings as both an erotic object and a skilled performer of music and dance. In a few deft pages, Calame gives the best single outline of the problem of the often misunderstood role of the hetaira), which oscillates between that of a close and beloved companion (*philê*) and a common prostitute (*pornê*) rented for the occasion, and he gives much more latitude to the representation of women at banquets and the functions they perform in the erotic life of the city. Precisely because Eros and Aphrodite are central to women's rites of passage from maiden to wife, Calame's analysis of the problematics of sexuality in conjugal relations, starting with the courtship and the wedding, gives a balanced and often corrective account of an ideology of Eros that has more recently stressed (perhaps to an extreme) the incompatibilities of maternity and sexuality in marriage and the severe disequilibrium between husbands and wives. Marriage is as much an affair of men, after all, as it is of women.

Yet if Calame demonstrates a "normative" view of ordinary sexual relations and the decorum of family life in the institutions of the city, he is cognizant too of the negative side, especially as manifested through the cult of Dionysos, particularly in the theater, whether with comedy and its bawdy licentiousness or with tragedy and its entire range of erotic images and attitudes in their associations with sacrifice, death, and entry into states of madness and destruction. In these "contestations of Eros," as he calls them, Calame well understands the dual role of Dionysos, both as an agent who integrates instinctual life into the city and, more often, as an instigator of erotic madness and transgression, who affords the context for articulating what is more ordinarily repressed in the course of civic life.

If I have singled out this section of the book for more detailed summary, I have done so because Calame's general view, arrived at with meticulous attention to texts, images, and historical data, insists finally that Eros is to be understood as a vital principle of organization and education, representing the force of reproduction through erotic desire in both biological and social terms. While myth and ideology about the dangers of Eros reveal the anxieties of sexuality, perceived as a power struggle for control over others and over oneself, Calame emphasizes the integrative function of Eros as an essential component of social and civic life. It is but a short step to the transformation of this role into a key element of philosophical training, especially in Plato.

In a book of this size, there are obviously omissions and abridgments. The focus is on the archaic and classical eras, which means that the Hellenistic and Greco-Roman culture of later periods, when the polis no longer operates with the same kind of central authority over its citizens, is not treated in systematic detail. Moreover, his interest, as I have emphasized, lies in the functional, not the dysfunctional, aspects of a system of desire and the control, even tyranny, this system exercises over social relations. Calame also does not engage in the heated debates undertaken in feminist or gay studies. Yet the book is truly instructive in the largest sense of the word; its arguments are subtle and well-founded, and its variety of materials, including the choice of notable texts for analysis (e.g., Homer, the lyric poets, tragedy and comedy, and Plato), brings the discussion into the heart of classical culture. Above all, I know of no other work that supplies this range of information in such a brief and readable form. I venture to say that it will readily become a standard in the field.

# PREFACE

P ORTIONS OF THIS BRIEF STUDY (first published in Italian, revised for the French edition, and now updated for the English translation) were presented successively as lectures at a colloquium on "Orphism and Orpheus" in Geneva (April 1989), at a conference on "Initiation" in Montpellier (April 1991), and subsequently at Brown, Columbia, Cornell, and Princeton Universities (February 1991 and November 1992), and also in the course of a number of seminars during my tenure as visiting Directeur d'Etudes in the Section des sciences religieuses at the Ecole Pratique des Hautes Etudes in Paris (January 1992). As a result, the present study has benefited greatly from the advice of numerous authoritative scholars and has also afforded me great pleasure in the very generous hospitality that was everywhere offered me. It has also profited from discussions with a number of students in Lausanne. The somewhat limited nature of its scope and technical modalities stems from my desire to reach beyond a small circle of scholars to a wider public.

The double index was composed by Annette Loeffler, in Lausanne, to whom I am most grateful. So am I also to Sandrina Cirafici for her help in collecting the photographs for the plates. The publication of the English version of this work, originally commissioned by the Laterza publishing house of Rome and Bari, would not have been possible without the continuous interest and friendly encouragement of Froma Zeitlin, at Princeton University. The generous conditions offered me by the Institute for Advanced Study in Princeton has allowed me to work on this new version of the book in close collaboration with Brigitta van Rheinberg, Joan Hunter, and Marta Steele at Princeton University Press. Finally, I would like to express my gratitude for the sensitive translation by Janet Lloyd.

# NOTE ON TRANSLATIONS

The following English translations of texts have been used. Where the name of a translator is not mentioned, the translations of the Greek result from a collaboration between the author and the translator.

Loeb Classical Library. Cambridge, Mass., and London: Harvard University Press–Heinemann:

*Aeschylus* I and II, translated by H. Weir Smyth, 1926

*Elegy and Iambics* I and II, translated by J. M. Edmonds, 1921

*Euripides* I, translated by D. Kovaks, 1994

*The Greek Anthology* IV, translated by W. R. Paton, 1948

*Greek Lyric* I, II, and V, translated by D. A. Campbell, 1988

*Hesiod*, translated by H. G. Evelyn-White, 1914

*Plato* I, translated by H. N. Fowler, 1953

*Plato* V, translated by W.R.M. Lamb, 1925

*Plutarch. Moralia* IX, translated by W. C. Helmbold, 1961

*Sophocles* I, translated by H. Lloyd-Jones, 1994

*Homer. Iliad*, translated by E. V. Rien. Harmondsworth: Penguin Classics, 1950

*Odyssey*, translated by E. V. Rien. Harmondsworth: Penguin Classics, 1946

*Theocritus* I, translated by A.S.F. Gow. Cambridge: Cambridge University Press, 1950

*Games of Venus: An Anthology of Greek and Roman Erotic Verse from Sappho to Ovid*, introduced, translated, and annotated by P. Bing and R. Cohen. New York: Routledge, 1991

# LIST OF ABBREVIATIONS

## Authors and Works

Ach. Tat.: Achilles Tatius
Ael.: Aelianus
    *Var. Hist.: Varia Historia*
Aeschin.: Aeschines
    *Tim.: Against Timarchus*
    *Amb.: On the Embassy*
Aeschl.: Aeschylus
    *Ag.: Agamemnon*
    *Eum.: Eumenides*
    *Pers.: Persians*
    *Prom.: Prometheus Bound*
    *Sept.: Seven against Thebes*
    *Suppl.: Supplices*
Alc: Alcaeus
Alcm.: Alcman
Anacr.: Anacreon
    *Epigr.: Epigrams*
*Anth. Pal.: Palatine Anthology*
Ap. Dysc.: Apollonius Dyscolus
    *Synt.: Syntax*
Ap. Rhod.: Apollonius Rhodius
Apoll.: Apollodorus
Apul.: Apuleius
    *Plat.: in Platonem*
Archil.: Archilochus
*Arg. Orph.: Orphic Argonautic*
Aristoph.: Aristophanes
    *Ach.: Acharnaians*
    *Av.: Birds*
    *Eccl.: The Women in Assembly*
    *Eq.: Knights*
    *Lys.: Lysistrata*
    *Ran.: Frogs*
    *Nub.: Clouds*
    *Thesm.: Thesmophoria*
    *Vesp.: Wasps*

Aristot.: Aristotle
>    *Ath. Pol.: Constitution of Athens*
>    *EE: Eudemean Ethics*
>    *EN: Nichomachean Ethics*
>    *Gen. An.: The Generation of Animals*
>    *PA: Parts of Animals*
>    *Poet.: Poetics*
>    *Pol.: Politics*
>    *Probl.: Problems*

Aristox.: Aristoxenus
Ath.: Athenaeus
Bacch.: Bacchylides
Bion
>    *Ad.: Lament for Adonis*

Call.: Callimachus
>    *Dian.: Hymn to Artemis*
>    *Epigr.: Epigrams*

Callin.: Callinos
*Carm. pop.: Carmina popularia*
Choeril. Sam.: Choerilos of Samos
Cic.: Cicero
>    *Tusc.: Tusculanes*

*Cypr.: Cypria*
Dem.: Demosthenes
Dem. Phal.: Demetrius of Phalerus
Dion. Hal.: Dionysius of Halicarnassus
>    *Compos.: On Stylistic Composition*

*EMag.: Etymologicum Magnum*
Emped.: Empedocles
Eph.: Ephorus
Eur.: Euripides
>    *Bacch.: Bacchae*
>    *Cycl.: Cyclops*
>    *El.: Electra*
>    *Hel.: Helen*
>    *HF: Hercules Furens*
>    *Hipp.: Hippolytus*
>    *IA: Iphigenia in Aulis*
>    *Med.: Medea*
>    *Phaeth.: Phaethon*
>    *Phoen.: Phoenissae*
>    *Suppl.: Supplices*
>    *Tr.: Trojan Women*

Eus.: Eusebius
    *Praep.: Praeparatio Evangelica*
*frag. mel. adesp.: fragmenta melica adespota*
Hdt.: Herodotus
Hecat.: Hecataeus
Hes.: Hesiod
    *Op.: Works*
    *Scut.: Shield*
    *Theog.: Theogony*
Hippon.: Hipponax
*Hhom.: Homeric Hymn*
    *Cer.: To Demeter (Ceres)*
    *Dion.: To Dionysus*
    *Merc.: To Hermes (Mercurius)*
    *Ven.: To Aphrodite (Venus)*
Hippocr.: Hippocrates
    *Aph.: Aphorisms*
    *Fract.: Fractures*
    *Gener.: On Generation*
    *Reg.: Regimen*
Hom.: Homer
    *Il.: Iliad*
    *Od.: Odyssey*
*HOrph.: Orphic Hymns*
Hsch.: Hesychius
Iambl.: Iamblichus
    *Vit. Pyth.: Life of Pythagoras*
Ibyc.: Ibycus
Long.: Longus
Lyc.: Lycophron
    *Alex.: Alexandra*
Mimn.: Mimnermus
Mosch.: Moschus
    *Eur.: Europa*
Nonn.: Nonnos
  *Dion.: Dionysiaca*
Olymp.: Olympiodorus
    *Vit. Plat.: Vita Platonis*
*Orph.: Orphica*
Ov.: Ovid
    *Met.: Metamorphoses*
Paus.: Pausanias
*P. Derv.: Derveni Papyrus*

Pherec.: Pherecydes of Athens
Pherec. Syr.: Pherecydes of Syros
Phot.: Photius
    *Bibl.: Library*
    *Lex.: Lexicon*
Pind.: Pindar
    *Isthm.: Isthmian*
    *Nem.: Nemean*
    *Ol.: Olympian*
    *Pyth.: Pythian*
Plat.: Plato
    *Crat.: Cratylus*
    *Gorg.: Gorgias*
    *Leg.: Laws*
    *Lys.: Lysis*
    *Phaedr.: Phaedrus*
    *Resp.: Republic*
    *Tim.: Timaeus*
Plin.: Pliny the Elder
    *Hist. Nat.: Natural History*
Plut.: Plutarch
    *Amator.: Amatorius*
    *Glor. Ath.: Glory of the Athenians*
    *Lyc.: Life of Lycurgus*
    *Pel.: Life of Pelopidas*
    *Praec. conj.: Conjugal Precepts*
    *Quaest. conv.: Quaestiones convivales*
    *Sol.: Life of Solon*
Poll.: Pollux
Procl.: Proclus
Sem.: Semonides
Serv.: Servius
Simon.: Simonides
    *Epigr.: Epigrams*
Sol.: Solon
Soph.: Sophocles
    *Ant.: Antigone*
    *Oed. Col.: Oedipus at Colonus*
    *Oed. Tyr.: Oedipus the King*
    *Trach.: Women of Trachis*
Stes.: Stesichorus
Strab.: Strabo
*Sud.: Suda*/Suidas

Theocr.: Theocritus
Thgn.: Theognis
Tim.: Timaeus
Tzetz.: Tzetzes
Verg.: Vergil
    *Aen.: Aeneid*
Xen.: Xenophon
    *Symp.: Symposium*
    *Mem.: Memorabilia*
Xen. Eph.: Xenophon of Ephesus
Xenoph.: Xenophanes


## COLLECTIONS OF TEXTS AND DOCUMENTS

*ABV: Attic Black-Figure Vase-Painters* (J. D. Beazley)
*ARV: Attic Red-Figure Vase-Painters* (J. D. Beazley)
*CEG: Carmina Epigraphica Graeca* (P. A. Hanson)
*FGrHist.: Fragmente der Griechischen Historiker* (F. Jacoby)
*IG: Inscriptiones Graecae*
*LfgrE: Lexikon der frühgriechischen Epos*
*LIMC: Lexicon Iconographicum Mythologiae Classicae*
*Paralip.: Paralipomena* (J. D. Beazley)
*P.G.M.: Papyri Graecae Magicae* (K. Preisendanz)
*P. Oxy.: Oxyrhynchus Papyri*
*SEG: Supplementum Epigraphicum Graecum*
*SGDI: Sammlung der Griechischen Dialekt-Inschriften* (H. Collitz and
    F. Bechtel)


## JOURNALS AND PERIODICALS

*Am. Hist. Rev.: American Historical Review*
*Am. Journ. Arch.: American Journal of Archaeology*
*Am. Journ. Philol.: American Journal of Philology*
*Arch. Begriffgesch.: Archiv für Begriffgeschichte*
*Arch. Rel.-Wiss.: Archiv für Religionswissenschaft*
*Bull. Corr. Hell.: Bulletin de Correspondance Hellénique*
*Bull. Inst. Class. Stud.: Bulletin of the Institute of Classical Studies*
*Class. Ant.: Classical Antiquity*
*Class. Mod. Lit.: Classical and Modern Literature*
*Class. Philol.: Classical Philology*
*Class. Quart.: Classical Quarterly*

*Et. Lettres: Etudes de Lettres, Lausanne*

*Freib. Zeitschr. Philos. Theol.: Freiburger Zeitschrift für Philosophie und Theologie*

*Harv. Stud. Class. Philol.: Harvard Studies in Classical Philology*

*Harv. Theol. Rev.: Harvard Theological Review*

*Ill. Class. Stud.: Illinois Classical Studies*

*Journ. Hell. Stud.: Journal of Hellenic Studies*

*Mat. Disc. Anal. Testi Class.: Materiali e Discussioni per l'Analisi dei Testi Classici*

*Mus. Helv.: Museum Helveticum*

*Par. Pass.: La Parola del Passato*

*Proc. Cambr. Philol. Soc.: Proceedings of the Cambridge Philological Society*

*Quad. Stor.: Quaderni di Storia*

*Quad. Urb. Cult. Class.: Quaderni Urbinati di Cultura Classica*

*Rev. Et. Gr.: Revue des Etudes Grecques*

*Rev. Hist. Rel.: Revue de l'Histoire des Religions*

*Rhein. Mus.: Rheinisches Museum*

*Stud. It. Filol. Class.: Studi Italiani di Filologia Classica*

*Trans. Am. Philol. Assoc.: Transactions of the American Philological Association*

*Wien. Stud.: Wiener Studien*

*Zeitschr. Pap. Epigr.: Zeitschrift für Papyrologie und Epigraphik*

THE POETICS OF

EROS IN ANCIENT GREECE

## Tragic Prelude

## THE YOKE OF EROS

THERE WAS NEVER any shortage on the attic stage of dramas about love. One that appears to have most affected the audience honoring Dionysus on the Acropolis hillside was that of the deadly passion of Phaedra. This was no doubt partly because Phaedra was married to the classical city's own founding hero, but partly also because of the somewhat gratuitous nature of her feelings for her stepson. Hippolytus, the son of the queen of the Amazons, for his part, certainly deserved to die by reason of his stubborn rejection of the pleasures of mature erotic desire offered by Aphrodite—a rejection that stemmed from his exclusive passion for Artemis, the virgin huntress. Phaedra, however, was simply a tool in the vengeful plan devised by the goddess of love. In Euripides' version of the story, the plot ascribes to her no personal blame for the destructive passion inflicted on her by Cypris.

By way of an introduction, I will first focus attention upon fifth-century B.C. Athenian drama consecrated to Dionysus the Liberator, sketching in the modes of action and the field of intervention of the force of love that is embodied in Eros and the goddess whom he assists. The close-knit web of social relations that these two combine to create for us in the poetic fiction of the tragedies composed for the Attic theater will provide plenty of illustrations for an approach, both discursive and anthropological, that I propose to adopt here. Starting with this tragic prelude, I shall then proceed to consider many other symbolic manifestations of the powers of love in ancient Greece from this twofold perspective.

In Aristophanes' comedy *The Frogs*, Aeschylus maligns his rival Euripides, accusing him of having created in Phaedra a model for prostitutes. Whatever the effect of such jibes, Euripides, the sophist poet, decided to write a second tragedy entitled *Hippolytus*, the one that has come down to us.[1] In this play, the honor—and consequently the heroic renown—of the unfortunate lovesick woman are saved by a double transformation of the plot. The revelations of the talkative nurse re-

---

[1] For the Aeschylus represented on stage by Aristophanes (*Ran.* 1040ff.), Phaedra is one of the noble wives of noble husbands whom Euripides condemns to dishonor and suicide. For an attempted reconstruction of the plot of the first *Hippolytus*, see Barrett 1964, 11ff.

garding the incestuous passion felt by her mistress make it possible for the heroine's suicide to be a death that is spared the dishonor of an open declaration. And the false accusations against her stepson are made indirectly, through the intermediary of writing. Not only does this recourse to a written message, attached to Phaedra's wrist before she hangs herself, prepare the audience for her suicide, but it also avoids any direct confrontation between the wayward Phaedra and her royal husband. The heroine perpetrated a lie through the tablets dangling from her wrist, but never actually through her own mouth. Even as he respected and reinforced the theological premise of the tragic consequences of Aphrodite's implacable power, Euripides contrived to stretch his plot to the limit in order to shield Theseus' spouse from general condemnation.[2]

At the turning point in this plot, at the very moment when Phaedra's nurse unjustifiably presuming to take the destiny of her mistress into her own hands instead precipitates it, the chorus addresses an anguished prayer to Eros:

> Eros, Eros, distilling liquid desire upon the eyes,
> bringing sweet pleasure to the souls
> of those you make war against,
> never may you show yourself to me for my hurt
> nor ever come but in harmony.
> For neither the shafts of fire nor of stars
> are more powerful than that of Aphrodite,
> which Eros, Zeus's son, hurls from his hand.
>     'Tis folly, folly, for the land of Greece
> to multiply the slaughter of cattle by
> the banks of the Alpheus and in the Pythian shrine of Apollo
> if we pay no honour to Eros,
> mankind's despot; who holds the keys
> to the sweet chambers of Aphrodite!
> He ruins mortals and launches them among every kind of disaster
> when he visits them.[3]

This prayer addressed in its cultic form to the god of erotic desire should be read in the context of the tragic irony that is introduced by the words of the nurse, for in her naivety that foolish woman is still

---

[2] See F. I. Zeitlin, "The Power of Aphrodite," in P. Burian (ed.), *Directions in Euripidean Criticism* (Durham, N.C., 1985), 52–111; now in Zeitlin 1996, 219–84; also C. Segal, *Euripides and the Poetics of Sorrow* (Durham and London 1993), 103ff.

[3] Eur. *Hipp.* 525ff., in D. Kovacs (trans.), *Euripides* I (Loeb, Cambridge, Mass. and London 1995); this hymn is echoed by the chorus at 1.1268ff; see below, ch. VII, §2.2, with the references given in n. 32.

relying on the goodwill and collaboration of Aphrodite. All the same, even if this hymn does condemn the destructive effects of divine intervention in the realm of love, it still uses the device of a religious prayer to evoke the characteristics of a poetic image of Eros. A specifically Greek representation of love is also discernible in the very earliest poems that have come down to us thanks to the Greeks' adoption of the Phoenician alphabet at the end of the eighth century B.C. That representation was, as we shall see, certainly not to remain untouched by historical variations. Nevertheless, by way of an introduction let us rapidly trace its broad outlines by adopting a synchronic perspective, just as the members of Euripides' chorus did.

In their hymn, the women of Troezen who make up Euripides' chorus sing of the modes of action of the deity to whom they are addressing their prayer. As is often the case in ancient Greece, the effects of love are portrayed not so much in terms of personal feeling as in terms of their physiological aspects. Eros distills desire (*pothos*), arousing pleasure (*kharis*) by its sweetness. His preferred medium is a gaze that can penetrate the soul (*psukhê*). But Eros' impact, which is conveyed in a military metaphor, is immediately perceived as an attack. The epiphany of Love in the form of a deity is ambivalent and may be unwelcome. Moreover this child of Zeus does not go into battle alone: it is Aphrodite who guides the darts shot by his bow, asserting her imperious power throughout the tragedy and laying low all the protagonists of the *Hippolytus*. Eros, the goddess of love's right-hand assistant, who holds sway over the whole of Greece, should thus command even more than all the divine honors of Delphi and Olympia put together. He is a tyrant who even holds the keys to the marriage chamber of Cypris herself.

In classical tragedy, the songs of the chorus are almost always functional. In the case of the chorus members of the *Hippolytus*, at the crucial turning point of the plot, they need to express their forebodings as to the fate reserved for the victims of Aphrodite. To illustrate the destructive reversals of fortune for which Eros and his mistress are responsible, the women sing of the tragic destinies of a number of heroines who struggled in the clutches of the goddess of love. Like Hippolytus, who rejects the yoke of marriage in the manner of a girl pledged to Artemis and is then strangled to death by the reins of his own horses, so too Iole, the untamed mare, was broken by Aphrodite, who coupled her with Heracles in a burning, deadly union. Semele likewise by the will of Cypris celebrated a union with Zeus which resulted in the birth of Dionysus; this union went up in flames, torched by the heavenly god's thunderbolt, before plunging the young woman into a deathly slumber. It is the stifling power of love that leads girls into marriage, which is thus shown to be one of the fields of intervention most favored by the goddess from Cyprus; but when Aphrodite takes a hand out of jealousy, her divine power can create a fusion of sexual fulfillment, sleep, and death. An appalled Phaedra is soon to hear Hippolytus, blinded by his hatred for womankind, launch into a wild tirade; but first Euripides produces one last metaphor: in her flight, Aphrodite is a bee that produces honey but mercilessly stings its victims. With this fleeting, paradoxical image the chorus's song returns, in accordance with the pattern of a typical ring composition, to the theme of the ambivalence of love, as embodied in Eros, the "soldier of pleasure."[4]

The above brief analysis of this chorus in Euripides' *Hippolytus* is designed to suggest the broad lines of the method and orientation to be followed in this study. The only available evidence that has come down to us over the centuries consists of texts and pictorial representations, so our image of Greece culture is almost entirely literary and aesthetic. Accordingly, let us first concentrate on the poetic representations of love in the Greek manner. A discursive analysis will make it possible to form a picture of both the divine personification of love with its modes of action and the physiology that relates to that figure's field of intervention. We shall thus be able to study not only a series of textual representations of love, but also, adopting the perspective of an anthropology of literature, to make out the whole network of social relations that is instituted by the power of Eros and Aphrodite through the poetic compositions that they inspire.

The second part of the present study is designed to add a historical dimension to this image of the deities who embody the power of amorous desire and also to the representations of the relationships that result from the deployment of that power. The configuration of love peculiar to melic or song poetry of the archaic period has neither the same features nor the same function as that forged by the literary writers, initially poets, then authors of romances, who were active in the Alexandrian and post-Alexandrian periods. A study of the pragmatic dimension of archaic poetry will lead on to a similar investigation into the rich images that, through their representations of legends or rituals, illustrate the various practices of Eros during this same period.

In ancient Greece, the practice of poetry and likewise the use of ornamented objects were linked with particular institutions. To sing of love was not only to represent erotic desire but also to establish it as a social practice; to sing of Eros and to admire his iconographical representa-

---

[4] The comparison of Aphrodite to a bee implies a probable allusion to the twofold effect of "bittersweet" love: the sweetness of honey and the sting of the bee; see Barrett 1964, 266, and below, ch. I, §1.

tions was first and foremost to revere the practices he instituted.[5] Provided caution is exercised, poetry and iconography may yield empirical and historical referents to their interpreters. For both encourage their readers to ponder on the functions of love in civic institutions such as the ritual gatherings of citizens, educational practices of an initiatory nature, marriage ceremonies, and so on. In the third part of this study, which likewise adopts an anthropological view of cultural phenomena, we shall move on from the symbolic products of culture to consider the institutional and social realities that underpinned them. We shall discover that Eros, with his power to create interactive relationships, in particular affects the establishment of the social sexual relations that are nowadays defined as matters of "gender." Gender will thus be understood, in the Anglo-American sense of the term, as "the manner in which the members of the two sexes are perceived, evaluated and presumed to behave," in each different culture. It is precisely through a fatal confusion in gender distinctions on two counts that Hippolytus, not content with behaving like a young girl wholly pledged to Artemis, goes on to reject Aphrodite and marriage altogether. Gender, which I take to be a phenomenon that is dependent on the process of the production of symbols, is here understood as a construct; it corresponds to a shared representation of the social relations between the sexes.[6]

To avoid the pitfalls of pure "naturalization" albeit probably still shocking some of the founders (both men and women) of the sociological notion of "gender," I shall be suggesting that distinctions relating to gender stem from a difference in perspective that is inseparable from the fact that there never will exist a man who himself lives through the physiological experiences of a woman. This factor explains why, in all societies but particularly in ancient Greece, social differences between the sexes are legitimated by an anthropology, a conception of the human being. As I shall several times have occasion to point out, those differences are rooted in a physiological view of men and women that is

---

[5] This practical, if not "performative" function of love was not understood by I. Grellet and C. Kruse, *La déclaration d'amour* (Paris 1990), despite the fact that one of the chapters in their book is entitled "Un geste de langage," 43ff. (to cite but one recent study on the words of love).

[6] According to the definition given following A. Schlegel, with a commentary by P. R. Sanday, "Introduction," in P. R. Sanday and R. G. Goodenough (eds.), *Beyond the Second Sex: New Directions in the Anthropology of Gender* (Philadelphia 1990), 1–19, at 5. See also the definition suggested by J. W. Scott, "Gender: A Useful Category of Historical Analysis," *Am. Hist. Rev.* 91 (1986): 1053–75; reprinted in E. Weed (ed.), *Coming to Terms: Feminism, Theory, Politics* (New York and London 1989), 81–100: "Gender is a fundamental element in social relations based upon the perceived differences between the sexes," so it is also "a primary way of signifying power relations." As for the idea of the symbolic process, let me refer the reader to my comments of 1996, 29ff.

very much a product of culture.[7] In this respect, I shall argue, antiquity was no exception to the rule which claims that this anatomical and biological image tends to constitute the basis of any ideological justification for the relations of power that are generally part and parcel of social relations between the sexes. By the end of the third part of the present study I hope to have shown, in the context of the cult addressed to Dionysus, that comedy and tragedy, which were ritual poetic practices, eventually formulated a bitter critique of the representations of love and the social relations between the sexes that stemmed from them. The hymn to Eros in the *Hippolytus* in itself surely bears out that point!

Moreover, despite his presence everywhere, Eros is more likely to manifest himself in certain particular places. Some of these are marked out by the institutions mentioned above, such as the ritual banquet, education in gymnastics and music, and marriage ceremonies. Others, however, are spaces that are elaborated symbolically by legends and their poetic manifestations such as lush, flower-filled "mythical" and poetic gardens, the study of which demands a semiotic sensitivity to symbolic construction and the effects of its meanings. It is particularly important to make a prudent transition from the real spaces where Eros operates to the imaginary ones where he is often to be found in the company of Aphrodite, for these imaginary spaces lead us back to the institutions. The fourth part of this study will show that those symbolic sites are sometimes matched by an equivalent in the spaces that are created by the religious practices dedicated to the deities of love.

With this extension to the spaces of his deployment, the social, poetic, and cultic imaginary representations of Eros will lead us finally, in a fifth and last part, toward cosmogony and philosophy. The more speculative thought of cosmologists from Hesiod to Plato, taking in the devotees of Orpheus, made use of both the demiurgic aspect of the power of love and the initiatory gifts embodied in Eros. Such reflections turned Eros finally into an essential ethical and mythical agent, one who operated through vision but also through speech, and whose bases of gender and sexuality were used by symbolic thought and figurative discourse as the vectors of an initiatory activity. This evolution by which Eros ac-

---

[7] The inquiry into sociological and anthropological concepts of the sexes has recently been pursued, on a comparative basis, by F. Héritier-Augé, "La costruzione dell'essere sessuato, la costruzione sociale del genere e le ambiguità dell'identità sessuale," in M. Bettini (ed.), *Maschile/Femminile* (Roma and Bari 1993), 113–40. On Greece itself, see in particular the contributions of S. Saïd, "Féminin, femme et femelle dans les grands traités biologiques d'Aristote," in E. Lévy (ed.), *La femme dans les sociétés antiques* (Strasbourg 1983), 93–123; M. M. Sassi, *La scienza dell'uomo nella Grecia antica* (Torino 1988), 81ff.; Laqueur 1990, 1ff.; A. E. Hanson, "The Medical Writers' Women," in Halperin, Winkler, and Zeitlin (eds.) 1990, 309–38; and G. Sissa, "Philosophie du genre," in Schmitt-Pantel 1991, 58–100.

quired a role in the revelation of truth remained, it must be said, more or less unaffected by any notion of "mastery over pleasure," as Michel Foucault would have it.

Through the representations that he inspired, and the attitudes adopted toward him by each of the sexes in their interrelations, Eros certainly opened the door to "sexuality." But in the present study, sexuality, like "gender," will be considered an operative concept. It will be regarded not so much as an "experience" as a modern construct by which we try to incorporate a whole body of psychosocial practices with a genital basis. The figure of Eros will thus be used to track down representations of "sexuality" rather different from the moral and philosophical experience that Foucault set out to discover in a study limited to the Greek orators and thinkers of the fourth century; a study surprisingly influential in the Anglo-Saxon countries.[8] Seen as symbolic practices, the erotic poetry and iconography of the archaic and classical periods reflect social relations and institutions as much as they reflect "sexual subjects"; furthermore, through these manifestations of the symbolic process and through its own dynamism, the carnal desire embodied in the power of Eros creates relationships that redefine the genders and at the same time call them into question. Instead of concentrating on the rather philosophical concepts and moral attitudes studied by Foucault, instead of relying on a philosophical and ethical notion of subject as "sujet de désir," which is not really relevant for Archaic and Classical Greece, I shall try to show how the divine force of Eros is at the core of representations that are active in the construction and practice of different institutions as well as of various symbolic manifestations such as poetry or iconography.

It may be objected that this is an idealizing view of the Eros of the Greeks, a purely academic and scholarly view of "sexuality." However that may be, it is certainly an inevitably euro- and androcentric view of words and a few images that were for the most part formulated by men. A male author is probably at a disadvantage when it comes to the feminine specifics of erotic desire and the sexual attitudes expressed in, for instance, Sappho's poems. At stake here is the asymmetrical aspect of the anthropological relationship.

---

[8] Foucault 1984, 10ff., which should be read taking into account the remarks of M. Piérart, "Michel Foucault et la morale sexuelle des Anciens," *Freib. Zeitschr. Philos. Theol.* 33 (1986): 23–43; M. Vegetti, "Foucault et les Anciens," *Critique* 371/2 (1986), 925–32; "Introduction" to Halperin, Winkler, and Zeitlin (eds.) 1990, 3–20 (see D. Cohen's "Review Article: Sex, Gender and Sexuality in Ancient Greece," *Class. Philol.* 87 (1992): 145–59); Kennedy 1993, 41ff.; and finally Goldhill 1995, 44ff. and 146ff., with the collection of essays published by D.H.J. Larmour and P. A. Miller (eds.), *Rethinking Sexuality. Foucault and Classical Antiquity* (Princeton 1997).

# PART ONE

## THE TOPICS OF EROS

# Chapter I

## THE EROS OF THE MELIC POETS

PRONE AS IT IS to an incoherence fostered by its excessive practice of criticism, our civilization has fragmented the notion of amorous feeling into the most contradictory representations of it. On the one hand a medical approach has led to isolating an instinct of a physiological nature, which the behavioral sciences promptly seized upon: love has thus been reduced to the taxonomy of interactive and determinist relations known as "sexuality." On the other hand, psychology inspired by psychoanalysis refers us to a libido that turns erotic desire into a series of affective reactions that are responses to an unconscious motivating impulse. Yet the desperate search for partners attested by the "lonely hearts" columns in the newspapers and fostered by the simplistic plots of televised soap operas and romantic tales told in photography indicates an aspiration oriented exclusively toward tenderness, sensuality, and affection, if not toward passion of the most romantic kind. We are thus presented with a total contrast between, on the one hand, a sexuality centered on "desiring man" and, on the other, an aspiration toward a relational type of love.[1] As we know, in ancient Greece love was essentially *erôs*, a force that this term tended to objectivize, a power of such an autonomous nature that writing it with a capital *E* can be enough, in modern usage, to express its divine nature. If Love was seen as an anthropomorphic deity, we should study it as a semiotic agent, with particular symbolic qualities and in consequence particular modes of meaning and action of its own, amid the forces that it brings into play; and we must relate it to the beneficiaries of its action and the web of social and symbolic relations in which it involves them, as well as to any sexual roles and gender functions that it institutes in situations of contrast and conflict. Our investigation into the social and semiotic means of action devised by Eros will focus synchronically upon

---

[1] Given the perspective adopted in this study, which is that of love expressed, no one has conveyed better the breaking up of contemporary love than R. Barthes: see *Fragments d'un discours amoureux* (Paris 1977; English translation by R. Howard, *A Lover's Discourse: Fragments*, New York 1978). As for the productivity of the recent application of the concept of sexuality to the reality of ancient love, see the pertinent remarks in the critical bibliography discussed by M. Arthur Katz, "Sexuality and the Body in Ancient Greece," *Mètis* 4 (1989): 155–79. By "desiring man," Foucault 1984, 11 and 18, means the "sexual subject," a matter I have touched upon in the introductory remarks above. See now F. I. Zeitlin, "Eros," in S. Settis (ed.), *I Greci* I. *I Greci e noi* (Turin 1996), 514–27.

first their literary and then their symbolic manifestations. The image that emerges will then be resituated in its historical context, at which point we shall turn our attention to the question of the function of the texts through which that image has been transmitted to us.

But why, some might ask, should we follow the scholarly tradition so closely as to begin chronologically with the poetry we mistakenly label "lyric"? For a number of reasons. One is the inevitably literary nature of most of the tradition about antiquity and consequently also about Eros. Another is that, although melic poetry cannot be said to mark the advent of the modern individual, it does allow a place of importance to the figure of the narrator or locutor, in that the one who speaks or sings the poem uses the grammatical forms of the first person; this linguistic or discursive figure tends to be all too readily identified with the real utterer of the poem, if not with its author.[2]

Yet these poems furthermore assume vis-à-vis their addressees a function that will offer us a means of understanding the social practice of love, as the Greeks understood it. It should also be acknowledged that, given the fragmentary form in which these poems have come down to us, they are naturally easier to divide into small units, so as to meet the requirements of the search for a paradigm.

## 1. THE ACTIONS OF BITTERSWEET EROS

In archaic poetry, the power of love is perceived most immediately through its sweetness, which flows through us, enchanting our hearts with a sense of ease. But this sensation of sweetness is certainly not conveyed solely through the faculty of taste. Sometimes, to be sure, it is aroused by a liquid such as water or wine. But it is a sweet pleasure that can also be brought on by sleep and, above all, by music in all its forms: a voice, a song, a flute melody, the sound of the phorminx, in short the Muse. On two occasions Pindar uses a crater, or mixing bowl, as a metaphor for a lingering song.[3] The sweet charm of the kind of love that is concrete enough to take on a human configuration and potent

---

[2] I shall adopt the convention of using "melic" to refer to all the various forms of archaic poetry except epic. This concept of "sung" poetry (to the accompaniment of the lyre or the flute) includes iambic and elegiac poems. The difficulties raised by the category of "lyric" poetry are described by Gentili 1984, 41ff.; on the question of the identity of the melic "I," see below, ch. III, §1, n. 1.

[3] Alcm. frag. 59 (a) Page, with my commentary of 1983, 560; on the Homeric meaning of the verb *iainein*, which refers to the feeling of relaxation, see Latacz 1966, 222ff. The sweetness of a liquid: Xenoph. frags. 18 and 133 Gentili-Prato; of sleep: Alcm. frag. 3.7 Page, Sappho frag. 63.3 Voigt, Pind. *Pyth.* 9.23; of a voice: Pind. *Pyth.* 10.56 or frag. 52 i

enough to act as a deity is to be found in the Eros that Theognis describes awaking at the moment when the earth is becoming carpeted
with flowers and then leaving Cyprus to go forth and spread his seed
among men. Alcman has a springtime Eros frolicking among the cyperus (galingale) flowers like a playful child. And Anacreon gives him
knucklebones to play with just as, much later, Apollonius Rhodius has
Ganymedes play with these in the flower-filled garden of Zeus.⁴ Such
scenes are frequently depicted in the pictorial imagery of a later age:
Italiot pottery, in particular, was prone to represent a winged Eros hov-
ering above a bed of flowers.⁵ But in the very same poem by Alcman
mentioned above this impish Eros is also an unstoppable force; and—
according to an interpreter of Apollonius Rhodius, who echoes Alcman's description—he is a "mad Eros" who is capable of communicat-
ing the full force of that madness to human beings. Similarly, for Anacreon, Eros' knucklebones represent his mad whims and refer us to the
chaotic conflicts in which he involves his victims. In a similar violent
contrast, in another of Anacreon's poems, Love invites the narrator to
play an altogether metaphorical game of ball with a young girl who is
wearing brightly embroidered slippers. She, however, invokes her aristocratic Lesbian origins and turns away from the poet, showering him
with her contempt.

> Once more Eros of the golden hair
> hits me with his purple ball,
> calls me out to play with the girl
> with the flashy slippers.
> But she, since she comes from noble
> Lesbos, scoffs at my hair,
> since it's white, and gapes for another girl.⁶

---

(b).13 Maehler; of a song: Pind. *Nem.* 5.2 or 9.3, *Ol.* 10.3; of a flute: Pind. *Ol.* 10.94 or
Bacch. 2.12; of a phorminx: Pind. *Nem.* 4.44. Singing and wine: Pind. *Ol.* 6.90f. and
*Nem.* 9.50.

⁴ Thgn. 1275ff.: see Vetta 1980, 71ff.; Alcm. frag. 58 Page: see Calame 1983, 555ff.;
Anacr. frag. 398 Page; see Ap. Rhod. 3.114ff. with the sch. *ad* 1.120 (p. 221 Wendel) and
the commentary by R. Pretagostini, "Le metafore di Eros che gioca," in *Lirica greca e
latina* (Rome 1990), 225–38, on the continuity of the "theme" of the game of Eros, and
also the remarks of Rosenmeyer 1992, 45ff.

⁵ See *LIMC Eros* 136–44 (Italiot vases of the second half of the fourth century B.C.); on
Eros playing knucklebones, see *LIMC Eros* 773. Frag. 18 of *P. Oxy.* 3695, attributed to
Anacreon, also seems to assimilate the effect of *erôs* to madness. As for the erotic significance ascribed to knucklebones, see B. Neutsch, "Spiele mit dem Astragal," in R. Herbig
(ed.), *Ganymed* (Heidelberg 1949), 18–28.

⁶ Anacr. frag. 358 Page, in P. Bing (trans.), *Games of Venus* (New York 1991); the
various interpretations that have been suggested for the Lesbian origin of the girl are
mentioned below, n. 29. On the metaphor of the play with the ball, see C. Pace,

Paradoxically, the sweetness that Eros inspires is also a burning. Sappho calls Eros "the bittersweet one," combining the two polar opposites in a single compound. But, in view of the arrows that Eros lets fly in Euripides, perhaps a more accurate translation would be "the sweet-stinging one" or, to confine ourselves to archaic poetry and, for now, to that particular couplet of Sappho's, it might be added that there Eros is compared to a creeping serpent against which there is no defense. In archaic poetry, penetration is the distinctive power attributed to arrows, and it can lead to a death that is itself sometimes described as bitter.[7] Some erotic lines of poetry attributed to Theognis convey the contrast even more specifically. For young people, love is both stinging and sweet, for it is both a torment and a delight. But, using an expression that is probably proverbial and that, with the same contrast, can be applied equally either to the relations between kin in a family household or to political situations, these lines also create a new, dynamic image of Eros. The fulfillment of love confirms its sweetness, but when pursuit ends in frustration love is an unwelcome affliction.

> Bitter and sweet, kindly also and harsh, Cyrnus, is love unto the young till it be fulfilled; for if a man achieve it, it becometh sweet, and if he pursue and achieve not, that is of all things the most painful.[8]

Eros is thus characterized by the same dynamism as that conveyed by our own concept of aspiration, aims, desire. Later in this semantic study, I shall try to define what this mobility involves. For now, though, suffice it to say that archaic poetry always dwells more upon the dissatisfying side of love. For example, the Theognidean corpus portrays Eros as a burden that is hard to bear: no longer to fell desire is to be freed from weighty sorrows, to escape the most painful of woes, and to rediscover the joys of life.[9] For Eros strikes hard, as one double, interwoven metaphor shows. He strikes his victim as would the mallet of a bronzesmith who then plunges his material into icy water. In this metaphor, both the

---

"Anacreonte e la palla di Nausicaa (Anacr. frag. 13 G. = 358 *PMG*, 1–4," *Eikasmos* 7 (1996): 81–86.

[7] Sappho frag. 130 Voigt, which should be read with the commentary by R. Schlesier, "Der bittersüsse Eros," *Arch. Begriffgesch.* 30 (1986/7): 70–83; using Homeric parallels, the author associates the sweetness of Eros with that of nectar, and consequently with immortality. See Mimn. frag. 23.8 Gentili-Prato and Pind. *Isthm.* 7.48.

[8] Thgn. 1353f., in J. M. Edmonds (trans.), *Elegy and Iambics* (Loeb 1921), the conventional character of which is demonstrated by Vetta 1980, 125ff.; see also Thgn. 301ff., and Sol. frag. 1.5ff. Gentili-Prato, where the respect or, on the contrary, the terror inspired by the sweetness or the bitterness are expressed in the gaze; see also Sappho frag. 5.6ff. Voigt. On the contrasts of Eros, see Carson 1986, 3ff.

[9] Thgn. 1322ff. and 1337ff.; Anacr., frag. 460 Page, also complained of the burden of Eros.

blows and the contrast are violent. Elsewhere, Eros, condemning his victim to insomnia, swoops in like a Tracian North Wind, with effects as antithetical as the work of the bronzesmith: at once blazing with lightning yet shrouded in darkness, shamelessly and with the utmost violence he shakes the lover's "diaphragm" to its very core; his gusts are sudden attacks of madness, winds that burn.

In Spring Cydonian
quince trees flower, watered by the sluice
of streams, where the Maidens'
untrimmed garden strands, and vineshoots
rise and bloom beneath the shading branches
of the vine. But for me desire
knows no season of rest:
ablaze with lightning —
a Thracian north wind —
    swooping from Kypris with
    searing frenzies, black, unabashed
he brutally wrenches my heart
at the root.

In this poem by Ibycus, the very action of Eros, who may strike whatever the season, is set in sharp opposition to the spring blooms of the garden (into which we shall be venturing a little farther on). For now, let us simply note that Sappho, too, compares Love to a wind that could well be the same Boreas, one that shakes the membrane surrounding the heart, like the blast that falls upon the mountain oaks.[10] Eros shakes the organs of the body with repeated flurries, shattering its very limbs. The main feature of Eros upon which these poets dwell is his implacable cruelty, all those violent onslaughts of his that successively led to the destruction of Troy, of Theseus, and of Ajax, son of Oileus. So destructive is his power that he seems to have thrived upon the attacks of madness to which Ibycus also refers. Even later when Pindar, in a more positive vein, evokes instances of a more noble love, he still considers it an advantage to be able to keep it under control.[11]

[10] Ibyc. frag. 286 Page, in P. Bing (trans.), *Games of Venus* (New York 1991); see below, ch. IX, §2, with n. 2; the poem is cited following the mention of Anacr. frag. 413 Page, who discounts the Homeric comparison of the description of Odysseus at the point when he blinds the Cyclops (Hom. *Od.* 9.391ff.); see O. Vox, *Studi anacreonti* (Bari 1990), 64ff. and 73ff.; Sappho frag. 47 Voigt; see Hes. *Op.* 509ff., where an analogous description designates Boreas. A reading of the form *etinaxe* in Sappho's text suggests a correction in Ibycus' text from the incomprehensible *phulassei* to *tinassei*. For the identity of the organ called *phrenes*, see below n. 15.

[11] Sappho frag. 130 Voigt, already cited above in n. 7. The adjective *lusimelês*, already

Eros prides himself on hitting his target at its emotional center. But as surely as it is through this particular organ that he can permeate the entire person, that person may then appropriate this erotic desire as his or her own. For example, the narrator of some lines attributed to Theognis proclaims, using the proverbial form of the *makarismos*: "Happy is he who, loving (*erôn*) a boy, knows not the sea"; Sappho, juxtaposing her "I" to the "you" that designates the beloved, declares "Once I loved (*eraman*) you, I, you, Atthis"; and Anacreon too, addressing Dionysus, concludes with a reference to his own situation, claiming as his own the domineering love that joins in the games played by Dionysus, Aphrodite, and the Nymphs. For the poet can experience erotic desire in its pure state, simultaneously sensitive to both the madness that it induces and its absence:

> Once again I love and I do not love,
> I am mad and I am not mad.

Reduced to a simple condition for the duration of the present tense, the contrasts in the nature of Eros become so strong that the poet uses contradictory terms rather than merely contrary or contrasting ones: now Eros is not simply both sweet and stinging, but is both active and absent, all at once. In similar fashion Sappho, or her enunciative substitute, seems, in one short opening fragment of a poem, to be feeling two desires at once.[12]

Eros thus delights in contradictions as much as in contrasts. Despite the frequent claims that the power of love is objectivized into a noun, Eros, when expressed in a verbal form, can equally well be taken over by the subject experiencing desire. But whether objectivized or embodied, Eros as an agent profoundly alters the state of his victim more than he impels him or her into action. But we must still investigate the modalities of this state of desire. We have already noted some of the organs affected by the action of Eros; now let us consider the preferred intermediaries that are employed, and then go on to examine the substance of that action, along with the various relationships it weaves around Eros' victim. In the guise of desire, *erôs* may also be designated by other terms, which enrich its semantic field, a field that may be extended to

---

used—as will be seen—by Hes. *Theog.* 120ff. and 190ff. is also used for Eros in the *Carm. pop.* 873 Page; Thgn. 1231ff; see also Simon. frag. 575.1 Page, and see the commentary by Müller 1980, 83ff. On the blind violence of the Erotes as archers, see also Anacr. frag. 445 Page, Ibyc. frag. 286 Page (above n. 10); Pind. *Nem.* 8.4ff., see also 3.30.

[12] Thgn. 1375, in D. A. Campbell (trans.), *Greek Lyric* II (Loeb 1988), with the examples of *makarismos* given by Vetta 1980, 60; Sappho frag. 49 Voigt; Anacr. frags. 357 and 428 Page (cited in translation): see Goldhill 1987, 12ff.; Sappho frag. S 282.2 Page, see frag. 51 Voigt where the locutor says: "my thoughts are divided."

take in love's affinities with other intense emotional states, such as the madness or intoxication to which I have already referred.


## 2. Physiologies of Erotic Desire

While the power of Eros may thus be wholly assumed by a person capable of expressing him- or herself as "I," it first strikes one of the specific organs that the ancient Greeks considered to be the seat of the emotions: for Alcman this was the heart (*kardia*); for Sappho and Ibycus it was the diaphragm (*phrenes*), and likewise for Pindar, who tells how Eros implants his stinging darts in a similarly selective manner.[13] Alcaeus' Helen, for her part, is struck by love in the "soul" (*thumos*) within her breast (*stêthea*): from that moment on she is beside herself, in the grip of madness. One of Anacreon's poems uses an equestrian metaphor (to which we shall return) in which love holds the reins that control the vital breath called *psukhê* by the Greeks. And Archilochus' description of the physiology of amorous feeling is even more specific:

> Such desire for love, coiled at my heart,
> Shed a thick mist over my eyes,
> Stealing the tender senses from my breast.[14]

It is certainly not easy to match these organs of feeling to our own nomenclature of affective physiology. However, Eros seems regularly to be kept separate from the organs of the intellect that, in the archaic view, constituted the seat of knowledge and will. He is to be found in neither the *noos* (mind) nor the *boulê* (will). This is not surprising since, precisely, the power of Eros cancels out all ability to understand or to make decisions.[15]

---

[13] Alcm. frag. 59 (*a*) Page; Ibyc. frag. 286 Page; Sappho frag. 47 Voigt; Pind. *Pyth.* 10.60. The same set of expressions for the effects of love are developed in tragedy: R. Padel, *In and Out of the Mind* (Princeton 1992), 114ff.

[14] Archil. frag. 191 West, cited following Alc. frag. 283.3f. Voigt and Anacr. frag. 360 Page, in P. Bing (trans.), *Games of Venus* (New York 1991). In Alcaeus' fragment, the subject of the verb *e[pt]oaise*, which is absent from the words transmitted by the papyrus, certainly corresponds to one of the figures in whom love is embodied (see l.9): on this, see D. Meyerhoff, *Traditioneller Stoff und individuelle Gestaltung* (Hildesheim and New York 1984), 76ff. and n. 40; see also Müller 1980, 90ff.

[15] Among the analyses of the psychological vocabulary of archaic poetry, it is worth citing those of S. Darcus Sullivan, in particular "The Function of *thumos* in Hesiod and the Greek Lyric Poets," *Glotta* 59 (1981): 147–55, and "An Analysis of *phrenes* in the Greek Lyric Poets," *Glotta* 66 (1988): 26–62; see also S. M. Darcus, "How a Person Relates to *noos* in Homer, Hesiod and the Greek Lyric Poets," *Glotta* 58 (1980): 33–44, and C. P. Caswell, *A Study of thumos in Early Greek Epic* (Leiden and New York 1990),

To overcome his victim, Eros resorts to his favorite medium: not touch or caresses, but one that operates from a distance: namely, the gaze that, fixing the desiring subject, now creates another subject, the one who inspires that desire. For it is in the eyes of the man or the woman who arouses the libido that Eros is most likely to dwell. Sometimes, as in Ibycus, he resorts to the ploy of substitution we have already noted at work in the case of the subject who is in love; and Eros, from beneath his own dark lids, casts the look that dissolves and ravishes its recipient, provoking in the narrator a reaction of anxious alarm. At other times, as in Alcman, this gaze, whose sweetness is more melting than even sleep or death, is attributed directly to the young girl who arouses the desire.[16] In the poetic language of Pindar's Spartan chorus leader, the verb that designates such gazing is marked by the prefix *pros-*, and the gaze is always cast in a particular direction. Focused on the desiring subject, it operates as a vector of amorous feeling.

> You must harvest desires at just the right moment, heart, at just the right age.
> But any man who has seen
> the dazzling rays
> of Theoxenos' eyes and does not swell with longing
> has a black heart forged of adamant or iron
>
> in an icy flame. Disgraced by Aphrodite of the roving gaze,
> either he struggles for money with all his might,
> or, a slave to female arrogance,
> is towed down every path. But me,
> I melt at her urging like wax
>
> of sacred bees stung by sunlight, whenever I see
> the fresh young limbs of boys. Yes, on Tenedos too
> Persuasion and Charm are at home
> in the son of Hagesilas.

Only a black heart, forged of steel or iron in an icy flame, could fail to respond to the shining rays of desire flashing from the eyes of the young Theoxenos of Tenedos, whom Pindar praises here and who is

---

who demonstrates the emotional connotations of *thumos* even when it refers to the capacity of the intellect; the organ designated by *phrenes* is described by Aristotle, *PA* 672b11; cf. Plat. *Tim.* 70a. On the meaning of *psukhê*, see J. Bremmer, *The Early Greek Concept of the Soul* (Princeton 1983), 14ff.

[16] Pind. *Pyth.* 10.59ff., Ibyc. frag. 287 Page; see also frag. 288 Page, where a soft look is attributed to Peitho, the companion of Aphrodite. M. Davies, "The Eyes of Love and the Hunting Net in Ibycus 287 P.," *Maia* 32 (1980): 255–57, has not understood the homology between Eros / the desiring subject and Eros / the inspirer of desire; but he gives the bibliography on this poem. Alcm. frag. 3.61f. Page; see also frag. 1.75 Page, together with my commentary of 1977 on it, II, 90ff., and that of 1983, 403ff.; complementary references may be found in Halperin 1986, 63 n. 5. See Hom. *Il.* 14.294: below ch. II §1, n. 8.

assisted by the equally bright-eyed Aphrodite.[17] It is clearly through sight that the recipient perceives the Eros emanating from the one who is desirable. Similarly, it is at the sight of her young friend bantering with her betrothed that Sappho is gripped by a feeling that, in all of its physical symptoms, certainly corresponds to that inspired by Eros.

Even discounting the etymology proposed in the associative tradition of the *Cratylus*, it seems fitting that Plato should conclude this physiological survey: "*Erôs* is so called because it flows in (*esrei*) from without and this flowing is not inherent in him who has it, but is introduced through the eyes."[18]

Eros thus emanates from the gaze of the one who is arousing desire and then invades the one who is desiring, enabling the latter to say first "I see," then "I love." Once Eros' piercing gaze is felt, its effect is to induce in the beholder an amorous state that he or she can assume as "my state." So it is that, in the prayer already mentioned above, Anacreon is in a position to entrust his love to Dionysus; and Pindar, as we have seen, likewise can express a wish to seize the right moment to love and give himself up to love. Similarly, Ibycus provides us with the first occurrence of the noun *erastês*: the *erastês* is the person who is seized by the emotion of love.[19] This state of erotic desire, which is aroused externally, is naturally fixed, in response, upon an object outside itself. That is particularly evident among the gods. Love for Thetis affects both Zeus and Poseidon; then Poseidon is seized by a desire for Pelops, while Zeus falls in love with Ganymedes. Likewise, when Ixion is received among the gods and his "diaphragm" is suddenly gripped by madness, he falls in love with Hera, thereby committing an unpardonable act of hubris. If justice consists in what is the most beautiful, and health in what is the most beneficial, must not obtaining what one desires (*erai*) be the sweetest of all things? And, in parallel with Theognis, could one not maintain, along with Sappho, that the most beautiful thing of all is what one loves? Whatever it may be, the object of one's desire is apprehended through the intermediary of vision.[20]

[17] Pind. frag. 123 Maehler, in P. Bing (trans.), *Games of Venus* (New York 1991); Sappho frag. 31.7f. Voigt; on the physical symptoms of love, see Lanata 1966, 76ff., and for the countless interpretations of this poem, from which I have hastily chosen a single example, see Burnett 1983, 229ff., and Lasserre 1989, 147ff.

[18] Plat. *Crat.* 420b, according to the theory of perception, especially vision, developed by the Presocratics: see Emped. frag. 31 A 86 Diels-Kranz, with the commentaries by D. O'Brien, "Empedocles' Theories of Seeing and Breathing," *Journ. Hell. Stud.* 90 (1970): 97–109. On the dissolving effect of a visual emanation, see also Plat. *Phaedr.* 250bc, and Plut. *Quaest. conv.* 681ab, with the comments of C. Brillante, "L'invidia dei Telchini e l'origine delle arti," *Aufidus* 19 (1993): 7–42.

[19] Anacr. frag. 357.10ff. Page; Pind. frag. 127 Maehler; Ibyc. frag. S 181.10 Page. For the role of the gate in Sappho's poems, see Hatherly Wilson 1996, 100ff.

[20] The following texts have been cited, in this order: Pind. *Isthm.* 8.29, *Ol.* 1.25, Thgn.

However the verb *eramai* is used, its complement is always expressed in the genitive case, a syntactical peculiarity that early on struck an Alexandrian grammarian who occasionally commented on Sappho and who produced an exegesis on her use of this word. *Philein*, to whose meaning we shall return, was regarded in the second century A.D., on the basis of its construction with the accusative, as implying an action affecting the beloved. In contrast, the construction with a genitive case required by *eran* seems to indicate passivity on the part of the designated individual, a state of dependency "that characterizes anybody whose reason has been impaired."[21] *Erôs*, which is provoked by another, is a passionate desire for that other person. Given that it turns whoever it strikes into what we would call a "desiring subject" or a "sexual subject," *erôs* at one stroke involves that person in a relationship with the "object" of his or her amorous desire.

It should be remembered that in archaic melic poetry, as later, the verb *eramai* certainly possessed a wider semantic field than *erôs*. But the field of application of *erôs* itself was not limited solely to sexual desire: *erôs* could also be a desire for war, and in one famous passage in the *Iliad* it is set in opposition to the sense of satiation that is induced by sleep, love, sweet singing, or faultless dancing. However, the melic poets, particularly Theognis in his compositions intended for symposia, excluded that love of war by using the negative form of the verb, as they also did for the longing for wealth and ambition for political power. They preferred to write of the desire for great worth or beauty. This brings us back to the eroticized desire of Alcman's young *choreutai* aspiring to please their chorus leader.[22]

Although he or she is aroused by a gaze, the one who falls in love is not invariably an entirely passive victim of his or her condition. The lover is not a victim of a purely passionate state, as is shown by An-

---

1345ff., Pind. *Pyth.* 2.25ff., Thgn. 255ff. (a distich cited as an epigram from Delos by Aristotle, *EN* 1.1099b26ff., and *EE* 1.1214a7ff., which turns the statement into a definition of happiness), Sappho frag. 16.1f. Voigt: see C. Brown, "Anactoria and the *Kharítôn amarúgmata*," *Quad. Urb. Cult. Class.* 61 (1989): 7–15.

[21] Ap. Dysc. *Synt.* II.418.9ff. Uhlig, mentioned in this connection by Lasserre 1989, 164ff. The construction in the genitive of the verb *erân* is now assimilated to the participative/partitive construction of verbs of (unsatisfied) desire: see R. Kühner and B. Gerth, *Ausführliche Grammatik der griechischen Sprache* II, 1 (Hannover and Leipzig 1898), 351ff.

[22] Hom. *Il.* 13.636ff. Rejection of the aspiration toward war: Thgn. 886 (but see, in a probably metaphorical sense, Archil. frag. 19.3 West) and Thgn. 1191. Positive aspirations: Thgn. 654, 1160 and 696 (in contrast to Sem. frag. 1.23 West); in the domain of the pleasures of the table: Alcm. frag. 17.5 Page, and Pind. frag. 52f. 59 Maehler (in the metaphorical sense); general aspirations: Pind. *Pyth.* 1.57 and *Nem.* 10.29; eroticized: Alcm. frag. 1.88 Page, Pind. *Pyth.* 3.20. See, in this connection, the (partly tentative) semantic analysis presented by Fischer 1973, 47ff.

acreon, who, as a result of the impact of Eros, claims to be as if borne up to Olympus on airy wings, or, better still, when under the influence of wine, does not hesitate to take on the god of love in a fist fight. The state of love may also take on the aspect of a quest, which, through the use of a verb such as *dizêmai*, implies seeking out the means to gratify what is felt to be a need: Anacreon deliberately sets out to catch the eye of the youth who, with his girlish air, seems able to strangle the poet's very soul.[23] For the archaic Greek poets, love also involved strategy.

## 3. STRATEGIES OF LOVE

As a strategist, Anacreon sees a way — or gets the interpreter of his poetry to see a way — to elude love, possibly after a fist fight such as that mentioned above, but in any event certainly with the intention of devoting himself, for preference, to the Dionysiac joke of a banquet. At other times he may take the opposite course of seeking out the object of his love, as in the case of Cleobulus, whose name he declines in various forms to fit in with the morphological interplay of the meanings of the verbs he uses: "I love Cleobulus, I am mad about Cleobulus, I gaze at Cleobulus."[24]

### 3.1. An Essential Asymmetry

A relationship between a person who arouses *erôs* and a person undergoing its effects is generally characterized by the latter having to play a kind of game of hide-and-seek. While the amorous poet seeks out and pursues (*diôkôn dizêmai*) the young adolescent to whom he addresses his verses, the latter on the contrary, instead of granting him his favors, eludes his lover like a mad (*margos*) Eros, with all the cruelty of a fickle kite bird.

This mismatch between the desire of the one afflicted by love and the elusiveness of the one who provokes that erotic passion is a feature that

[23] Anacr. frags. 378 and 396 Page (in so far as the formulation of the statement is not negative, implying a rejection of the fight with Eros: see Gentili 1984, 128, but also Rosenmeyer 1992, 46ff.); frag. 360 Page (see Goldhill 1987, 11ff., who points out the reversal in the image of the reins); see also Thgn. 1299ff. It is not hard to imagine that this physiological concept of Eros is evoked in the use of charms and love philters: see Winkler 1990, 71ff.; reprinted in C. A. Faraone and D. Obbink (eds.), *Magika Hiera* (New York and Oxford 1991), 214–43.

[24] Anacr. frag. 359 Page, cited after frags. 400 and 346.4 Page, in D. A. Campbell (trans.), *Greek Lyric* II (Loeb 1988); this incomplete text is provided with a useful commentary by Gentili 1958, 202ff., who relates the fight evoked here to the one mentioned in frag. 396 Page (see above n. 23); on the meaning of the verb *dioskein*, attested only here, see the gloss by Hesychius, s.v. (*D* 1926 Latte).

pervades all archaic poetry. It stems from the fleeting nature of the gifts that Aprhodite bestows upon those who, in youth, arouse desire. For the author of the *Iliad*, the ensnaring gifts of the goddess of love are constituted by luxuriant locks and beauty such as those of the young shepherd Paris. In Bacchylides, too, it is those that inflame the heart of Minos when he sets eyes on one of the girls who, along with Theseus and others, belongs to the group of adolescents sent as tribute for the Minotaur. But even if the gifts of Aphrodite are bestowed at the fleeting moment of youth's flowering, as the years slip away whoever is favored by them will become the victim of another. He will then find that the gifts of Aphrodite have become her "deeds" (*erga*)![25]

As conceived by the melic poets, love is doomed to create an asymmetrical and unhappy relationship, but it nevertheless involves an exchange. If to ask is not shameful for me, to yield is noble for him. According to a symposium poem attributed not to Theognis but to Anacreon, for Eros whatever is just (*dikaia*) is beautiful. At the heart of this poetic concept of love lies the archaic notion of justice regarded as the redressment of inequalities that have been brought about by a wrongly disturbed equilibrium.[26] The author of one poem attributed to Theognis draws from the legend of Atalanta just such a moral, intending it for the boy who, by eluding him with cunning and deceit, does him an injustice. Fair-haired Atalanta, though ripe for love, vainly seeks to elude the charms of marriage and the gifts of golden Aphrodite by devoting herself to hunting in the mountains, but despite all her subterfuges she ends up accepting the constraints of desire. In the same way, the poet will eventually catch up with the fleeing youth, probably as a result of turning the tables against him by adopting the very same cunning ploys, just as Melanion overcomes Atalanta's resistance by means of the stratagem of the golden apples.

> Wrong me not, lad (still would I fain to be to thy liking), but understand this
> with good shrewdness;

[25] Thgn. 1299ff.: on the kite bird as an image of fickleness, see 1260ff.; the adolescent with the *thumos margos* who sets the poet's heart aflame is clearly reminiscent of Eros, the *margos* child of Alcm. frag. 58 Page (see above n. 4). The same topos with regard to an amorous situation is formulated at 1329ff.: see in this connection the commentary by Vetta 1980, 87ff. and 106ff., and also n. 28 below. On the gifts of Aphrodite, see Hom. *Il.* 3.54ff. and 64, and also *Hhom. Cer.* 2 and *Hhom.* 10.2; Bacch. 17.8f.: see C. Brown, "The Power of Aphrodite," *Mnemosyne* IV.54 (1991): 327–35; on the transformation of the gifts of Cypris into *erga Aphroditês*, see Thgn. 1305f.; see also Sol. frag. 24 Gentili-Prato, and Hom. *Il.* 5.427ff. and *Hhom. Ven.* 9 and 21.

[26] Thgn. 1329; Anacr. frag. 402 (*b*) Page. This concept of justice is explained by Gentili 1984, 58ff. (with the references given in his n. 64).

[thy wiles] shall not circumvent me nor deceive me; thou hast won, and thine
    is the advantage hereafter,

but yet will I wound thee as thou fliest me, even as they tell me that the
    daughter of Iasius once fled [the young Hippomenes],

refusing wedlock for all she was ripe to wed; ay, girded herself up and accom-
    plished the unaccomplishable, forsaking her father's house,

the fair-haired Atalanta, and was away to the high tops of the hills,

flying from delightful wedlock, gift of golden Aphrodite; yet for all her refus-
    ing, she came to know the end.[27]

It is no doubt in the same vein as that Theognidean poem that we
should interpret the well-known lines in which Aphrodite herself responds to Sappho's prayer:

> But you, O blest,
> a smile on your immortal face,
> asked what was wrong this time, why
> was I calling this time,
>
> what did I most want to happen to me
> in my raging heart? "Whom shall I sweet-talk this time
> and lead back to your love? Who, Sappho,
> is doing you wrong?
>
> For if she runs, she'll soon be chasing;
> if she won't take gifts, well, she'll give them;
> and if she doesn't love, soon she will love —
> even unwilling."

Or better still: though the girl now feels no attachment, in the future it
is she who will be faithful, even against her will. As I shall again have
occasion to point out, by using the verb *philein* (love), which occurs
here in the next to last line, the Greeks emphasized not so much the
libidinous side of love (for this term could also suggest filial love or
simply friendship), but rather the aspect of trust in the mutual relationship that it established. Not to respond to love felt for you was to reject
or break the contract of trust established by *philotês*, particularly when

---

[27] Thgn. 1283ff., in J. M. Edmonds (trans.), *Elegy and Iambics* I (Loeb 1931); Apollodorus, 3.9.2, gives the complete version of the plot of the myth of Atalanta: see Detienne 1977, 82ff., Gentili 1984, 62ff., and J. M. Barringer, "Atalanta as Model: The
Hunter and the Hunted," *Class. Ant.* 15 (1996): 48–76. Contrary to what Vetta declares,
1980, 77ff., the cunning ploys of the adolescent do not necessarily imply an "infidelity"
on his part: see the parallel situation described in 1279ff. Lewis 1985, 214ff., relates the
example of the marriage of Atalanta to the process of socialization initiated by the relationship established by the *erastês* with the *erômenos*.

this was an erotic attachment; it was therefore to commit an injustice.[28]
The injustice to which Aphrodite refers in these somewhat ironical lines
by Sappho has naturally been associated with the erotic relations that
developed between the poet and the aristocratic girls who, until they
reached the status of mature women, attended her music classes on the
island of Lesbos. In this context the injustice is interpreted as a violation
of the contract on which Sappho's "school" was based. However, although Aphrodite certainly does ask Sappho which of the girls it is that
she should lead back to her "love" (philotês), all the rest of the goddess's remarks are devoted to the same mismatch that we have noted in
other poems: justice will not necessarily be restored by the girl actually
returning to Sappho's hypothetical circle of pupils, but rather because,
like Atalanta, she in her turn will, through love, come to experience the
full force of the goddess's power. The reparation that is demanded is
thus above all that the loved one, through the almost magic intervention
of the goddess, will herself one day become subjected to passion.

The equilibrium that dike demands can only be restored when the
young beloved comes to experience the fullness of adult love for herself.
Erotic discrepancy is an essential feature of the asymmetry of the amorous relationships presupposed to exist in Sappho's poems.

It is true that sometimes the relationship of trust to which erotic desire aspires is destroyed by the youth or girl coming under the influence
of a new lover. For instance, the young member of Alcman's female
chorus might have turned to Aenesimbrota had she not been yearning
for Hagesichora, the chorus leader, in a relationship that is the reverse
of the others so far mentioned (in that here it is the younger girl who is
in love with an older woman); or, to take another example, the well-
built young Lesbian girl who took Eros' role and aroused in Anacreon
the desire to play metaphorical games with her scorned the old poet's

---

[28] Sappho frag. 1.13ff. Voigt, in P. Bing (trans.), *Games of Venus* (New York 1991); on
the by now traditional interpretation of this passage, which proposes to link the negative
use of *philein* with a breach of the contract into which the girls entered when they joined
Sappho's "circle," see Calame 1977, I, 367ff., and Burnett 1983, 254ff., who gives the
references to studies that show the incantatory aspects of Aphrodite's intervention (see in
particular Segal 1974, 146ff.). The expression *dôsei*, "she will give (the gifts that she does
not accept)," presents the same absolute use as the forms *didont'* or *didoun* (on this
textual problem, see Vetta 1980, 106) in 1.1329 of Theognis, which is explained later in
the poem: these are the gifts that the adolescent boy or girl receives when he or she
accedes to maturity and can grant before becoming him- or herself the asker; see also the
lines 1381ff. A. Giacomelli, "The Justice of Aphrodite in Sappho Fr. 1," *Trans. Am.
Philol. Assoc.* 110 (1980): 135–41, rightly saw that in a relationship between a female
lover and her female beloved, justice can only be reestablished with the passing of time.
However, Stehle 1997, 297ff., has come back to the idea of "(political) reciprocal attachment" within Sappho's circle.

white locks but gaped with admiration for "another one."[29] However, more usually love in archaic melic poetry remains unrequited. That is no doubt because of the inevitable mismatch in the asymmetrical relationship that would regularly develop between a young man or woman and an older person. This asymmetry is further emphasized by the equestrian metaphor of yoking or taming that is frequently employed in this erotic poetry.

Anacreon, in particular, dreams of bridling and reining in the Thracian filly who eludes him with her sidelong glances. For while the girl or youth who arouses desire plays freely in the meadows, it is the person filled with desire who feels the yoke of subjection. In the poem cited above, it is the adolescent with his girlish gaze who holds the reins that control the poet's "vital breath." In consequence, the youth, when subjected later to the yoke himself, will in turn experience the bondage of love, the constraints imposed by the domineering Eros whom we have already glimpsed. In Theognis' poetry, the girl and the youth, respectively, become a fine racing filly, which would like to shatter the bit and so escape from her cruel driver, and a horse, which, sated with oats, submits to whoever is riding it. The relationship that is established at the fleeting moment when the adult subjected by Eros at last becomes the tamer of the adolescent who inspires him is designated by the verb *philein*.[30] But does that necessarily mean that this is a mutual love? Even when the object of desire becomes a subject of *philein* in his adolescent youth, never — at least in the poems that have come down to us — does he become the subject of the verb *eran* (desire).

## 3.2 Mutual Commitment

The fact is that, for a Greek, to enter into an amorous, if not sexual, relationship was necessarily to feel desire. Archilochus makes this perfectly clear: the blindness we have noted is provoked by an erotic desire for loving commitment (*philotêtos erôs*), not solely by *philotês*. It is

[29] Alcm. frag. 1.73ff. Page, with my commentary 1983, 337ff.; Anacr. frag. 358 Page: there is some doubt about the identity of the object (*allên tina*) before which the girl from Lesbos remains speechless: hair, pubis (as is suggested in particular by Gentili 1984, 16ff.), or another girl (see the humorous remarks of Goldhill 1987, 16ff.). The fact that in archaic Greece a woman's head of hair was regarded as erotic, and also the coupling of *tina* with *allên*, make me favor the last of those solutions; but that does not mean that the Lesbian origin of the woman of whom Anacreon sings is an allusion to the homosexual nature of the implied relationship; see most recently in this connection, H. Pelliccia, "Anacreon 13 (358 PMG)," *Am. Journ. Philol.* 86 (1991): 30–36. On the last development of the concept of Lesbian women, see Lardinois 1989, 15ff.

[30] Anacr. frag. 417 Page, with the exegesis proposed by Goldhill 1987, 14ff., and the commentary by Kurke 1997, 113ff.; frag. 360 Page (see above n. 23); see also frag. 346.1.8f. Page; Thgn. 257ff., 1249ff., and 1267ff.

clear that the person who feels the desire for a mutually amorous obligation of this kind is the poet or narrator, and that he addresses himself to an adolescent.

So often, once the relationship of trust is established, it specifically finds expression in the verb *paidophilein* or in the noun *paidophilês* (one who loves the boys). To give one example of the enchantment of love that involves boys, Theognis refers to Zeus' abduction of Ganymedes and the boy's subsequent metamorphosis into a *daimôn* (or demigod). But when such a love is denied fulfillment, the poet expresses the hope that the boy who has eluded him will never find anyone else susceptible to love at the first sight of a boy. For to be a *paidophilês* is to suffer for the sake of the *philotês* of a youth, to set a yoke upon one's own neck. Elsewhere — proving that the relationship established by *philotês* is a cruel one even when it is asymmetrical — the young man of whom Theognis' symposiast sings may, like a ship that founders on a rock, slip or break the moorings of the relationship; and in another poem, Anacreon's narrator expresses the wish that boys should enter into a commitment with him. Conversely, though, the subject who is in love and expresses his love may repudiate the relationship of *philotês*, if the boy mixes with others (*philoi*!), thereby incurring blame and reproach. Even if it is against his will that the poet does so, in the end it will prove advantageous to him: the social sanction that is implied here testifies to the institutional nature of the relationship of *philotês*. If a boy betrays such a relationship, it is in order to become the *philos* of other men. Every such relationship between a man and a youth can be defined as one of trust (*piston*); it makes the boy the adult's companion (*hetairos*). For a woman, on the other hand, it is not possible to secure a reliable companion (*piston hetairos*); she can only commit herself (*philei*) to the man of the moment. It is also possible to betray *philotês* in contexts other than that of erotic love, which is no doubt why relationships of mutual trust are sometimes said to involve not only an affective center such as the "diaphragm," but also an intellectual organ such as the *nous* (mind).[31]

[31] Thgn. 1345ff., 1311ff., 1357ff.; 1361 ff. (for the naval comparison, see the interpretation formulated by Vetta 1980, 130ff.; in the use of *peisma*, moorings, rigging, there may be a play of words on derivatives from *peith-* that refer back to trust); Anacr. frag. 402 (*c*) Page; Thgn. 1377ff., 1311ff., 1367ff.: anyone unfaithful to the bond of *philia* is associated with the *deiloi* (cowards), who are themselves opposed to the *agathoi* (brave): see Lewis 1985, 218ff.; see also Thgn. 1097ff. and 87ff. B. Gentili, "Amore e giustizia nella 'Medea' di Euripide," in Calame 1983b, 159–70, transfers to these lines the idea of a just, loving reciprocity, which is only valid in relations between adults: see Sem. frag. 7.83f. West (below ch. VI, §1.3, n. 20). On the emotional reciprocity implied by a relationship of *philia*, see L. Edmunds, *Theatrical Space and Historical Places in Sophocles' Oedipus at Colonus* (Lanham, Md., and London 1996), 121ff.; see also, for a contrasting analysis of *phileô*, Adrados 1995, 29ff., and for *philos*, Konstan 1997, 44ff.

The amorous relationships of Greek melic poetry thus seem to have to be between an adult (of either sex) and an adolescent (of either sex). With the relationship doomed to asymmetry, only the adult partner is abandoned to pitiless Eros, who stirs up the emotions so chaotically. No reciprocity can be expected here, but perhaps there is a hope that once the youth or girl who arouses such passion reaches adulthood, he or she will, in turn, fall prey to the torments of Eros. It is virtually inevitable that the subject of *erasthai* be a person of mature years. However, it is possible for Eros to prompt a form of *philotês* in which an adolescent may be attached to an adult in a relationship of mutual trust that has the approval of the community. To break this trust is to commit an injustice.[32]

## 4. A VARIETY OF PASSIONS

In the examples considered so far, the power embodied by Eros has been no more than a desire for love. Does this mean that, given the asymmetry of its effects, such a passion can lead only to platonic relationships? On the contrary, when Mimnermus expresses a wish for a death that will save him from an old age that would dishonor him in the eyes of youths and women, he describes the pleasures to be derived from the ravishing flower of youth: these include secret relationships (*philotês*), the sweet gifts of Aphrodite, and bed. Borrowing a Homeric expression, he declares that, with the aid of Aphrodite, *philotês* can lead to an amorous union. For, as we shall see, in all archaic Greek poetry, both *eunê* (couch) and *lekhos* (bed) are used metaphorically to designate a union in which love is physically consummated. Similarly, in an all too brief passage by Solon, relations with boys (*paidophilein*) find expression in a violent desire (*himeirôn*) for a boy's thighs and all the sweetness of his mouth.[33]

---

[32] This asymmetry in the erotic relations between an adult and an adolescent is reflected in the iconography (especially at the end of the archaic period) in both scenes of erotic courtship and scenes of sexual caresses: see below, ch. IV, §1.2, and the references given in ch. V, §1.3, n. 22. It also marks the speech acts represented in votive inscriptions: in Athens at the end of the sixth century B.C., an adult could swear to go to war out of love (*erastheis*) for a boy (*IG* I².920 = *CEG* 47), but an adolescent, it seems, could only declare his *philia* for the adult whose bravery (*andreios*: *IG* I².924) he admired: see Dover 1978, 123ff.

It is also worth noting that the analyses devoted to *philotês* by Benveniste 1969, I, 341ff., and by H. J. Kakridis, *La notion de l'amitié et de l'hospitalité chez Homère* (Thessaloníki 1963), 7ff., show that this term may designate relationships of kinship, of subordination, and of hospitality, which imply on the part of both sides, by mutual consent, reciprocal duties; bonds of affection may spring from these: see below ch. V, §1.1, n. 9.

[33] Mimn. frag. 7 Gentili-Prato; in Hom. *Il.* 6.161, the expression *kruptadiê philotês*,

Erotic union is discreetly veiled by metaphorical expressions, as we shall see, and is led up to through various verbal and physical approaches, most frequently a touching of the beloved's hand. For Archilochus, taking hold of Neboule's hand is an opening gambit in the game of love. The members of the female chorus trained by Alcman express their love of the chorus leader by voicing a wish to seize hold of her soft hand. With his heart aflame, thanks to the socially sanctioned gifts of Aphrodite, the king Minos represented by Bacchylides reaches out to touch the cheeks of the young Athenian girl who, in the group of boys and girls accompanying her, has been sent to satisfy the voracious appetite of the Minotaur. And in the "Cologne Epode," whose recent publication has provoked passionate discussion, Archilochus (once again), having laid the girl of his dreams upon a bed of flowers and covered her with his soft cloak, kisses the nape of her neck, tenderly caresses her breasts, strokes her glowing, youthful skin, and at last gathers her whole body into his arms and takes his pleasure with an ejaculation the exact mechanics of which continue to inspire ingenious conjectures on the part of interpreters.[34]

Ancient Greek uses two terms in particular to convey intermediary stages of desire. In association with *epithumia*, which denotes specifically erotic desire, and *hêdonê*, which designates physical pleasure or enjoyment — two words that date from a later period — Socrates, in Plato's *Cratylus*, recalls the existence, alongside Eros, of *pothos* and *himeros*. In this dialogue, *pothos* means desire for something absent, something that is somewhere (*pou*) else; in contrast, *himeros* is assimilated to the current (*rhei*) that impetuously (*hiemenos*) carries the soul toward an object that is present.[35]

---

combined with the verb *migêmenai*, denotes the furtive relationship that Anteia, the wife of Proetus, would like to have with the young Bellerophon; on the meaning of a couch/bed in epic poetry, see below ch. VI, §2.3; Sol. frag. 16 Gentili-Prato with commentary by P. Roth, "Solon fr. 25 West: 'Der Jugend Blüten,'" *Rhein. Mus.* 136 (1993): 97–101; see also, similarly, Pind. *Pyth.* 4.92 and, on contact with a boy's thighs, Archil. frag. 119 West: see below ch. III, §1.

[34] Archil. frag. 118 West is generally read from the viewpoint of frag. 119; Alcm. frag. 3.80 Page; Bacch. 17.10ff. (see above n. 25); Archil. frag. 196a.42ff. West: the meadow in which this first meeting takes place is purely metaphorical (see below ch. IX, § 1 with n. 3), and the relationship between the poet as *neos anêr* and the girl abides by precise social rules: A. Aloni, *Le Muse di Archiloco* (Copenhagen 1981), 139ff., and J. Henderson, "The Cologne Epode and the Conventions of Early Greek Erotic Poetry," *Arethusa* 9 (1976): 159–79. On the nuptial significance of the cloak, see below ch. IV, § 1.2; as for the industry deployed by interpreters of this poem to define the modes of union that are described, one of the latest attempts is that by J. Latacz, " 'Freuden zur Göttin gibt's ja für junge Männer mehrere . . .' Zu Kölner Epode des Archilochos (fr. 196a W)," *Mus. Helv.* 49 (1992): 1–12!

[35] Plat. *Crat.* 419b f.; see Vernant 1989, 140ff., who bases his entire sematic analysis on this philosophical definition.

Quite independently of this passage in which Plato proposes a number of bold etymological comparisons, in archaic poetry, too, *pothos* and *himeros* belong with a semantic field that is very close to that defined by *erôs*. Pothos, like Eros, chokes the subject who is filled with desire, breaking his limbs and leaving the poor victim gasping for breath, his bones literally shattered. Like Eros, Pothos flutters around the girl, overcome by the sight of the dress of one of her companions; and, again like Eros, he both lodges himself in a gaze and is solicited by one; and, like Eros, *pothos* may take as its object a youth who, designated in the gentitive case, constitutes its grammatical complement. Like Eros then, Pothos seizes you to fill you with langorous desire for a girl or boy you cannot possess. Yet the arrival upon the scene of the person for whom you are yearning is enough to cause an icy grip upon your ardent heart.[36] Sometimes, however, particularly in Sappho, that ardent desire can be satisfied, for instance on a bed (whose metaphorical meaning will be discussed later). For the *pothos* that overcomes a girl who is in love with a young man is itself subject to the power of Aphrodite:

> Truly, sweet mother, I cannot weave my web,
> for I am overcome with desire for a boy because of slender Aphrodite.[37]

*Himeros*, which is related to *pothos*, seems to refer to a more pressing desire that comes even closer to fulfillment. This kind of desire is also aroused by a face that is desirable, or by a laugh. Sweet it may be, but it strikes at the very organs of feeling, choking and consuming the diaphragm, the heart, and the breast. Sometimes it is a desire for boys, but in the case of one beautiful and tender girl it is an acute longing for consummation with an adult. A late-fifth-century hydria represents Himeros as a young boy who is present at the judgment of Paris: while Eros concentrates on winning over the young shepherd, Himeros and Pothos flank Aphrodite, indicating that this is the goddess upon whom

---

[36] Archil. frags. 196 and 193 West, see also Alcm. frag. 3.62 Page, Sappho frag. 22.11f. Voigt (on the use of the verb *ptoeô*, see above n. 14); Stes. frag. S 227 Page and Pind. frag. 123.3 Maehler; Simon. *Epigr.* 67.8 Page (on Anacreon); Sappho frag. 48 Voigt, with the commentary by Lanata 1966, 78ff.: see also the very brief frag. 36 Voigt, in which the verb *potheô*, formed from *pothos*, is coupled with the same verb *maiomai*, "to seek with ardor." In a line paraphrased by Plutarch, the Eros of Anacreon (frag. 444 Page) seems to have shone with desire (*pothôi*); see also Pind. frag. 123.3 Maehler. Like *erôs* and *eramai*, *pothos* and *potheô* may designate desires that are not restricted to the erotic field: see below n. 50 and also Tyrt. frag. 9.28 Gentili-Prato (funerary context), Anacr. *Epigr.* 3 Page (homesickness), Simon. *Epigr.* 74 Page (erotic connotation), Pind. *Ol.* 13.64 (desire to tame Pegasus), etc.

[37] Sappho frag. 102 Voigt, in David A. Campbell (trans.) *Greek Lyric* I (Loeb 1988), preceded by an allusion to frag. 94.21f. Voigt; see Lanata 1966, 70ff.

his choice will fall. And a famous black-figure plaque dating from as early as the mid-sixth century shows Aphrodite holding in her arms two wingless children named, respectively, Pothos and Himeros.[38]

But whether it is represented as a langorous need in the form of Pothos, or embodied in Eros, or in the guise of the more pressing Himeros, the erotic desire of archaic poetry ultimately depends on the intervention of the goddess of love. If the girl described by Sappho is suffocated by *pothos*, this sensation has been brought about by tender Aphrodite; if sweet Eros inflames the hearts of the girls in Alcman's poem, it is through the will of Cypris; and if desire (*erôs*) floods the lovely (*himertos*) face of the young wife of whom Sappho sings, again that is a gift that Aphrodite offers to her sweetheart. For the goddess of Cythera has the power to deliver a poet from the desire that grips him: when she does so, the boy he used to love loses all his appeal (*kharis*). That appeal, or charm, that arouses desire (*himeroessa*) is clearly a gift bestowed by the goddess born in Cyprus, and it is something that the boy upon whom it is showered may then grant to the adult who is courting him. As an expression used by Pindar conveys, to desire (*eran*) is already to abandon oneself to Eros and respond (*kharizesthai*) to him.[39]

Aphrodite generally acts through the mediation of these other powers of desire, but sometimes she intervenes directly, and with the same effects as those attributed to Eros. The function that Zeus has allotted her is precisely that of gaining a stranglehold on men's hearts, a hold from which not even a sage can escape. That is why Sappho appeals directly to this deity, begging her not to submit her own heart to further suffering. Ibycus, too, is well aware that when Eros directs his tender gaze at him, the purpose of its manifold charms is to ensnare him in the meshes of Cypris.[40] But Aphrodite, the hatcher of plots, is fond of company. Sometimes her playmates are Dionysus, Eros the subduer, and the Nymphs, as in the symposium poem by Anacreon mentioned earlier, in

---

[38] Archil. frag. 188 West, Sappho frags. 31.5ff. and 96.15ff. Voigt, Pind. *Ol.* 1.41; Simon. *Epigr.* 67.4 Page, Archil. frag. 196a.5 West (in which, after *himere[i]*, one can restore *lekheos* or *gamou*). *Himeros* and *himeirô* can also designate nonerotic desires: Alcm. frag. 27 Page, Alc. frag. 130B.3 Voigt, Sappho frag. 137.3 Voigt, Pind. *Ol.* 3.33, etc.; on *himeros* as irresistible desire, requiring immediate satisfaction, in epic poetry, see *LfgrE*, s.v. Pinax of the Acropolis, Athens, Mus. Nat. 15131 (= *LIMC Aphrodite* 1255 = *Eros* 1007); hydria of Vulci previously Berlin, Staatl. Mus. F 2633 (*ARV*² 1187.32 = *LIMC Aphrodite* 1429); other representations collected by A. Hermary, "Himeros, Himeroi," *LIMC* V.1 (Zurich and Munich 1990), 425–26.

[39] Sappho frag. 102 Voigt, Alcm. frag. 59 (*a*) Page, Sappho frag. 112 Voigt; Thgn. 1339ff., 1203ff. (see above n. 25, in particular on the gifts of Aphrodite), 1319ff., 1331ff., also 1372; Pind. frag. 127 Maehler. The role of *kharis* in erotic interplay is well defined by B. MacLachlan, *The Age of Grace. Charis in Early Greek Poetry* (Princeton 1993), 56ff.

[40] Thgn. 1386f.; Sappho frag. 1.1f. Voigt: cf. Burnett 1983, 247ff.; Ibyc. frag. 287 Page.

which she collaborates with the shining Graces and fair-faced Persuasion to encourage the blossoming of a handsome youth. In the above-mentioned case of Theoxenus of the flashing eyes, in Tenedos, the situation is similar: the reason why the very thought of him melts the poet as though he were wax is that it is not only Aphrodite who is at work on the island, but also Peitho and Charis, who are with her and are assisting her. Behind the look that kindles love is Cypris, the goddess who brings forth the youthfulness and beauty that inspire desire.[41] For whether the bonds that mythological representation weaves between Aphrodite and Eros are genealogical or social, whether she is his mother or his mistress, the goddess always dominates the young Eros, who is either represented as a deity or, toward the end of the archaic period, in a number of other forms. For Alcaeus, Eros is the son not of Aphrodite and Ouranos, as he is in Sappho's poems, but of Iris and Zephyr, and he is the most fearful of all the gods.[42]

## 5. METAPHORS FOR THE ASSUAGING OF DESIRE

From the visual evocation of love through its consummation on a soft bed, every stage in the evolution of love in the Greek manner is placed under the responsibility of Aphrodite. Just as pressing desire (*himera erga*) is at work behind the behavior by which one satisfies one's love by spending the entire night lying alongside a boy or a girl in the flower of youth, so too does Aphrodite have her "working methods." The donkey woman criticized by Semonides employs such methods to ensnare the first of any *hetairoi* who comes to hand. As for the weasel woman, who is devoid of beauty, desire (*epimeron*), charm, or grace (*erasmion*), her total ignorance of such methods would prove a sad disappointment for any man who deposited her on "the couch of Aphrodite." Later, even the technical language of Hippocratic medicine resorted to terms derived from the name of the goddess of love to designate sexual intercourse: the expression *ta aphrodisia*, in particular, was assured of a long future among philosophers as well as doctors.[43]

[41] Anacr. frag. 357 Page (see also frag. 346.4); Ibyc. frag. 288 Page; Pind. frag. 123 Maehler (see above n. 17) and *Ol.* 10.99ff.

[42] Sappho frags. 159 (Eros, servant of Aphrodite) and 198b Voigt (Eros, son of Aphrodite and Ouranos): see below ch. X, §1; Alcm. frag. 327 Voigt; Bacch. 9.73f. (Cypris, the mother of pitiless Erotes), Pind. frag. 122.4 Maehler (Aphrodite Ourania, mother of the Erotes; see also frag. 118 Maehler); see also Alcm. frag. 58 Page, and on this subject, Rosenmeyer, 1951, 14ff.

[43] Thgn. 1063f.; Sem. frag. 7.48f. and 51f. West. In *Les Enfants d'Athéna* (Paris 1981), 106ff. (English translation: *The Children of Athena* [Princeton and Chichester 1993]), N.

A wide field of metaphorical expressions is used to convey the fulfillment of erotic desire. In poetry, particularly archaic poetry, the sexual
act is always referred to indirectly, in striking contrast to the practice of
the contemporary iconography and, a few decades later, the crudely explicit manners of Old Comedy. Within the limits of the present work, it
is not possible to undertake an exhaustive investigation into these metaphorical expressions for coupling, but we can focus upon two that are
both common and significant.

It is on a bed that the whole erotic process guided by golden Aphrodite is consummated and completed. There, with Aphrodite's permis-
sion, the adolescent courtesans of Corinth pluck the flower of tender
youth. And it is also on a soft bed that young Apollo mates with the
nymph Cyrene in a mutual union that Aphrodite herself veils with
obliging modesty. For when the archer god declares his wish "to garner
on the bed of this brave huntress a grass as sweet as honey," the Centaur, a wise counselor, tells him that, for gods as well as for men, it is
not seemly to make directly for "the soft bed." Persuasion holds the key
to the lovemaking (*philotêtes*) that is sanctioned by the goddess.[44] The
most honored of all beds are clearly those that provide a discreet haven
for the lovemaking of Zeus and whomever takes his fancy: the bed of
desire in which the god is united with Semele, the couch to which he
flies with Aegina, surrounded by *Erotes* dispensing the gifts of Aphrodite, the pallet used for his union (*migeisa*) with Europea, to engender
Minos. But it is a bed that he is denied by the other gods when, having
been struck by Eros, as Poseidon's rival he tries to make Thetis his wife
(*gamos, alokhos*), as we have seen above. That was a union that had to
be prevented to thwart the oracle who had predicted that a union (*mis-
gomena*) between the sea goddess and Zeus would result in the birth of
a son more powerful than his father.[45]

A man and a woman finding themselves in the same bed could also be
a sign of a betrayal of a conjugal union that could itself be indicated by
the same metaphor. Jealous slander drove Hippolyte to spread the false
rumor that by being united with her in the bed (*en lektrois*) of her
husband Acastus, the young Peleus had undermined his own conjugal
bed (*numpheia eunê*). The beds that Ixion coveted because Zeus and

---

Loraux has shown that these animal women are distinguished from the bee woman by
their lack of productive *kharis*. Hippocr. *Reg.* 3.73.1, *Fract.* 35, *Aph.* 6.30, etc. On the
fortunes of the term *ta aphrodisia* and its derivatives in a philosophical and ethical perspective very different from that of the archaic period, see Foucault 1984, 47ff.

[44] Mimn. frag. 7 Gentili-Prato (see above n. 33); Pind. frag. 122.5f. Maehler: see Calame 1989, 104ff.; Pind. *Pyth.* 9.9ff. and 36ff.; see below ch. VIII, §2.

[45] Pind. *Pyth.* 3.99 (*lekhos himerton*); Pind. *Nem.* 8.5f. (*lekhos*); see also Bacch. 9.55ff.;
Bacch. 17.30ff. (*lekhos*); Pind. *Isthm.* 8.27ff. (*eunê*): see above n. 20.

Hera had found pleasure together (*polygêtheis eunai*) upon them became beds that were prohibited (*paratropoi eunai*) when the mortal hero tried to infiltrate himself there. The bed in which Coronis was unfaithful to Apollo and "lay" with a stranger (*eunasthê lektroisin*) was a bed of deception; so was the bed that, like Eros, overcame Clytemnestra by leading her astray into nocturnal unions with Aegisthus; and so too was the richly covered bed that Helen, distracted by love, abandoned.[46] In mythology a bed is essentially a metaphor for a union between two young adults. As an institutional reality such a bed was described as *homophrôn*, in that it "brought feelings together." In a matrimonial context, Sappho expressed a wish that such a bed was "younger" for a male friend (*philos*) who was her junior. And on just such a bed children were procreated, even if the wife was a foreigner. Only the primordial beings Deucalion and Pyrrha had no need of a bed (*lekhos*) to procreate the race of stones from which the human race originated.[47]

As the reader will have noticed, the sexual act that takes place on this nuptial bed is discreetly designated by a second metaphor, based on the use of verb *meignusthai*, to be united. Most such unions are fruitful. They produce the Muses, Apollo, Heracles and Iphicles, Hermes, even Eros himself! When it comes to referring to the sexual act, even Archilochus abandons the customary coarseness of his diction and resorts to metaphor, calling sexual union a "divine affair."[48] But it will also have been noticed that the image of the bed has led us away from the love of a poet, usually an adult, for some youth or girl, and has landed us right in the midst of conjugal love and its attendant procreative function.[49] And, at the same time, the erotic states and practices of the poets have been left behind and replaced by the love affairs of legendary figures and deities. Does this mean that the Greeks of the archaic period drew a firm distinction between the *erôs* of the poets and the love involved in legendary unions? Before addressing that question, let us consider the

---

[46] Pind. *Nem.* 5.25ff.; *Pyth.* 2.25ff., 3.24ff. (the term *koitê*, used here, in tragedy assumes the same metaphorical significance as *lekhos* or *eunê*: see Aesch. *Suppl.* 805, Soph. *Trach.* 922, etc., and below ch. II, §1, n. 2); Alc. frag. 283.7ff. Voigt (see above n. 14).

[47] Pind. *Ol.* 7.6; Sappho frag. 121 Voigt; Pind. *Pyth.* 4.51 (on the subject of Euphremos) and *Ol.* 9.42ff.

[48] Alcm. frag. 8.9ff. Page, with commentary by Calame 1983, 385ff., Sapph. frag. 44A.2ff. Voigt (verb object of a restoration), Pind. *Pyth.* 9.84ff., Alc. frags. 308 and 327 Voigt; Archil. frag. 196a.15 West. On the meaning of the expression *theion khrêma* (divine thing) as *mixis* (coitus), see E. Degani, "PAREX TO THEION KHREMA nel nuovo Archiloco di Colonia," *Quad. Urb. Cult. Class.* 20 (1975): 229.

[49] By the end of the archaic period, a series of terms compounded from *eunê* could refer to marriage: see for example *eunaioi gamoi*, "conjugal union" (Aesch. *Suppl.* 331); *eunastêrion*, "the marriage chamber" (Aesch. *Pers.* 160); *eunêteira*, "the wife" (ibid. 157); *eunêtor*, "the husband" (Aesch. *Suppl.* 665), etc.

representations of a number of states that complement and are associated with the state of Greek erotic love, namely sleep, death, and, finally, poetic inspiration.

## 6. The Erotic Charms of Poetry

In Greek literary culture, sleep and death, along with Eros and the secondary condition that he induces, share features in common that have been widely studied and discussed. In melic poetry, such associations are by no means absent. They are detectable in particular in the passage in Alcman's second *Partheneion*, in which, arousing a desire of such force as to loosen the limbs (*lusimelês pothos*), the girl about whom the chorus trained by the Spartan poet sings shoots him a look even more melting than sleep or death. Likewise Archilochus, to describe the secondary state into which amorous desire plunges us, does not hesitate to borrow an expression from epic language that designates the mist that clouds the warrior's sight when he falls in combat, as his legs crumple beneath him. As for Sappho, the state of physical atrophy to which Eros reduces her leads on to a sense of death—a death that she ardently (*himeros*) yearns for in another poem, where she seems to find herself "falling in love." Meanwhile, in a poem by Theognis there is a risk that his *philotês* for an adolescent boy will lead the narrator into the abode of Persephone. For a poet intoxicated with love (in Greece, intoxication constituted yet another of those states in which an individual was no longer in control of himself), the only solution left was to leap from the top of the Rock of Leucas, from an erotic trance into death.[50]

Although love has the power and control to drive us out of our minds, it nevertheless gives the poet one power of his own, that of ex-

---

[50] Alcm. frag. 3.61.f. Page, with the parallels I cited in 1983, 403ff. It is worth noting that in Homer *Od.* 20.57 and 23.343, the adjective *lusimelês* qualifies sleep, whereas it describes death in Euripides *Suppl.* 47 (see also Homer *Il.* 4.469: death); Archil. frag. 191 West: see Homer *Il.* 5.696 or 20.421, Homer *Od.* 22.88 (death); Sappho frags. 31.15ff. and also 94.1 and 95.11ff. Voigt, with intelligent commentary by Lanata 1966, 71ff.; Thgn. 1295ff.; Anacr. frag. 376 Page, with comments by G. Nagy, *Greek Mythology and Poetics* (Ithaca and London 1990), 228ff. We should note that the sense of a lack inspired by *pothos* may also be related to someone who has died: Callin. frag. 1.18 Gentili-Prato, Pind. *Ol.* 6.16; and on epic poetry Vernant 1990, 41ff. On the enervating power of the characteristics of drunkenness, see for example Pind. frag. 124a.b.11 Maehler. The correspondences established by the Greeks between sleep and death (particularly in the iconography) have been studied in particular by C. Mainoldi, "Sonno e morte in Grecia antica," in R. Raffaelli (ed.), *Rappresentazioni della morte* (Urbino 1987), 9–46: on the affinities with *erôs*, see most recently E. Vermeule, *Aspects of Death in Early Greek Art and Poetry* (Berkeley and London 1979), 145ff.; Carson 1986, 138ff.; and Vernant 1989, 134ff.

pressing himself in verse. His rhythmic words are addressed to a particular girl or boy who arouses Eros. In a fragment included in the *Theognidea*, the poet recognizes that he cannot delude himself that his love will be returned. On the other hand, he can at least respond to the love that he feels through his poetic speech, a speech of enchantment and persuasion that affects both the heart (*kardia*) and the mind (*noos*). Aphrodite's gift of the grace that evokes amorous desire is thus matched by the spellbinding words of the poet.[51]

In melic poetry in general, it is the vast semantic field of music that most often provides the metaphorical vocabulary not only for descriptions of the youthful or springlike charm of both individuals and places but also for evocations of amorous desire. Eros can be evoked by the sound of a lyre, the singing of a chorus of young people, the melody of a flute, or the song of a poet. The sound of flutes that arouses *himeros* fires the heart of a poet attending a symposium just as the adorable (*himertai*) songs of his fellow citizens honor the victor of the Olympic Games who was also the cofounder of Syracuse. It is above all to Alcman that we are indebted for a definition of the three components of the Muse's art. Each of them is described in erotic terms. Calliope, the Beautiful Voice, is represented as the inspiration for words that are desirable (*erata*), melodies that convey *himeros*, and dancing that is full of grace (*kharieis*).[52] In our very first encounter with Eros in the present study, we found him to be the inspiration for a sweetness that was also associated with pleasure derived from music and poetry.

If I may be allowed a diversion by way of a literary genre that was contemporary with melic poetry but took epic form, it is worth noting that the best example of this erotic power of song is the famous account that the *Homeric Hymn to Hermes* gives of Hermes' invention of the lyre. Here, the desirable (*eratos*) voice of the instrument skillfully played by the infant Hermes arouses sweet desire (*glukus himeros*) in Apollo's heart (*thumos*) just before invisible Eros slips into his breast. Apollo, who until that moment had encountered only the beguiling (*himeroeis*) sound of flutes, has to admit that the cithara is capable of inspiring a divine joy (*euphrosunê*), love (*erôs*), and sleep. For Solon and Anacreon, that divine joy is exactly what is produced when the gifts of charming Aphrodite are combined with the works of the Muses. Plutarch, who

[51] Thgn. 1235ff. and 1365ff.; see also Anacr. frag. 402 (*c*) Page.

[52] Stes. frag. 278 Page, Bacch. 17.125, Pind. frags. 140b.16ff. and 124a.b.1 Maehler; see also Anacr. frag. 373.2 Page (harp), Thgn. 531ff., Pind. *Ol.* 6.6ff., or frag. mel. adesp. 955 Page; Alcm. frag. 27 Page (Calame 1983, 483ff.); Pind. *Pyth.* 5.107 also uses *kharieis* to designate singing. In the Hellenistic period, Eros might, together with the Muses, become the inspiration for poetry in which bucolic themes and amorous subjects tended to become confused: see for example Bion frags. 3.9 and 10 Gow; see Lasserre 1946, 207ff.

cites Solon's distich, observes in his moralistic way that it is peaceful matrimonial love and the practice of philosophy that are characterized by such moments of divine joy, in sharp contrast to tempestuous pederastic love![53]

The very activity of producing Greek poetry, quite apart from its contents, seems to have created erotic desire and pleasure, and this spellbinding power possessed by poetry leads us on to consider the function of the poet's words of love and how that function related to the circumstances in which the words were uttered. This will involve moving from a semantic analysis of the expressions used in poetry to a study of the practices that may have provided the basis for those symbolic linguistic constructions. But before adopting that method to tackle the major theme of Part Two of the present work, we must complete our discursive inquiry by giving it a comparative dimension capable of revealing the specificity conferred upon melic poetry by its particular concepts of erotic love and the symbolic forms in which it expressed them. In the form in which they have come down to us, various manifestations of epic poetry were roughly contemporary with melic poetry, and these offer a whole range of love scenes upon which a comparative inquiry may be based.

[53] *Hhom. Merc.* 409ff.; see L. Kahn, *Hermès passe ou les ambiguïtès de la communication* (Paris 1978), 134ff. In Homeric poetry, desire aroused by song is provoked by the magical charm that it exerts (*thelgô, kêlêthmos*): see *Od.* 12.40 and 44 (song of the Sirens), or 17.514ff. (Odysseus' story), *Hhom. Ven.* 161 (song of the Deliads); see Z. Ritoòk, "The Views of Early Epic on Poetry and Art," *Mnemosyne* IV.52 (1989): 331–48; G. B. Walsh, *The Varieties of Enchantment* (Chapel Hill and London 1984), 14ff.; H. Parry, *Thelxis: Magic and Imagination in Greek Myth and Poetry* (New York and London 1993), 149ff. and 173ff.; C. Segal, *Singers, Heroes and Gods in the Odyssey* (Ithaca and London 1994), 113ff., and (1974) 143ff.; P. Pucci *Ulysse Polutropos* (Lille 1995), 263ff. (English version: *Odysseus Polutropos* [Ithaca and London 1987]); Anacr. frag. eleg. 2 West and Sol. frag. 24 Gentili-Prato cited by Plut. *Amator.* 751e, who associates this thought with the maturity of Solon, in contrast to frag. 16 (see below ch. III, §1, n. 4), believed to have been composed when the poet was still young.

*Chapter II*

## THE EROS OF EPIC POETRY

IN OUR ANALYSIS focused on signifiers we have so far concentrated on Greek melic poetry. Now let us carry that study of poetical and symbolic representations of erotic desire farther, turning our attention to the Homeric texts and others that adopted the same diction, recognizing however, that the terms selected by no means exhaust the lexical field of poetic love in the archaic period. The investigation that follows is not intended to be as exhaustive as that into melic poetry.

### 1. SCENES OF MUTUAL LOVE

How best to counter the reproaches of Helen, led to her lover by Aphrodite of the beautiful bosom, breasts of desire, and flashing eyes? Paris has just suffered a humiliating defeat at the hands of Menelaus. He now tells the heroine, who is the epitome of love, that they should forget the pains of war in the bed that he proposes to share and enjoy (*terpein*) with her: the sharing of the bed is conveyed as much by the dual form of his invitation as by the term *philotês* that is used to designate the relations of love to be consummated there. Paris' intention is to satisfy a desire (*erôs*) that has literally enveloped the hero's diaphragm, as sleep sometimes does, in a repetition of the first union (designated by the verb *meignumi*) that took place between the young shepherd and the woman stolen from Menelaus, on a bed (*eunê*) on which their relationship of *philotês* was lovingly established. Paris is the subject of the desire aroused by Helen (*seo eramai*), and certainly he alone is the victim of the sweet passion that grips him (*me himeros hairei*); but when he makes for the bed, followed by his wife, it is again the dual form that is used to designate the erotic sleep of the two lovers:

> "Come let us go to bed together and be happy in our love. Never has such desire overwhelmed me, not even in the beginning, when I carried you off from lovely Lacedaemon in my seagoing ships, and we spent the night on the isle of Cranae in each other's arms — never till now have I been so much in love with you or felt such sweet desire."

As he spoke, he made a move towards the bed, leading her to it. His wife followed him.[1]

The desire here is ambivalent: first it submerges its victim, then it is assumed by him as his own; and although the erotic desire is felt only by its subject, its satisfaction leads to a mutual relationship through a *philotês* that finds fulfillment in a doubly sexual metaphor of intimate contact on a soft bed. This epic concept of love seems very close to the models to which the melic poets refer. But there is one difference: the Homeric text refers explicitly to the pleasure derived from the interplay of love that takes place on a bed. When manifested in a relationship of *philotês*, the pleasure of love is generally enjoyed by both partners, as suggested by the dual or plural forms that epic poetry employs in such cases.[2]

Similarly, in *The Shield*, an epic text attributed to Hesiod, the desire (*pothos*) that takes possession of Amphitryon, who for many years has been denied the pleasures of conjugal love (*ater philotêtos ephimerou*), leads him straight to his wife's bed where he consummates his love in a long night of passion, enjoying all the gifts of Aphrodite: *terpesthai* and *dôra Aphroditês*—which is yet another way of referring to carnal love. Zeus, who has joined Alcmene in her bed shortly before the arrival of her husband, is for his part content to be united with the young woman "on her bed and in mutual commitment," as the conventional formula puts it (*eunêi kai philotêti migê*); the desire that he satisfies there is no more than an *eeldôr*, a longing or wish. And when the plot of the *Odyssey* is at last resolved in a peaceful ending, and Odysseus can once more invite the wife he has won back to partake of sweet sleep at his side, their dual (!) enjoyment of desirable (*erateinê*) *philotês* is complemented by the pleasure of exchanging (*pros allêlous*) words of love. The pleasure of love is combined with the pleasure of words, and, sure enough, the verb *terpein* (enjoy) used to designate both in this passage is also the

[1] Hom. *Il.* 3.441f., in E. V. Rien (trans.), *Homer. Iliad* (Penguin Books 1950); see also 3.390ff. in a scene reminiscent of the amorous meeting of Zeus and Hera in *Il.* 14.313f.: see Janko 1992, 170ff. and 201ff., and also below n. 8. It should be pointed out that the desiring subject, referred to by *eramai*, could be a man just as well as a woman: see *LfgrE* s.v., and Wickert-Micknat 1982, 99ff.

[2] Hom. *Il.* 14.314 (Zeus and Hera); Hom. *Od.* 5.227 (Odysseus and Calypso), 8.292 (Ares and Aphrodite), but at 23.345ff., where all that is mentioned is a *eunê* and sleep, the only person who experiences this delight is Odysseus! See also *Il.* 9.336ff. where the unshared enjoyment of Agamemnon has the ring of a reproach. On all these passages, see now F. Zeitlin, "Figuring Fidelity in Homer's *Odyssey*," in B. Cohen (ed.), *The Distaff Side: Representing the Female in Homer's Odyssey* (Oxford 1995), 117–52 (rpt. in Zeitlin 1996, 19–52), with an important distinction between *eunê* and *lekhos* (125ff. = 27ff.). For an analysis of *terpein* and its field of application, see Latacz 1966, in particular 184ff. and 203ff. on sexual pleasure.

verb used to describe the spellbinding effect of poetry.[3] Clearly, epic verse and melic poetry share the same power to enchant, and it is a power that is also possessed by Eros.

Better still, the first union of Helen and Paris in a bed together is designated by a formulaic expression whose uses and variations illuminate the meaning of *philotês*. The expression "to be united in amorous exchange in a bed" is one that is used, in either the complete or a shortened form, to denote the paradigmatic relationship between Zeus and Hera, and it indicates a close relationship that, whether or not it is sanctioned by marriage, is likely to lead to the generation of a descendant. Hesiod, in particular, uses it frequently when tracing the genealogy of the cosmos and the gods. Although Earth produces the very first elements, namely the sky, mountains, sea, and waves, by parthenogenesis — that is to say without any mutual relationship fostered by pressing desire (*ater philotês ephimerou*) — she then lies (*eunêtheisa*) with Ouranos to engender Ocean, the Titans, their sisters (Rheia, Mnemosyne, and others), and the charming Tethiys. This is also the form taken later by the fruitful love affairs between the monstrous Echidna and arrogant Typhon, Ceto and Phorcys, and Chrios and Eurybie, to name but a few; and in the *Catalogue of Women*, the unions between Pandora and Zeus, Philonis and Hermaon, and Alea, the mother of Telephus, and Heracles likewise all take that same form.[4]

Although repetitive, the expression is by no means redundant. It establishes a careful balance between the sexual aspect of the union to which it refers — expressed either separately or jointly by the ideas of bed (*eunê*) and intercourse (*meignumi*) — and the aspect of trust that is conveyed by *philotês*. When Circe offers Odysseus her bed, she is trying to establish a relationship of mutual trust (*philotêti pepoithomen allêloisin*) there, and places it under the sign of *philotês*. The use of the linguistic form of the dual in her speech and the inclusion of Odysseus in the metaphorical bed that Circe now regards as *their* bed (*hêmeterê eunê*) is a syntactical way of affirming the enchantress's view of what

---

[3] Hes. *Scut.* 15 and 30ff.; Hom. *Od.* 23.254ff. and 300ff. This rare use of *pothos* in an erotic context (see also Hes. *Op.* 66) confirms the general sense of a "lack," "desire for someone who is absent" (see also Hom. *Od.* 14.144); see also the rare uses of *eldomai* with this sense of erotic desire: Hom. *Il.* 14.276 and *Od.* 5.210.

[4] Hom. *Il.* 14.295 and 15.32f.; see 6.25 (a shepherd and a nymph) or 24.130ff.; *Od.* 23.219 (Helen and Paris); 19.266 (Odysseus and Penelope), 8.271 (Ares and Aphrodite). Hes. *Theog.* 132ff. (see already 125), 306, 333ff., 375, etc.: see below ch. X, §1, n. 4; note that at line 374, the relation of *philotês* that is established between Hyperion and Theia, engendering Sun, Moon, and Dawn, results from a "taming." Hes. frags. 5.3, 64.17, or 165.8ff. Merkelbach-West; see also frag. 17 (a), 5 Merkelbach-West, and *Hhom. Merc.* 3ff., with the interpretation of Homeric *philotês* given by Plut. *Amator.* 769a.

she considers to be a situation that involves both of them together. Odysseus' reluctance, in contrast, is conveyed in his reply by his omission of any mention of *philotês* and his pointed reference to *her* bed (*sê eunê*). It is true that their union was to be consummated after all, but it was to involve no mutual amorous commitment. Elsewhere, when Agamemnon defends his breaking his promise not to sleep with the captive Briseis, he similarly makes no mention of any *philotês* in that extramarital relationship, despite the fact that, in the Homeric world, both women and men were traditionally considered to have the right to indulge in such affairs.[5]

In truth, the establishment of a relationship of trust seems to have depended not so much on the union being of a conjugal nature as on the consent of both partners. In the false accusations that Proetus' wife brings against Bellerephon, the desire for *philotês* is attributed to the young man, who is represented as having been the one who wanted an erotic relationship that the woman claims to have refused (*m'ethelen philotêti migêmenai ouk ethelousêi*). On the other hand, in the version of the birth of Helen given by the epic poem in the *Cypria*, the union into which Zeus forces Nemesis after a long pursuit is marked by the reciprocity that is introduced by *philotês*, for here the point is that, though fleeting, their relationship is fruitful, leading to the birth of the Dioscuri and their sister.[6]

Like the relations of desire in melic poetry, the sexual relations of the Homeric heroes and heroines may develop into an institutional and affective solidarity that stems from the services (mutually) rendered that are implied by the term *philotês*. Whatever the circumstances in which a relationship of *philotês* is established, it is never devoid of affection. Even the highly erotic relationship that develops between Ares and Aphrodite is placed under the sign of close reciprocity: the god ardently desires the *philotês* of Cypris; the goddess, for her part, "loves" (*phileei*) Ares, and together they climb into Hephaestus' bed, to lie there *en phi-*

---

[5] Hom. *Od.* 10.334ff., 340ff., and 347; Hom *Il.* 9.132ff. and 274ff. The relations between Odysseus and Calypso reveal the same dissymmetry in expectations as those between the hero and Circe: see *Od.* 5.118ff., 153ff., and 23.334ff., together with the remarks of Konstan 1994, 170ff., and the sensitive commentary by Luca 1981, 177ff., which provides yet further Homeric examples of unshared relations. See, in contrast, the potential relationship that Odysseus would like to establish with Nausicaa (*Od.* 7.303f.) together with the comments of S. Goldhill, *Language, Sexuality, Narrative: The "Oresteia"* (Cambridge 1984), 187ff. On the vocabulary used in these scenes of amorous relations, see Wickert-Micknat 1982, 100ff.

[6] Hom. *Il.* 6.163ff.; finding himself in precisely the opposite situation with Calypso, Odysseus does not make any direct reference to *philotês* in the union into which he is forced: *Od.* 5.154.ff. (*ouk ethelôn ethelousêi*). *Cypr.* frag. 9 Bernabé.

*lotêti*, setting the seal upon their mutual love, which is appropriately expressed using a dual construction (*phileonte*):

> Ares grasped her hand and saluted her fondly: "Come, my beloved," he said, "let us go to bed and lie in each other's arms, for Hephaestus is no longer about. He has gone to Lemnos, I think, to visit his Sintian friends and listen to their barbarous talk." Aphrodite desired nothing better than to sleep with him. So the two went to the bed and lay down.[7]

## 2. Scenes of Seduction

But before such lovemaking there must be seduction and desire. The famous scene in the *Iliad* which Hera manages to persuade Zeus to leave the battlefield of Troy presents us with the epic manner of feeling love. As soon as the king of the gods sees his wife, when she joins him on the summit of Mount Ida, his diaphragm is enveloped by desire (*erôs*). Zeus immediately puts his feelings into words, using the same formulae as those encountered above, on Paris' lips. Like him, Zeus speaks of enjoyment (*terpein*) on a bed shared in *philotês* in order to satisfy a desire (*eramai* and *himeros*) that he both feels and inspires. While this passionate union puts the narrator in mind of the very first amorous meeting of these two spouses, in the description of which dual constructions predominate (*emigesthên philotêti, eis eunên phoitôntê*), it makes the god himself think of his erotic encounters with other goddesses and mortal women; these are evoked in a rhetorical *preambulum* whose effect is to enhance his present passion. For although those dalliances were characterized by desire (*erôs*) that overwhelmed the god's heart (*thumos*) in his chest, and did for the most part engender descendants, they seem in general to have been devoid of *philotês*. For the

---

[7] Hom. *Od.* 8.291ff. in E. V. Rien (trans.), *Homer. Odyssey* (Penguin Classics 1946); see also the lines 288, 309, 313, and 316; on this subject, see the decisive commentary by Zeitlin (above n. 2), 131ff. (= 1996, 33ff.), compared with the love of Penelope. The very exclusive yet classical concept of a *philotês* based on mutual self-interest developed by A.W.H. Adkins, "'Friendship' and 'Self-Sufficiency' in Homer and Aristotle," *Class. Quart.* 56 (1963): 30–45, may be contrasted to the more nuanced analyses by Benveniste 1969, I, 345ff., and B. Snell, *Dichtung und Gesellschaft* (Hamburg 1965), 24ff. and 43ff.: see in particular Hom. *Il.* 9.340ff. in which Achilles says that he loved Briseis *ek thumou*, "wholeheartedly." P. Mauritsch, *Sexualität im frühen Griechenland* (Vienna and Weimar 1992), 61ff. and 88, rightly points out that from the point of view of the terms used, Homeric poetry makes no distinction between legitimate sexual unions and extraconjugal ones, yet this observation destroys the pertinence of the typology of sexual relations through which he sets out to interpret the epic world.

moment it is Hera who overwhelms Zeus and eventually gets him to fall asleep, just as she has planned.[8]

But Hera is not the only one to seduce Zeus; nor does she operate alone. The god's passion is aroused by finery that has earlier been referred to as an *eidos*, an essentially generic external appearance of beauty. Lack of space precludes any analysis of the variety of ways that poetry represents this essentially erotic concept. Suffice it to recall that Hera's seduction plan involves her paying careful attention to her skin and to her hair, which is treated to a lengthy combing; then richly embellished apparel is added, a betassled belt, sparkling jewels, a white veil, and fine sandals — in a word, a whole *kosmos*, an outfit that, for all its brilliance, would still be ineffectual were it not accompanied by the desire (*himeros*) and commitment (*philotês*) bestowed by Aphrodite. Both *himeros* and *philotês* are accompanied by words of love and winning talk that affect the mind, the *noos* that we have already noted being beguiled in a poem by Theognis, even when the poet is spared the direct effects of *erôs*. The concrete manifestation of these two, *himeros* and *philotês*, is the breastband of seduction and charm that Cypris entrusts to Hera. This ornament has been the subject of much scholarly discussion, but at this point let us simply note the power to enchant, *thelgein*, that it shares with music. A brief *Homeric Hymn* addressed to Aphrodite suggests that clothes prepared by the Hours, combined with jewels, are in themselves enough to complete the *eidos* of the goddess born from the sea spray and to inspire each of the gods, who are gathered together into a charming (*himeroeis*) chorus, with a desire (*êrêsanto*) to make her his wife. So impressed was Plato by the means of seduction employed by Hera that, in the *Cratylus*, he even attempted to incorporate *erôs* into the goddess's (Hera's) name![9]

[8] Hom. *Il.* 14.292ff., with commentary by Janko 1992, 198ff.; see also the lines 159ff. and 237. It should be added that, to deceive first Aphrodite (1.200ff.), and then Zeus (1.301ff.) about her true intentions, Hera pretends that she wishes to commit Ocean and Thetys to a reconciliation in *philotês* in a bet that has been long forsaken: physical love between adults certainly does lead to the reestablishment of the bond of trust. The meaning of *philotês* thus cannot be limited to the sense of "Beischlaf" still attributed to it by Müller 1980, 15 and 66ff.

[9] Hom. *Il.* 14.166ff. and 214ff., with the parallels indicated by Janko 1992, 173ff.; Luca 1981, 187ff., also provides a few bibliographical references for the breastband of Aphrodite; it could be likened to the ribbons that Erotes are sometimes seen to be holding on classical vases: cf. Greibenhagen 1957, 11ff. Plat. *Crat.* 404b; see also Plat. *Resp.* 390bc. where the desire by which Zeus is seized is expressed as *hê tôn aphrodisiôn epithumia*.

On the meaning of the verb *thelgein*, see *LfgrE* s.v. and above ch. I, §6, n. 53; its most striking erotic use comes in Hom. *Od.* 18.212ff., where this verb designates the feeling of amorous enchantment that seizes the hearts of the suitors, loosening their knees at the sight of Penelope adorned by the gifts of Aphrodite (1.190ff.). *Hhom.* 6.5f.; see also *Cypr.*

Hesiod calls specifically upon Eros and Himeros to escort the goddess born from the sperm of the castrated Ouranos. But he also attributes to her the chatter of young girls and all their smiles and wiles as well as easy delight (*terpsis*) and sweet tokens of love (*philotês*). According to Sappho, the methods of seduction and tricks inspired by Aphrodite, the hatcher of cunning plots, lead both the poet herself and others into mutual commitments. The causal link that engenders the mutual commitment of *philotês* from the wiles of seduction illuminates one of the more surprising aspects of the logic of deception that governs the Hesiodic legend of Pandora. Adorned (*kosmêse, kosmôi*) by Athena in the same finery as that worn by Aphrodite herself, Pandora, the beautiful evil, is regarded by men as cunning incarnate. The longer version of the account of her creation that is to be found in the *Works and Days* spells out her methods, which depend upon lies, deception, and a scheming heart. This appears to amount to an irreversible condemnation of women. Yet in the genealogy of the *Theogony*, Deception is represented as the sister of Philotes! The tricks of erotic seduction thus constitute a necessary prelude — of which, to be sure, Hesiod is bitterly critical — to the formation of a conjugal union that, provided certain precautions are taken, may turn out happily after all.[10] The beautiful body (*eidos*) of Pandora, the girl in the legend of origins, thus changes into the figure of a wife who is faithful to the family hearth, as society would have her be.

The *Homeric Hymn to Aphrodite* provides a representation of the ultimate example of this dialectic between seduction and happiness. According to the Muse, whom the poet begs for inspiration, Aphrodite rules as sovereign over this passion (*himeros*) that she knows how to arouse in the gods and with which she also subjugates both mortals and all the animals of the earth and the sea. Yet it falls to the king of the gods, whose own mind and heart are so often led astray by the goddess of love, to inspire Aphrodite herself with sweet passion together with an urgent desire to be united (*mikhthêmenai*) with a mortal man. In accordance with the double motivation that the Greeks of the archaic period considered to rule the actions of men generally, Zeus introduces into the heart of the goddess a tender passion for Anchises. At the sight of the

frag. 4 Bernabé, in which the clothing of Aphrodite is made by the Hours and the Charites, and frag. 5 Bernabé, in which the goddess is surrounded by the Charites and the Nymphs who are also to be found alongside Cypris in Anacr. frag. 357 Page.

[10] Hes. *Theog.* 201ff. (note that in its other theogonic use at line 917, *terpsis* designates the pleasure afforded by singing: see below n. 12); Sappho frag. 1.2 Voigt; Hes. *Theog.* 573ff. and *Op.* 60ff.: cf. P. Pucci, *Hesiod and the Language of Poetry* (Baltimore and London 1977), 88ff.; the relations in Hesiod between the qualities attributed to women in general and the figure of Pandora are described by J. Rudhardt, "Pandora: Hésiode et les femmes," *Mus. Helv.* 43, 1986, 231–246; see also Hes. *Theog.* 224 and *Op.* 695ff, and Zeitlin 1996, 11 and 53ff.

young shepherd, desire for him grips the "diaphragm" (*phrenes*) of Aphrodite, who is overcome by passion (*êrasato*). Then, when Anchises beholds the beauty (*eidos*) of the goddess, who has assumed the shape of a spirited young girl with a marvelous figure and brilliant attire, he, too, in his turn, is seized by desire (*erôs*). The false story about herself that Aphrodite tells him, pretending to be an innocent girl who knows nothing of *philotês*, has the effect of doubling the *erôs* and *himeros* that engulf Anchises. The young hero takes the young woman by the hand and leads her to the bed, where he gently removes her apparel (*kosmos*). Then he fulfills his desire to share the bed (*eunê*) with her in a union of mutual love. The union between the mortal and the goddess, which is conveyed exclusively in metaphors relating to the bed, ends in a sleep for which, Anchises passionately declares, he would willingly pay with death and being plunged into the abode of Hades.

> When she had so spoken, the goddess put sweet desire in his heart. And Anchises was seized with love, so that he opened his mouth and said: "If you are a mortal, as you say . . . and are to be called my wife always, then neither god nor mortal man shall here restrain me till I have lain with you in love right now; no, not even if farshooting Apollo himself should launch grievous shafts from his silver bow. Willingly would I go down into the house of Hades, o lady, beautiful as the goddesses, once I had gone to your bed." So speaking, he caught her by the hand. And laughter-loving Aphrodite, with face turned away and lovely eyes downcast, crept to the well-spread couch.[11]

Aphrodite the seductress, driven to distraction by her very own methods of seduction, is affected not only in her heart, as Anchises is, but also in her mind (*noos*), just as Zeus is by the words of love in the passage from the *Iliad* noted above, and as is the addressee of Theognis' beguiling words. In this instance, the reciprocity of the erotic relationship that is to lead to the birth of Aeneas is reflected in the reciprocal way that vengeance is answered by deception.

## 3. BEGUILING WORDS

The *Homeric Hymn to Aphrodite*, better than any other poem, represents a seduction accomplished by means of false words spoken by the goddess, who has just assumed the appearance of a young mortal

---

[11] *Hhom. Ven.* 143f., in H. G. Evelyn White (trans.), *Hesiod. The Homeric Hymns* (Loeb 1914); see also lines 1ff., 33ff., 81ff., 131ff., and 252ff. For a comparative analysis (particularly of the scene in Hom. *Il.* 14.292f.), see C. A. Sowa, *Traditional Themes and the Homeric Hymns* (Chicago 1984), 67f., and the bibliography cited by I. de Jong, "The Bitter Bit," *Wien. Stud.* 102 (1989): 13–26.

woman as yet untamed by love. Aphrodite's lies affect Anchises with a force that equals that of the effects of Eros produced by the sight of the girl's beauty, which itself is artfully contrived. The erotic nature of the words of love that continue to be murmured even after the contract of *philotês* has been concluded returns us to the subject of the erotic nature of the poetry that tells of those words.

In connection with first Penelope, then Hera, we have already noted words of love that have the power to produce a pleasure or rapture (*terpein, thelgein*) that coincides with the effects that epic recitation itself produces on its audience. It is a correspondence to which the *Iliad* itself refers in general terms, when Menelaus contrasts the insatiable desire (*erôs*) for war that characterizes the Trojans with the satisfaction that stems from sleep, words exchanged in love, or singing and dancing. Thus, in the brief lines of invocation in the short *Homeric Hymn to Aphrodite*, the pressing desire aroused by the smiling face and blooming beauty (both described as *ephimertos*) of the goddess who bestows sweet gifts is reflected in the erotic (*himeroessa*) quality that the poet begs Cypris to confer upon his song. Similarly, as the reader no doubt hardly needs reminding, the Hesiodic Muses, who embody archaic poetry, in the company of Himeros and the Charites sing a melody and produce a rhythmic accompaniment for a dance whose echoes arouse *erôs*; this peculiar quality in their song is personified in the very name of the Muse Erato, who awakens desire.[12] And conversely, the Attic painters of the early classical period frequently depicted Eros holding a lyre or a pair of pipes, thereby indicating the musical skills that the winged adolescent was later to develop in the Dionysiac *thiasos*.[13]

In the religious representations of archaic poetics, love and poetry thus share affinities that are bound to be of interest to a scholar seeking to discover the function of erotic poetry.

This detour by way of the strategies of love has led us back to the seductive effects wrought by poetic discourse as conceived by the

---

[12] Hom. *Il.* 13.636ff.; *Hhom.* 10; Hes. *Theog.* 65ff. and 78 (see also 916ff.). On amorous *terpein*, see above n. 2; and on the eroticism of words of love, see the texts cited by Müller 1980, 53ff. On the *thelxis* of love, see Soph. *Trach.* 355, Eur. *Hipp.* 1274, etc., and above all Ap. Rhod. 3.1ff. who, playing on the meaning of the name *Eratô*, explicitly links the charm of poetry with that of love: see R. L. Hunter, *Apollonius of Rhodes. Argonautica III* (Cambridge 1989), 85ff. References to the pleasure to be derived from music or dancing may be found in Latacz 1966, 208ff., and for the charm of singing see above ch. I, §6, n. 53; the link between erotic charm and poetic charm also becomes clear from a comparison between Bacch. 17.130 and Alcm. frag. 59(*a*) Page. Note that in epic poetry, as in melic, the adjectives *eratos* and *eroeis* generally qualify either the beauty of a woman, or the charm of a song: see *LfgrE* s.vv. and also s.v. *himeroeis*, "which arouses desire" (often said of the Muses or of Aphrodite).

[13] Corpus of images put together by Hermary 1986, 907ff.

Greeks. Thus, we are now in a position to seek an answer to the question that was left up in the air when we embarked upon this foray into epic narratives. Even when the melic poets were in thrall to their erotic aspirations, the very act of poetic composition seems likely to have afforded them a certain pleasure, if not a positive satisfaction commensurate with the seductive power of their own verses.

## PART TWO

### THE SYMBOLIC PRACTICES OF EROS

# Chapter III

## THE PRAGMATIC EFFECTS OF LOVE POETRY

S I HAVE ALREADY stated, I am anxious to avoid the illusion of realism. The amorous relationships of the epic heroes and the melic poets are literary and symbolic creations that can no doubt help us to reconstruct a particular representation of love; however, they certainly do not provide a basis for any reconstruction of real sexual practices. Nevertheless, the modes of utterance and the meaning of the texts that represent those amorous relationships do offer a possible means of breaking out of the circle of internal reference and opening up a way of approaching extralinguistic, or extradiscursive, matters. Particularly promising for this purpose are the differences between the modes of utterance employed by these different kinds of texts. At the risk of oversimplification, it seems fair to say that in this respect the melic mode does appear to differ from the epic mode. By focusing on the mode of utterance of the erotic poems that we have studied and some of their functions, we shall perhaps gain access to the institutional aspects of Greek sexual practices in the domain of what we would call "sexuality."

If we adopt the enunciative distinction elaborated by Plato and subsequently adapted by Aristotle in their respective attempts to define the various forms of mimesis, the epic mode may be said to coincide with representation of a narrative type, while the melic mode turns out to be close to dramatic representation. A measure of qualification is called for, however: whereas in epic the narrator effaces himself behind the actors in his narrative, in melic poetry, because the various forms of "I" are never delegated to other actors—as they are in tragedy and comedy—the narrator becomes the principal protagonist in the action that is narrated. That is why this "I" poetry that is melic poetry is ultimately written off by both Plato and Aristotle! In melic poetry, where the narrator-locutor himself, by using various forms of "I," assumes some of the actions described in the utterance, the discourse lacks the distance that the narrative introduces in epic and that representation on the stage does in tragedy. Strictly speaking, it thus no longer belongs to the category of mimesis or, in consequence, to that of poetry. The discourse becomes confused with action: it becomes an action poem, if not an act of language, a speech act. Not only is the poet who says "For my part, I desire Cleobulus" liable really to be gripped by Eros; but furthermore, he is using those words to try to seduce the young man whom he loves. This means that the pronouns that refer to the narrator-locutor (the speaker), which are simple textual entities, may refer to an "extra-linguistic" poet—a historical figure or an imagined author whose role may be assumed by a number of performers. It also means that the modes of utterance may imply that the spoken verses are efficacious.[1]

## 1. THE EROTIC FUNCTIONS OF MELIC POETRY

From the point of view of erotic modalities, the difference between epic and melic poetry seems to be determined by whether or not the love is realized. On the one hand, epic represents a love that finds satisfaction on a soft bed in a reciprocal relationship; on the other, melic poetry tells of desire doomed to frustration, given the asymmetric nature of the amorous relationship that it postulates. In both the genres, all the protagonists are subjected to the dominating power known as Eros, a force that is terrible and allows no escape, as epic poetry itself states.[2]

However, upon careful examination, it transpires that the distinction between loves that are requited and loves that are left unsatisfied coincides with the difference between two modes of utterance: on the one hand narrative (usually epic, but sometimes melic); on the other, statements made by an "I" (essentially melic). In narrative, the actors are either gods or heroes—Zeus and Hera or Paris and Helen in the *Iliad*, but also Zeus and Europe or Peleus and Hippolyte in Pindar. For them, Eros rapidly becomes an urgent desire (*himeros*) that is satisfied by union on a soft bed. Melic poets, in their role of narrator-locutor, are for the most part obliged to accept being subjected to the damaging

---

[1] Plat. *Resp.* 392c.ff. and Aristot. *Poet.* 3.1448a.19ff. and 24.1460.5ff. The Aristotelian reorientation, which tends to confuse the two narrative modes distinguished by Plato, is well described by R. Dupont-Roc and J. Lallot, *Aristote. La Poétique* (Paris 1980), 160ff.; on the modes of enunciation of archaic poetry, see *Le récit en Grèce ancienne* (Paris 1986), 1ff. and 31ff. (English translation: *The Craft of Poetic Speech in Ancient Greece* [Ithaca and London 1995], 3ff. and 27ff.). The question of terms in the debate on the biographical or fictional identity of the narrator-locutor has recently been raised, in connection with "monodic" poetry, in the work edited by S. R. Slings (ed.), *The Poet's I in Archaic Greek Lyric* (Amsterdam 1990).

[2] Hes. frag. 298 Merkelbach-West (Theseus' love for Aigle), *Hhom. Merc.* 494 (the desire aroused in the heart of Apollo by the music of the lyre: see above ch. I, §6, n. 53). In the *Theogony*, Eros plays a particular founding role, and a study of his qualifications for it forms part of the last chapter in the present work: see below, ch. X, §1. The semantic difference that Lasserre 1946, 21ff., draws from the morphological distinction between *eros* ("the desire to") and *erôs* ("desire," probably personified) has not been appreciated by scholars (see Dover 1978, 43), with the possible exception of Fasce 1977, 10ff.

effects of a lacerating Eros that they do not succeed in satisfying. Whereas the actors of narrative feel only a force that unfailingly impels them into action, melic poets apprehend a power with whom they enter into dialogue, as they might with a god. The former are young adults, men and women, endowed with Aphrodite's gifts and responsive to her charms, who together enjoy the pleasures that she offers, in a relationship between the two genders that in most cases proves fruitful. From an erotic point of view, here the relationship between the two genders is remarkably symmetrical. Sometimes it takes the form of a legitimate marriage; but in the archaic period, it should be remembered, that was by no means the only way of forming a couple.[3] The latter are adult poets who are in love with adolescents, usually one of their own sex. From such a partner they cannot expect the shared and fruitful kind of enjoyment that is reserved for mature men and women. It is thus within relationships limited to the male — or indeed to the female — gender that the essential asymmetry and mismatch that we have noted appear.

Not that all hope of amorous fulfillment is ruled out for melic poets. The longed-for relationship may be achieved, as it is on the bed described by Mimnermus or amid the flowers of which Archilochus sings. But where the realization of desire was concerned, the Greeks of the archaic period appear to have distinguished clearly between the sexual behaviour that was *de rigueur* in their relations with adult women and the practices appropriate to the love of boys. The allusion to a desire for thighs in the fragment by Solon that suggests "paedophilia" is widely confirmed by Greek iconography. In sexual relations with adolescent boys, a particular position had to be adopted. Standing facing the boy, the adult would bend his knees slightly in order to take his pleasure between the thighs of the finally consenting beloved. Archilochus, in contrast, lays down the girl with whom he is going to make love upon a flowery meadow, and it is worth pointing out that, through this union, the coveted *parthenos* becomes a woman (*gunê*).[4]

---

[3] Vernant 1974, 55ff., in which he has clearly shown not only the diversity of the modes of cohabitation for a couple in ancient Greece, but also the absence of a definite category of marriage.

[4] Mimn. frag. 7 Gentili-Prato (see above ch. I, §4, n. 33); Archil. frag. 196a.44ff. West (above ch. I, §5, n. 34 and n. 48, where the union of the girl with the narrator is the subject of an account in the past tense), Sol. frag. 16 Gentili-Prato. This position, exclusively adopted in sexual relations between adults and adolescents, is mentioned by Aristophanes, *Av.* 669, using the technical term *diamerizein*; it seems to be implied by the homophile relationship between Achilles and Patroclus, which was set on stage by Aeschylus in the *Myrmidons*: frags. 135 and 136 Radt, with the commentaries by W. M. Clarke, "Achilles and Patroclus in Love," *Hermes* 106 (1978): 381–96, and Halperin 1990, 86ff. It is repeatedly attested by the iconography: see the collection of documents in

The protagonists of legend enjoy a relationship of mutual commitment (*philotês*) sealed by union on a shared bed, while the narrators of melic poetry generally have to make do with hoping that such a relationship will develop in response to an erotic desire that the young adolescent may in some cases satisfy by adopting a particular physical position, but that he cannot feel himself. The reciprocal nature of the relations of the gods and the heroes thus stands in contrast to the already mentioned asymmetry of the relations evoked in poetry and no doubt, experienced by the melic poets or those who sang their verses. Does that mean that there were two, clearly distinct ways of making love, the one in the heroic, the other in the human mode? In truth, the difference that we have noted relates only partly to the quality of the protagonists of the amorous relationships in question: relationships, on the one hand, of mutual love between young adults, as also existed in the social practice of people in the archaic period, and, on the other, asymmetrical love between adults and adolescent boys or girls. It also stems from two distinct ways of representing love, from two different poetic genres, which depend on different circumstances of utterance.

Yet the language used in different literary genres and above all for dissimilar poetic situations, and even for specific physical positions adopted in the sexual act, is a language that is shared in common. That is the paradoxical finding that emerges from a comparative linguistic reading of epic poems and melic compositions. Apart from certain nuances that we have already noted, the passionate desire that Homer's Paris feels for Helen is formulated in the same way as the yearning that burns in the hearts of Alcman's young *choreutai* members. Even within the confines of melic poetry, the very same amorous language is used by protagonists who occupy altogether different enunciative positions. While the partner evoked through the figure of Eros in the two erotic poems by Ibycus is of unspecified sex, Anacreon, or his narrator, is as likely to fall in love with an adolescent boy as with a girl. The erotic verses composed by Theognis are regularly addresses to a *pais*, which probably indicates the male gender, while Sappho, for her part, expresses her love for young girls who, under her tuition, are acquiring precisely the charms appropriate for women destined for marriage. Mimnermus attributes a preoccupation with bed, the gifts of Aphrodite, and secret pledges to men and women for whom the flower of youth is desirable; and in the indirect perspective adopted by his narrator-locutor, that desirable youthfulness is as likely to be embodied by boys

---

Dover 1978, 98ff., and Reinsberg 1989, 194ff.; see in particular the inscription "in exchange grant me your between-thighs" on an Attic lecythos, coll. Lord Guilford (*ABV* 664, *Paralip.* 317), representing athletes.

as by women. And in Alcman's poetry, amorous relationships are represented in a doubly different perspective in that here an adult poet puts into the mouths of young girls words of love that are in all probability addressed to a woman on the threshold of adult maturity.

It is clearly pointless to seek to draw a decisive distinction, in the erotic language of poetry in archaic Greece, between heterosexual and homosexual relations; and similarly, still at the linguistic and poetic level, differences of gender seem obscured to the extent that men and women adopt exactly the same language when confronted with the effects of Eros. Any attempt to draw a firm distinction would smack of anachronism and Eurocentricity. All the same, to refer to the particular nature of relations between adults and adolescents of either sex, let us from now on use the term *homophilia*, rejecting *homosexuality*, which is too general, and also *pederasty*, which is limited by linguistic convention to masculine relationships.[5] Our use of such a distinctive term, however, should not obscure the fact that the passion aroused in an adult male by an adult female adorned by all the charms bestowed by Aphrodite is expressed in just the same manner as the desire produced in a person of ripe maturity by the tender bloom of an adolescent: in both cases Eros leads to *philotês* or *philia*.

On the other hand, such relationships do differ not only in the manner in which they reach fulfillment, as has been noted above, but above all in their respective modes of enunciation. The former culminate in a union involving mutual commitment. Their enunciation always takes the form of a narrative, although this may be either epic or melic. So they stem, through literature, from the narrative past constituted by legend, and, as has been noted, they thus refer us back to the world of heroes and gods. Relationships of the latter type, particularly where the couple is homophile and masculine, only occasionally find satisfaction, so they are constructed solely on the basis of the desire expressed by the speaker, in the present tense, at the very moment of the enunciation of his poem. It is as if, in default of full physical realization, the poet's words were substituted for the act, so as—so to speak—to sublimate its impossibility.

Archaic erotic poetry, blessed with the same powers of seduction as

---

[5] Halperin 1990, 30ff., has strongly drawn attention to the irrelevance, in classical Athens, of the distinction between "homosexuality" and "heterosexuality." He replaces this by a distinction between an active role and a passive one, which corresponds to neither the love affairs of legend nor even the sexual reality of relations of homophilia: see below ch. V, n. 18. It is worth noting that a sacred law from Cos dating from the fourth century B.C. (151.A.42 Sokolowski) refers on the same level to the impurities that result from heterosexual and homosexual relationships: see the philological commentary by Parker 1983, 86 and 94.

music, could therefore be regarded as a possible means of correcting the imbalance inherent in any relationship between a person of riper years who is full of desire and an adolescent (either a boy or a girl) who provokes that love and at the same time foils it. All the rhetoric of the love poetry of the melic poets seems designed to get this linguistic act to compensate for the crippling effects of the amorous mismatch. The strategy employed by melic poetry is essentially a strategy of poetic speech, with its repetitive and to some extent formulary response to a searing desire that seems to recognize no distinction between the genders.[6] Amorous fulfillment seems to find a substitute in poetic delight, a compound of seduction and magical charm both for the poet and for any of his listeners who are also preyed upon by the torments of love. It is a substitution that is facilitated by the close association that links both love and poetry with that magical charm.

## 2. THE LOVES OF ALEXANDRIAN WRITERS

This pragmatic function of archaic erotic poetry is surely one that it is fair also to assign, at the other end of the spectrum represented by ancient literature, to the Hellenistic and subsequently to the Roman epigram. The erotic epigrams of poets such as Asclepiades, Meleager, or, much later, Strato are all short poems comprising elegiac distichs similar to the verses of Theognis, and they all constitute poetic manifestations of an "I" grappling with the torments of love; they are addressed to an implied addressee in a situation that is made very specific even if it is probably fictitious. Furthermore, they all similarly seem to constitute either attempts at seduction or poetic substitutes for it in situations of unrequited love. The similarity is emphasized by all the references that

---

[6] Most recently, Carson 1986, 117ff., has returned to the collection of the countless erotic poems that begin with the adverb *dêute*, which refers the lived experience described in the poem in the present tense back to past experiences; but at the time of Alcman and Sappho, such a reference to the past could not be considered as a written objectivization of Eros. Poetic eros was an act because it was preferred and repeated, apparently independently from any categories or points of view of gender. In this respect, the study by M. B. Skinner, "Woman Language in Archaic Greece, or, Why Is Sappho a Woman?," in N. S. Rabinowitz and A. Richlin (eds.), *Feminist Theory and the Classics* (New York and London 1993), 125–44, is too crude at the level of linguistic analysis to justify the detection of a typically feminine perspective in the poetry of Sappho. See, most recently, through a critique of Foucault, duBois 1995, 152ff., with the balanced chapter, entitled "Sexuality and Ritual," in M. Williamson, *Sappho's Immortal Daughters* (Cambridge, Mass. and London 1995), 9ff., and the sensitive observations of Hatherly Wilson 1996, 103ff. Contrary to those studies, Stehle 1997, 289ff. and 323ff., sees in some of Sappho's poems *Rollengedichte*, creating fictional characters and situations not by sung performance but by writing.

these poems make to a physiology of desire whose tradition was introduced by archaic poetry.

## 2.1. Thematic Variations

For Meleager of Gadara in particular, Eros was still—in the eastern
Mediterranean of the first century B.C.—that same wild, terrible,
winged child armed with his bow and arrows, babbling on amid sweet
tears mingled with smiles but at the same time capable of striking down
his victims with shots both swift and bold. On the basis of his physical
effects, he was still perceived as a god of contrasts. Erudite poets now
felt a need to comment as well as to play upon the meaning of his
attributes. One reason why Eros is called bittersweet, Meleager explains, is that he mixes honey with bitterness, in that the darts that he
shoots ignite a love that burns; for the honey tasted by unhappy lovers
burning with a love of boys is indeed bitter, and that fire can only be
doused by icy water. Admittedly, elsewhere the same Meleager expresses
astonishment that, with origins such as hers, Cypris was capable of engendering such ardor amid the element of water.[7]

In all the epigrams evoked here, the stinging erotic bitterness embodied by the fiery arrows of Eros is associated with the gaze. Either a torch
burns in the eyes of the provocative boy, or Eros the archer, with a
penetrating gaze himself, hides in the eyes of the beloved, or else the
archer shoots a steely firebrand into the eyes of the narrator himself,
whose heart (*kardia*) eventually goes up in flames. For, as in archaic
poetry, the heart is Eros' favorite target. Once struck, it acquires such
autonomy that, metaphorically, it can become the ball that the playful
Eros tosses into the camp of the beloved, who is at play there with her
companion Pothos. Ultimately, love affects the very breath of life
(*psukhês pneuma*). Reproducing the contrasting effects of Eros' action,
the gaze of the beloved, which is capable of speaking even to the blind,
is just as likely to bring the clouds of winter as the flowers of spring:

> My life's cable, Mysicus, is made fast to thee;
> in thee is all the breath that is left in my soul.

[7] *Anth. Pal.* 5.177 and 178: see Lasserre 1946, 205ff., who remarks that these descriptions fit with the "theme" of the antagonism between the winged child and Aphrodite (see
Ap. Rhod. 3.91f.); 12.154, 109, 81 and 5.176: A.S.F. Gow and D. L. Page, *The Greek
Anthology* II (Cambridge 1965), 663, 641, 654, 611, etc., constantly point out the traditional nature, despite a number of variations, of these descriptions of Love in Meleager;
see also Rosenmeyer 1992, 181ff. One could also refer to *Anth. Pal.* 12.84, where the
poet compares the fire of Eros that seizes him to the wave of Aphrodite that crashes upon
him, even more bitter and salty (*pikroteron*) than the seawater from which he has just
emerged: third metaphorical use of the polysemic *pikros*.

For by thy eyes, dear boy, that speak even to the deaf,
and by thy bright brow I swear it,
if ever thou lookest at me with a clouded eye I see the winter,
but if thy glance be blithe, the sweet spring bursts into bloom.[8]

Often, there is nothing to distinguish Eros the archer from the boy who is so desired. For example, the object of Meleager's love, young Myiscus himself, with his gaze, directs the arrows aimed at the poet's chest (*sterna*). This particular epigram ends by comparing the adolescent to the Eros who gained a hold even on Zeus. Elsewhere the poet declares that his only means of distinguishing between Eros and his young beloved are the wings and bow possessed by the former: were it not for these, Aphrodite herself would be unable to tell them apart.[9] Furthermore, for Meleager as for his predecessors, Asclepiades of Samos and Alcaeus of Messene, love for these boys who so resemble Eros is marred by exactly the same discrepancy as in the archaic period. The youthful Diodorus who used literally to bowl young men over with his flashing eyes, is now, in his turn, in thrall to the eyes of Timarius, and is himself a victim of the shots of bittersweet Eros. Hearing Alcaeus of Messene declare that the handsome Protarchus, who now refuses to bestow his favors, soon will be longing to do so, we are put in mind of Sappho and her remarks about the fleeting nature of the flower of youth. The boy to whom Asclepiades addresses his verses likewise eventually becomes the "asker"; by now his cheeks are covered by a light down:

Now you offer yourself, when the tender bloom is advancing under your
    temples
and there is a prickly down on your thighs.

---

[8] *Anth. Pal.* 12.159 (W. R. Paton [trans.], *The Greek Anthology* IV [Loeb 1948]), 12.63 (where the narrator is affected by the visualized or internal inflaming words of two boys at the same time!), 5.177 and 178, 12.83 (see also 5.179 and 12.82 on the characteristics of Eros or, for the active gaze of the lover, 12.60) and 5.214; see also the epigram 12.161, attributed to Asclepiades, in which the eye of the boyish girl projects flashes of desire (*himeros*); on the affinities between Eros and Hades, see 16.213; but the gaze that arouses desire may also be conceived as a sweet, moist wave: 12.68. H. Maehler, "Symptome der Liebe im Roman und in der griechischen Anthologie," in H. Hoffman (ed.), *Groningen Colloquia on the Novel* III (Groningen 1990), 1–12, notes a number of cases where psychological explanations have been offered for this traditional physiology of love; see also K. J. Gutzwiller, *Poetic Garlands* (Berkeley 1998), 122ff. and 276ff.

[9] *Anth. Pal.* 12.101; 12.76, 77, and 78 (the epigram 12.75 of Asclepiades introduces the same assimilation; see also 12.97, attributed to Antipater of Thessalonika): see W. Ludwig, "Die Kunst der Variation im hellenistischen Liebesepigramm," in *L'épigramme grecque. Entretiens sur l'Antiquité classique* XIV (Vandoeuvres and Geneva 1968), 299–334. For a collaboration between Eros, Pothos, and Cypris, see also 12.167; as for the name Myiscus, see below ch. V, §2.3, n. 35.

And then you say "I prefer this." But who would say
that dry stubble is better than the eared corn?[10]

Alexandrian poetry revived traditional ways of expressing love and representing its effects, while introducing its own variations. But in this
erudite poetry, so prone to witticisms, the play on meanings in which it
delighted may also become explanatory exegesis. In one famous epigram by Callimachus, poetry that becomes a substitute for love is said
to have the function of a charm. The Alexandrian poet almost certainly
found the inspiration for this attribution in the *Idyll* composed by his
colleague Theocritus. In this, Polyphemus, the shepherd burning with
love for Galatea, discovers that the art of the Muses works like a *phar-
makon*, a cure for the wound inflicted by the arrows of Cypris. For
Callimachus, too, poetic speech is the best antidote — an effective rem-
edy and magic formula — for the wounds of Love. Used as a substitute,
a poem has the effect of a catharsis, but it can also be used as currency
in a trade-off: in a prayer that Alcaeus of Messene addresses to Zeus, a
poem that is a gift from the Muses is offered in exchange for the love of
the latter-day Ganymedes, with whom the poet is in love.[11]

Did Hellenistic erotic poetry, which reinforced a conception of Eros
that was already well established, gain in efficacy through the variations
that it introduced?

## 2.2. Erotic Games

To claim that Hellenistic poetic speech was directly efficacious would be
to overlook the crucial distancing effect that the art of irony introduces.
For Eros was quite likely and clever enough to block the appeals of any
poet. At the end of the Alexandrian period, Meleager was complement-
ing the corpus of his predecessors' epigrams with productions of his
own, and was thereby reorienting the traditional concept of love. Now
a poet was likely to hesitate between the love of the mother, the adult
Aphrodite, and that of the son, the adolescent Eros. An equivalence was

---

[10] *Anth. Pal.* 12.36 (where there is probably a pun on the word *aitês*, in W. R. Paton
[trans.], *The Greek Anthology* IV [Loeb 1948]); see also 12.109 and 29; at 12.144, Eros
himself, in a subtle wordplay is somehow the victim of this same amorous timelag.

[11] Theocr. 11.1ff. and 80ff.: see H. Erbse, "Dichtkunst und Medizin in Theokrits 11.
*Idyll*," *Mus. Helv.* 22 (1965): 232–36. Call. *Epigr.* 46 Pfeiffer = *Anth. Pal.* 12.150, with
the commentary by Gow and Page, above n. 7, 157ff., and the remarks of G. Giangrande,
"Kallimacheische Beiträge," *Hermes* 91 (1963): 151–59; see also 12.100. Alcaeus of Messene: 12.64; the poet's comparison between Ganymedes and the boy whom he loves is one
that occurs frequently in Alexandrian erotic epigrams: see S. L. Tarán, *The Art of Variation in the Hellenistic Epigrams* (Leiden 1979), 7ff.

now explicitly postulated between love in the feminine and love in the masculine, even if in the shaft of irony that rounded off the epigram Aphrodite herself ended up by giving the advantage to the young Eros. Thanks to the identical vocabulary that continued to be used to describe both modes of love, their respective functions were no longer distinguishable. If one was struck by the lightning blast of masculine ardor rather than by desire aroused by a woman, it was simply because that was the will of Eros. But it was also possible for the narrator to turn his back on lewd creatures with hairy backsides, leaving them to goatherds who were even prepared to mount their own goats, and instead devote himself for preference to the love of women (*stergê thêlun erôta*). In that case his goal would be a beautiful wife, a bedfellow fit for epic heroes. In the vocabulary that we shall find in Old Comedy, "homosexual" pleasure in sodomy replaces the specifically homophile pleasure to be derived from between-the-thighs lovemaking.[12] The identity of the vocabulary used in the archaic and the classical periods to express two completely different kinds of erotic desire later evolved into an equivalence between interchangeable terms that could be used to express either love for boys or love for a woman (although the latter seems to have been considered likely to lead to a more lasting relationship).

At the same time, the amorous relationship between an adult poet and the youths that he pursued lost its asymmetry. To be sure, particularly in Meleager's poetry, the gaze remains Eros' preferred weapon, but it sometimes turns into a wink that may be accompanied by a furtive kiss.

> Save me, good sirs! No sooner, saved from the sea,
> have I set foot on land, fresh from my first voyage,
> than Love drags me here by force, and as if bearing a torch in front of me,
> turns me to look on the loveliness of a boy.

[12] *Anth. Pal.* 5.176; 12.86 and 87; 12.41 and 5.208 in W. R. Paton (trans.), *The Greek Anthology* IV (Loeb 1948): other parallels can be found in Gow and Page, above n. 7,613 and 658. With the same sense of a joking rejection of either young men or young women, see also 12.17 (the desire felt for a man is proportionate to his physical strength), 12.90 (the narrator, who remains anonymous, is engaged in amorous combat with a courtesan, a girl, and a young man), or 5.277 (the love of a woman, which is founded on *philia*, is more lasting). The change of position adopted by an adult making love with a boy is also noticeable at 12.7, 38.206, 245, etc.; misled by his synchronic perspective, Dover 1978, 99ff., wrongly sets these "homosexual" practices on the same level as those of the satyrs who, in the classical period, formed a quite separate category (see below, ch. IV, §1.2); a similar confusion is evident in Cantarella 1988, 44ff. On Ancient Comedy in the classical period and sodomy, see below ch. VII, §1.1. The art of the barbed remark in the Alexandrian erotic epigram is demonstrated by D. H. Garrison, *Mildfrenzy* (Wiesbaden 1978), 33ff.

I tread in his footing, and seizing on his sweet image, formed in air,
I kiss it sweetly with my lips.
Have I then escaped the briny sea but to cross on land
the flood of Cypris that is far more bitter?

Sometimes the poet addresses his own eyes, those boychasers that end
up being roasted in a fire of beauty, by decree of Eros, the cook. Descriptions of the lover's gaze hunting down its quarry contain a hint of
reciprocity: when the boy is all seductive winks, the covetous gaze that
responds to those winks may lead to paralysis for the lover.[13] The glance
that inspires desire is matched by the gaze of the one who sought it out.

A hitherto unknown reciprocity is certainly suggested by Dioscorides
when he warns of the kisses that his very youthful beloved will be giving his lovers once he reaches the age of maturity. This new development, which was detectable by the beginning of the Alexandrian period,
continued in the centuries that followed. For a poet such as Strato, age
group from twelve to seventeen possessed its own particular charm. But
whoever sought out the desire of an older boy, he suggested (using a
Homeric expression that indicated a verbal reply), was in quest of a
response and therefore of reciprocity. At this point, love for a boy became the very real equivalent of love for a woman.[14]

Expressing these shifts, the erotic epigram seems to have become a
purely literary game, designed to entertain intellectual groups on the
lookout for sophisticated poetic amusement. No doubt a love poem
might still be based on a real sentimental situation, but it is hard to see
how the allusive and erudite style of these scholarly poets could have
produced upon the poet's young masculine partners or upon a loved
woman the same seductive effect as that of the elegiac distiches of archaic poetry. The charm of erotic verses continued to weave its spell,
but on a different public and with a different function.[15]

---

[13] *Anth. Pal.* 12.84; see also 12.68. On the paralyzing effects of the gaze of boys, see
also 12.93 (Rhianos), 12.92 and 94; see also 72. For constant characteristics of the amorous gaze in post-Alexandrian literature: M. Bettini, *Il ritratto dell'amante* (Turin 1992),
167ff.; in the novel in particular: F. Létoublon, *Les lieux communs du roman* (Leiden,
New York and Cologne 1993), 137ff.

[14] *Anth. Pal.* 12.14 and also 12.4 on masculine love that is prolonged beyond adolescence; see also 12.10; see Cantarella 1988, 58ff. Expected reciprocity: 12.183. For play on
the absence of reciprocity, deplored in particular by Sappho: 12.203. Paul Silentiarius, at
5.255, goes so far as to describe the embrace in an amorous union. D. Konstan, "La
rappresentazione dei rapport erotici nel romanzo greco," *Mat. Disc. Anal. Testi Class.* 19
(1987): 9–27, points out that later, in the novel, under the effect of the equality introduced into amorous relations between men and women, the sexual roles tend to become
equivalent.

[15] G. Giangrande, "Sympotic Literature and Epigram," in the work quoted above in n.

Probably even more significant was the change in the homoerotic act implied by a poet dreaming not of a boy's thighs but of anal sex of the crudest kind. Might not this change in sexual behavior constitute a physical sign of the rejection of relations of *philia*? Such relationships, constructed in melic poetry, were rendered null and void by love that, though still of a pederastic nature, had lost its erstwhile educational aspect (which will be discussed later). Plutarch, writing after the Hellenistic period, was no doubt affected by this tendency, and his reaction was to transfer to conjugal relationships all the values attached to mutual trust and education that the archaic poets had attributed to an *erastês*'s love for an *erômenos* — to the lover's love for a beloved one.[16]

## 2.3. Love in the Novel

The most striking — albeit late — confirmation of this change of attitude toward relations of homophilia, and also of the concomitant shift in the functions of those relations, is without a doubt to be found in the novels written under the Roman Empire, such as, to give one example, Longus' *Daphnis and Chloe*. Although love constitutes the moving force of the plots of all the Greek novels that have come down to us, homophilia and homosexuality play only a marginal part, of an accidental, or anecdotal nature.

In Longus' novel, the love that Gnathon, the bearded city dweller feels for Daphnis, a young and tender goatherd, serves merely to slow down the plot that eventually leads to conjugal union between the handsome adolescent and the graceful, innocent Chloe. To be sure, when speaking of his feelings and justifying them, Gnathon refers back to mythical models: Apollo's love for Branchus, Aphrodite's for Anchises, Zeus' for Ganymedes, all three immortals who fell in love with young shepherds. Going one better, apparently inspired by memories of Plato, he claims to be in love with the beauty imprisoned within the body of this simple goatherd. What is important is beauty, which is associated with the condition of free men, never mind how it is embodied, even if it be by a slave. It is a beauty given material form by hyacinth-like curls, shining eyes, precious gems set in gold, and a mouth with ivory teeth that cries out for kisses. Gnathon's apologia is con-

---

9, 93–174, reveals the many thematic and stylistic resemblances between the Alexandrian and post-Alexandrian epigrams and the tradition of archaic symposiac poetry, but he also shows that the intended audiences of the two were not the same.

[16] Plut. *Amator.* 751cd, 767e, and 769a in particular; these passages are the subject of a brief commentary in M. Foucault, *Histoire de la Sexualité* 3 (Paris 1984), 224ff. (English translation: *The History of Sexuality* 3 [New York 1986]); see also Cantarella 1988, 102ff.

demned as that of a "sophist," all the more easily given that he has already been described as an inveterate drinker and a glutton. Quite apart from an allusion that assimilates him to a Homeric beggar, his very name suggests that essentially he is just a jaw or a belly, as befits his status as a parasite.[17] Gnathon, who is a keen participant in banquets and carousels, behaves somewhat like a satyr, which makes it all the more believable that his love for the goatherd of servile status is of a bestial nature and that his aim is to violate Daphnis just as a ram mounts a she-goat. With its allusion to sodomy, this very degradation of the city dweller into an animal is itself condemned as unnatural since bucks have never been seen to mount other bucks, nor rams to mount other rams, nor cockerels to mount other cockerels. By the second century A.D., nature had its rules and already served as the basis of fantasies about a new civilization in which *technê* (skill or art) would draw its inspiration from *phusis* (nature). With its tendency to set the highest value upon conjugal love, which had rediscovered its natural roots, Longus' novel inevitably used the very failure of all Gnathon's efforts to suggest that any relations between the adult *erastês* (city dweller) and the young *erômenos* (goatherd) must err on the side of the "unnatural," and so to condemn them. The relationship of homophilia was reduced to the level of homosexual practice, which was contrary to nature.[18]

Many contemporary critics have declared *Daphnis and Chloe* to be the novel of initiation par excellence. Actually, it is probably not an allegorical account of a ritual initiation into a mystery cult; nevertheless, the plot certainly is designed to set love on a pedestal. The narrator himself explains that its purpose is to serve as a means of *propaideusis*, to provide a lesson for readers still innocent of amorous experience.[19]

[17] Long. 4.10ff. and 16ff.; the Homeric allusion implied in the reference to Gnathon's *gastêr* has been recognized by O. Schönberger, *Longos. Daphnis und Chloe* (Berlin ⁴1989), 122ff.; the Homeric figure of the beggar who is all stomach has been studied in particular by J. Svenbro, *La parole et le marbre* (Lund 1976), 50ff.

[18] This is why this relationship is condemned, just as in the classical period, already, homosexual relationships between adults were mocked: see Goldhill 1995, 48ff.; and below ch. VII, §§1.1 and 1.2. D. Teske, *Der Roman des Longos als Werk der Kunst* (Munich 1991), 43ff., has clearly shown the interaction between the two concepts, *tekhnê* and *phusis*, in the construction of the space of the novel and in the very concept of the work.

[19] The most recent initiatory interpretation of *Daphnis and Chloe* was presented as a palinode by R. Merkelbach, *Die Hirten des Dionysos* (Stuttgart 1988); see, in this connection, the critical remarks of R. Turcan, "Le roman initiatique," *Rev. Hist. Rel.* 143 (1963): 149–99, on the first version of a mystic interpretation of the work. The idea of a *paideusis* for the protagonists of the action and also for the reader does provide a framework for Longus' novel: *Praef.* 3 and 4.40.3. The aspects of an initiation to love and marriage of this propaedeutic work have been studied by H.H.O. Chalk, "Eros and the Lesbian Pastorals of Longus," *Journ. Hell. Stud.* 90 (1960): 32–51; see also Winkler 1990, 101ff.

However, the agent of this adolescent's initiation to erotic love is no longer an adult man who in this way contributes to the boy's education; instead it is the townswoman Lycanion (!). Once this urban seductress has taught him the various moves and caresses that can excite her sexual ardor and the "technical" means (*entekhnôs*) to elicit a sexual response from her, all Daphnis has to do is heed the instructions of Nature.[20] Under the aegis of Eros, the whole novel boils down to a heterosexual initiation into the gestures, words, and ways of arousing the kind of love whose permanence can be assured by marriage. The love of boys, which is rejected as satyresque bestiality that is contrary to nature, has lost all the educative functions that — as we shall see — the poetry and institutions of the archaic period attributed to it. The learned prose of Longus certainly operates by recreating the effects of the magical charm characteristic of archaic poetry, effects that give the novel a propaedeutic power,[21] and in this way the much later novel reproduces the archaic combination of an experience of amorous desire and an erotic utterance. However, the love of boys is here presented as a purely parodic element in that combination.

But there is more to the function of Greek poetry than *terpein* (enjoy), which constitutes but one of its effects. To formulate and support the hypotheses on the function of erotic poetry that have been suggested above, we must now turn our attention to other forms of symbolic expression.

[20] Long. 3.15ff.; on the combined influence of *phusis* and *tekhnê* in the amorous education of Daphnis and Chloe, see Teske, above n. 18, 35ff., and above all the study by F. I. Zeitlin, "The Poetics of Eros," in Halperin, Winkler, and Zeitlin 1990, 417–64. The marginalization of homoerotic love in the Greek novel thus depends not so much upon the reference to the Homeric model, as is maintained by B. Effe, "Der griechische Liebesroman und die Homoerotik," *Philologus* 131 (1987): 95–108, as upon profound changes in the concepts of love (and education) at this period. The Greek novel promotes above all mutual love in marriage; the paradigm, since the time of Callimachus, being the myth of Acontius and Cydippe (*Aetia* frag. 67 Pfeiffer): see M. Fusillo, *Il romanzo greco* (Venice 1989), 56ff., 186ff., and 228ff.; see also Konstan 1994, 79ff.

[21] These effects are well described by Zeitlin, above n. 20, 425ff., and Kennedy 1993, 77ff.

*Chapter IV*

# THE PRAGMATICS OF EROTIC ICONOGRAPHY

IN ADDITION TO literature, there was another medium that produced symbolic representations of ancient Greek culture and that can convey an image of Greek love to us. Iconography, particularly that of the late archaic period, offers a great wealth of representations that, in my view at least, provide extremely concrete, albeit symbolic, information about sexual approaches, contacts, and relations. It is altogether deliberately that I introduce the modern concept of sexuality at this point. The iconic nature of these symbolic representations affords us a view that is the polar opposite of that provided by the literary representations: on the one hand, we see love reduced semiotically to the most concrete indications of sexual stimulation; on the other, we see love transfigured by the possibilities of literary "fictionality." Does this mean that the pictorial images show us extremely directly and crudely what poetry merely evokes metaphorically? The frequent intervention of Eros, represented as a winged figure, in the love scenes depicted on pottery would seem to suggest not. The archaic and classical iconographic corpus is so vast—ranging from scenes of divine love marked by the presence of Eros to erotic bed scenes at banquets—and presents such a varied figurative spectrum that we must content ourselves with a rapid overview of the collections of pottery that have been assembled to date. As we do so, we should above all bear in mind that these images of vase paintings that exist alongside the plastic representations of sculpture constitute a separate and specific symbolic order. It is certainly possible to compare it to that of the textual representations, but only provided we do not expect to find within the latter the origins and foundations of the former.[1]

## 1. FIGURATIVE REPRESENTATIONS OF LOVE

In default of any key that might enable us to detect signs of a less obvious nature, the iconography of love reveals itself to us either

---

[1] See the methodological suggestions made by C. Bérard, "Iconographie-Iconologie-Iconologique," *Et. Lettres* 4 (1983): 5–37; to mention but one example taken from one of the studies used here, see Kaempf-Dimitriadou 1979, 48ff., who appeals repeatedly to the development of the dramatic forms to account for the reorientations to be found in the erotic iconography of the gods.

through signs of sexual arousal (which are, of course, very evident in the case of men) or by figurative representations of Eros himself (although these are not always very clear, as he may easily be confused with a number of other winged creatures). Amid this abundant body of erotic imagery, let us first mark out a particular historical period. What has been called "the erotic art of the Greeks" seems to have appeared and peaked in the late archaic period. In Laconian iconography, examples of it are attested as early as 570–560 B.C., but in Attic pottery such images (some of them seemingly pornographic) first make their appearance around 530 and are at their peak around 470.[2] The overview attempted here will essentially be bounded by those two turning points, since they coincide not only with the final period in the development of melic poetry, but also with important shifts in the content of the representations.

## 1.1. Pursuits, Abductions, and Couplings

The first point to make, a paradoxical one when the texts are recalled, is that in the figurative imagery it is mortal men who actually make love, not the gods! However, this is an observation that calls for immediate qualification.

In epic poetry, gods and heroes are frequently to be found on a soft bed, enjoying the pleasures of Aphrodite with an adult partner, in a symmetrical and reciprocal relationship. By the end of the archaic period, pottery offers us a profusion of scenes in which a god or even a goddess, such as Eos, is pursuing a young girl or boy. These have customarily been classified as scenes depicting the abduction of a mortal male or female by a deity. But in most cases a better description would be "a pursuit scene": the pursuit of a girl, often a nymph, or a boy, who is likely to be a hero. Where inscriptions or distinctive emblems make positive identifications possible, we know that these images show Zeus chasing Aegina, the daughter of Asopus, the Nereid Thetis, or the Cadmean Semele, and also, very frequently, Ganymedes. These pursuits sometimes end with an actual abduction. Apollo is also seen to be active in the harassment of young nymphs whom it is tempting to identify as Marpessa, Creusa, or Cyrene. And in the pictures ornamenting the Amyclean throne, it was Poseidon who was at Zeus' side when the daughters of Atlas—Taygete and Alcyone—were carried off. The god with the trident occasionally shows an interest in boys, but in preference pursues adolescent girls such as Amymone, the daughter of Danaos in Argos, or

---

[2] For these dates, see Brendel 1970, 19ff.; Hermary 1986, 934ff.; and Reinsberg 1989, 105ff.

Aithra, the daughter of Pittheus in Troezen. But we also find Poseidon in pursuit of the woman destined to become his legitimate wife, Amphitrite.[3]

So could it be said that, in the iconography at least, the gods reenact the game of pursuit and flight in which the locutors of archaic melic poetry engage with their beloveds? In truth, the coincidence is no more than partial. It is true that the age difference between the adult god and the boy or girl who is his prey reproduces the asymmetry familiar from the texts. But, on the other hand, in the iconography the pursuit or abduction represented does—if we are to believe the texts—in many cases lead to a union that, although it does not necessarily assume the form of conjugal permanence, is generally productive. Semele becomes the mother of Dionysus, Cyrene gives birth to Aristeus, and Aithra to Theseus.[4] The creators of these images consistently represent sexual relations that lead into adulthood, even if they draw the line at depicting coupling in the cases of gods and heroes.

It is as if the iconography of the early classical period avoided representing the sexual unions of legendary beings, that is to say the gods and the heroes, and instead concentrated on the preliminary phases that led up to them. In their erotic courtships, the gods resort to constraint and are more successful in achieving their ends than men are, and the iconography for preference depicts the love affairs of those gods, leaving the texts to describe those of human beings. But this shift, which is linked as much to the switch to a different semiotic medium as to historical variation, is accompanied by a far more distinctive variation. In the melic poetry of the late archaic period, Eros manifests himself to mortals only as unfulfilled desire. In contrast, in the depiction of human beings, the pottery of both the archaic and the classical periods displays a rich variety of representations that are so direct that the vases concerned are frequently banished to the basement underworlds of the museums that acquire them. As is well known, from the mid-sixth century on the Greeks depicted by the painters of pottery appear to be in com-

[3] See the corpus put together, with a commentary, by Kaempf-Dimitriadou 1979, 7ff. and 76ff., and H. Hoffmann, *Sexual and Asexual Pursuits* (London 1977); for the texts, see Lyons 1997, 77ff. In a more complete catalog of the scenes of the abduction of Ganymedes by Zeus, K. W. Arafat, *Classical Zeus* (Oxford 1990), 64ff., points out how frequently these scenes relate to the symposium. The representations that adorn the throne of Amyclae are described by Pausanias 3.18.10; while the corpus of images presented by Kaempf-Dimitriadou goes back no farther than 490 B.C., the Laconian monument is generally dated to the late sixth century B.C.: see D. Musti and M. Torelli (eds.), *Pausania. Guida della Grecia* III (Milan 1991), 236.

[4] The meaning of these scenes of pursuit and abduction is discussed below ch. VI, §2.1. One could add to them the specifically Attic scene of the abduction of Oreithyia by Boreas: see below ch. VIII, §1, n. 3.

petition to see which of them can devise the most sophisticated positions to adopt in their lovemaking. The vase painters provide us with an extensive range of erotic play every bit as varied as that of the Kamasutras taken over by our own pornography, although, in truth, given the public character of these scenes, it might be more appropriate to assign them to the category of obscenity (or even derision).[5]

## 1.2. Polymorphic Sexuality

However — at first sight — this unbridled sexuality is not entirely free either in the forms that it assumes or in the choice of the spaces where it takes place. For example, the frieze on a black-figure Attic bowl dating from about 540 B.C. draws one decisive distinction in this respect. The positions adopted by the four heterosexual couples that it aligns are set in opposition to that adopted for the union of a couple comprising an adult man and an adolescent boy. The latter conforms with the "between-the-thighs" model, seemingly confirming that this was a particular feature of homophile relations.[6] Whereas the glance that is in many cases exchanged by the partners of heterosexual couples seems to indicate that their erotic pleasure is equally shared, the standard iconographical depiction of homophile couples seems to be placed under the sign of asymmetry. On a black-figure Attic vase from Vulci, dating from the mid-sixth century, a series of representations juxtaposed in the manner of a comic strip depict three moments leading up to homophile sexual union. In each, it is the adult who dominates the youth: first, he tries to win him over by presenting him with the gift of an animal; then he appeals to his affection by caressing his chin and his genitals; then he takes his enjoyment between the youth's thighs. On another very fine black-figure amphora on display in Princeton, the two images depicted on the vase correspond to the second and to the third phase of this iconographical courtship plot. The paintings show clearly that, in these three typical situations, it is only the adult who is aroused sexually and has an erection.[7] On the other hand, even when only one of the partners

---

[5] Along with the repertory compiled by J. Boardman and E. La Rocca, *Eros in Grecia* (Milan 1975), see the recent collections published by Keuls 1985, 153ff. (placed under the sign of prostitution), by Peschel 1987, *passim* (related to the symposium and the *kômos*), by Reinsberg 1989, 80ff. (placed under the sign of the *hetaira*), and most recently by M. Kilmer, *Greek Erotica on Attic Red-Figure Vases* (London 1993), with the comments of A. Stewart, *Art, Desire, and the Body in Ancient Greece* (Cambridge 1997), 156ff. and 255ff. See also Henderson 1991, 6ff., who subtly distinguishes between the extraverted nature of obscenity and the introversion of pornography.

[6] Attic black-figure cylix, Berlin, Staatl. Mus. 1798 (pl. I); for the iconography of "between-the-thighs," see above ch. III, n. 4.

[7] Attic black-figure amphora, London, Brit. Mus. W 39 (*ABV* 297, 16; pl. II); Attic

feels sexual enjoyment, occasionally the exchanged glance that passes between them possibly suggests a relationship of *philotês* such as the poets sought to establish; and if that is the case, the adolescent is not limited to a purely passive role. This may well be the correct interpretation of the scenes depicted on another vase, in which an adult and an adolescent are to be seen sheltering under a cloak together. There is nothing in the iconography to distinguish this cloak from the *khlaina* that frequently symbolizes nuptial intercourse. So the shared cloak might well indicate some degree of (sexual?) sharing between the two *philoi* (friends).[8]

It is, however, worth noting that, in the archaic period, scenes depicting the seduction of a woman also sometimes showed gifts or erotic caresses being bestowed upon her in the same way as they are frequently bestowed upon adolescent boys, although in the cases where women are represented the scenes are not worked into a sequence of images showing the progressive stages of seduction, as they are in the example discussed above. Apart from the images that depict carnal lovemaking, vase paintings do thus present "lexical" analogies that recall features we have noted in the texts. All the same, where the representation of both the heterosexual and the homophile lovemaking of mortals is concerned, iconography certainly employs an expressive "language" that is more direct than that of poetry. In the vase paintings, the discreet, polysemic evocations of literary metaphor are replaced by gestures that are totally unequivocal. Yet all the partners in the erotic scenes of iconography, whether they be adult men, beardless youths, women, or girls, and whether they be clothed or naked, are in general given the same harmonious physical features as those that characterize the representations of gods and heroes.[9]

However, the range of iconic representations of sexuality is not limited to the relatively regular courting procedures and sexual activity of couples of graceful mortal women and charming young men. While the

---

black-figure amphora, The Art Museum, Princeton University, L. 1990.60 (pl. III and pl. IV); see also the Attic cylix of about 500 B.C., Berlin, Staatl. Mus. 2273 (*ARV*² 115.2 and 1626, *Paralip.* 332; pl. V). For other scenes of the same type, see Koch-Harnack 1983, 147ff.; Keuls 1985, 279ff.; and Reinsberg 1989, 165ff.

[8] Scenes of union under a shared cloak: Arrigoni 1983, 8ff.; Koch-Harnack 1989, 138ff.; and below ch. VI, §2.2, n. 19 and n. 22. But the scene analyzed by Dover 1978, 98ff., in fact represents a man and a woman.

[9] See in this connection the iconographical parallels established for the gaze by Reinsberg 1989, 189f.; see also Schnapp 1984, 71ff. The contrast between the direct expression of iconography and the metaphorical language of the texts needs qualification to the extent that, for example, the sexual union of a couple may be suggested by an embrace under a shared cloak; this mode of representation, which corresponds approximately to the textual metaphor of the bed, also corresponds to the textual custom of drawing a veil over sexual activities under a *khlaina* by using a metaphor relating to weaving; see above n. 8.

relations of these handsome couples are certainly inventive, they do at least conform to certain persistent conventions that the painters impose upon them. In contrast, again from the mid-sixth century on, Greek vase painters were perfectly prepared to ascribe to satyrs practices that we ourselves should regard as dissolute. The satyrs depicted on the François vase are characterized by an ithyphallism, appropriate to their semianimal nature; they are beings close to donkeys and share their lechery. This leads them into every kind of debauchery: phallic games, sexual harassment, masturbation, exhibitionism, zoophilia, fellatio, and cunnilingus (even with animals!), not to mention—between satyr couples—anal coitus, something that in this same period is carefully avoided in the representations of sexual relations between adult males and boys. In the archaic and classical periods, sodomy appears to have been exclusively reserved for satyr bestiality.[10]

So perhaps we should distinguish between three different categories of erotic images in archaic and classical iconography: first, the preliminaries in which the gods engage; second, the imaginative sexual relations of mortals; and third, the exuberant couplings of satyrs. Satisfying though that would no doubt be to the academic's craving for clear classification, such a cut-and-dried nomenclature could not accommodate the scenes in which satyrs appear to be sharing a somewhat more measured erotic pleasure with maenads. Nor could it do justice to the images in which human beings are to be seen indulging in sexual excesses similar to those to which the satyrs are partial: not just fellatio and anal coitus, but also dildo play and group sex, if not sadomasochistic practices. The feature that tends to distinguish these images from other sexual scenes that are no less crude, but seemingly somewhat more restrained, is the size of the monstrous erections of these mortal men, which bestows upon them a priapic quality that sets them in the same category as the satyrs.[11] But to raise the matter of these examples that cannot be contained within the three categories suggested above is al-

---

[10] See, for example, the crater of Cleitias (known as the "François Vase"), which dates from about 560 B.C., Florence, 4209 (*ABV* 76.1), or the red-figure cylix, Berlin, Staatl. Mus. 1964.4 (*ARV*² 1700, *Paralip.* 334; pl. VI), together with the dossier accompanied by a commentary by Lissarrague 1987; see also Keuls 1985, 357ff. Dover 1978, 127ff., gives a detailed description of the phallic features that are characteristic of the satyrs of iconography. On the treatment reserved for sodomy, see below, ch. VII, §1.2.

[11] See, in particular, in contrast to the scene of moderate satyrical love on the red-figure Boston amphora MFA 76, 40 (*Paralip.* 144.1), the scenes represented on the cylix dating from about 510 B.C., Paris, Louvre G 13 (*ARV*² 86, *a*; pl. VII), and the cylix dating from twenty years later, Florence Arch. Mus. 3921 (*ARV*² 372.31): see Peschel 1987, 61ff. and 118ff., and also Reinsberg 1989, 98ff. with 11, 50 and 51, and the remarks by C. Bérard, "Phantasmatique érotique dans l'orgiasme dionysiaque," *Kernos* 5 (1992): 13–26, intended to modify the radical opposition constructed by Lissarrague 1987.

ready to adopt the perspective of the context of such orgies, a context that is as much psychocultural as institutional and spatial. In this connection, the painters were quite generous in their provision of telling signs. Suffice it for the moment to make the following observation: a satyr has only to pose as an *erastês* and present a youth with a gift of a pederastic nature for that young man to produce an erection that would be conspicuously absent from scenes of seduction involving him with a mortal adult.[12] If the satyr thereby becomes humanized, the young mortal for his part is "satyrized."

## 1.3. Interventions by Eros and Aphrodite

What is the role reserved for Eros in the figurative representations of these polymorphic unions? The iconography certainly honors him by depicting him in as concrete a fashion as could be desired. At first sight, the presence or absence of the adolescent deity or, later, of the mischievous winged child seems to distinguish the first of the three approximative iconic categories suggested above from the other two.[13] Eros is most prone to appear in the scenes of pursuit or abduction that imply the presence of a deity and a heroine or even a young hero. A typical example is provided by the scene depicted on an alabaster vase dating from the early fifth century, in which Zeus, literally stabbed in the back by a winged Eros, is laying hold of Ganymedes, who is engaged in playing with a cockerel. Eros is depicted in flight and is of the same adolescent stature as the young victim of the besotted Zeus. The clutching hand of the king of the gods has thus clearly been impelled by the action of the power who is the embodiment of passion. By the early fifth century, it was Aphrodite's turn to be depicted, sometimes in collaboration with Eros, in similar scenes of amorous pursuit.[14] Here too, the presence of Eros alongside the figure who is engaged in pursuit and is therefore the one who is in love has the effect of underlining the asymmetry by which the relations between the narrator-locutor and his addressee are characterized in the texts.

[12] Pelike, Leningrad 734 (*ARV*² 531.33); a scene mentioned by Lissarrague 1987, 77, although he does not draw attention to the adolescent's erection.

[13] Even distinguishing Eros from other winged figures raises problems of identification, as has been pointed out by Hermary 1986, 933ff.; to fall back on the context in this case seems a circular argument. See also Greifenhagen 1957, 34ff., who shows that the representation of Eros may alternate with that of Pothos or Himeros.

[14] White alabaster with black figures, Berlin F 2032 (pl. VIII), see Kaempf-Dimitriadou 1979, 7ff. and 27ff., and H. A. Shapiro, "Eros in Love: Pederasty and Pornography in Greece," in A. Richlin (ed.), *Pornography and Representation in Greece and Rome* (New York and Oxford 1992), 53–72; images attesting to the intervention of Aphrodite: A. Delivorrias, "Aphrodite," *LIMC* II.1 (Zurich and Munich 1984), 1–151 (142ff.).

But, to show how pointless it is to try to lay down hard and fast distinctions, it should be added that in a few scenes Eros appears to be on his own as he attacks a woman or a youth: in these scenes of pursuit or seduction, Eros takes the place of the lover by, for example, himself offering a gift to his quarry. In such cases the context is that of the life of human beings (rather than gods); for example where, on one Attic crater with little columns, Eros becomes double and flutters behind both the woman and the man who are here engaged in amorous conversation. In this plural form, which is attested by the beginning of the fifth century, the winged boy can even embody desire that is reciprocated.[15]

In contrast, to continue to limit ourselves to the period under consideration here, it is noticeable that Eros intervenes neither in bed scenes nor in the unbridled affairs of satyrs. And it is not until after 420 B.C. that he is to be found playing a direct role in the Dionysiac domain.[16] Were it not for the fact that the same applies to Aphrodite, it might be imagined that, as the embodiment of desire, Eros only has a place in scenes depicting the preliminaries of love: seduction, pursuit, abduction. Does this mean that neither Eros nor Cypris have any part to play in sexuality in the strictly limited sense of copulation? An explanation might be found in the Greek idea that urgent desire is a secondary state, akin to sleep or death. By the moment of erotic fulfilment, the powers of love have already attained their goal; so there is no longer any need for them to intervene.

## 2. The Functions of Erotic Images

Whatever the implications of this tentative summary of the iconographical nomenclature of, first, attitudes toward love in the late archaic period and, second, the circumstances in which an appeal is made to Eros, these erotic representations raise the same question as that posed above by melic poetry: namely, what was the purpose of these symbolic images? What was their function? Plenty of interpretations have been suggested for the most obscene of these images: a desire to represent reality, an expression of masculine aggression, a means of social satire, if not — as one tradition that has unfortunately become well established would

---

[15] Attic red-figure column crater, dating from about 485 B.C., Rome, Villa Giulia 1054 (*ARV*² 275.50; pl. IX; with a scene of seduction on the other side of the vase: pl. X): see Greifenhagen 1957, 40ff., who interprets it as the personification of Eros and Anteros; other attestations in Hermary 1986, 902ff. On the multiplication of Erotes, see above ch. I, §4, no. 42.

[16] Cf. Hermary 1986, 922ff., and, for the scenes representing satyrs, Lissarrague 1989, 78ff.

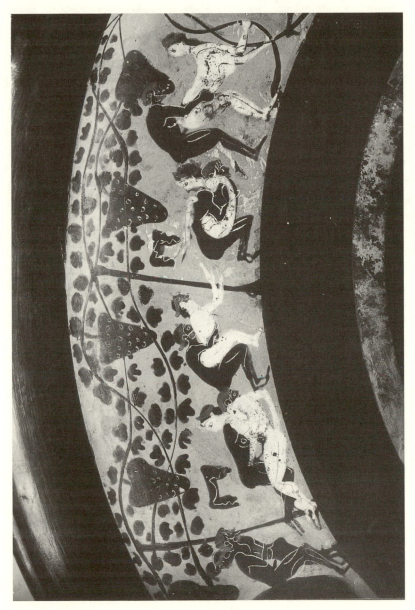

Pl. I. Attic black-figure cylix, around 540 B.C. (see n. 6).

Pl. II. Attic black-figure amphora, sixth century B.C. (see n. 7).

Pl. III. Attic black-figure amphora, around 540 B.C. (see n. 7).

Pl. IV. Attic black-figure amphora, around 540 B.C. (see n. 7).

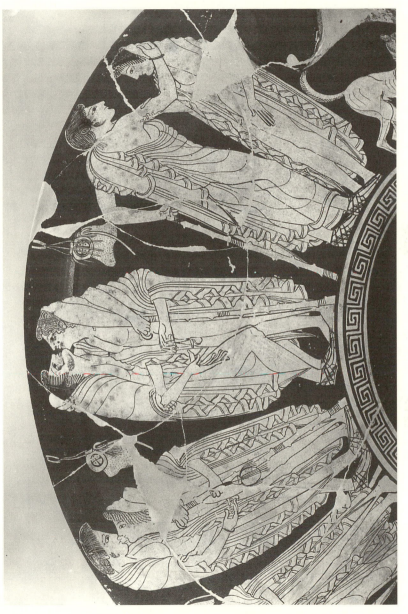

Pl. V. Attic red-figure cylix, around 500 B.C. (see n. 7).

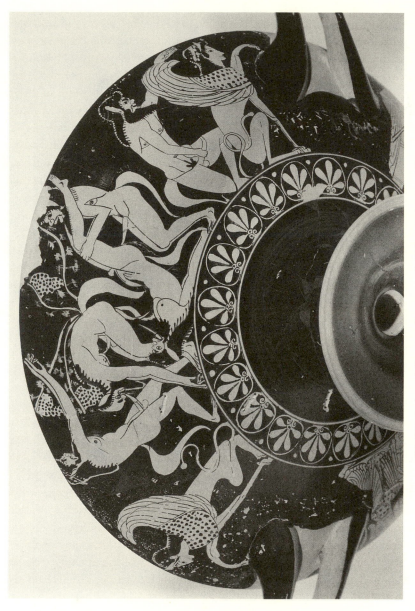

Pl. VI. Attic red-figure cylix, around 500 B.C. (see n. 10).

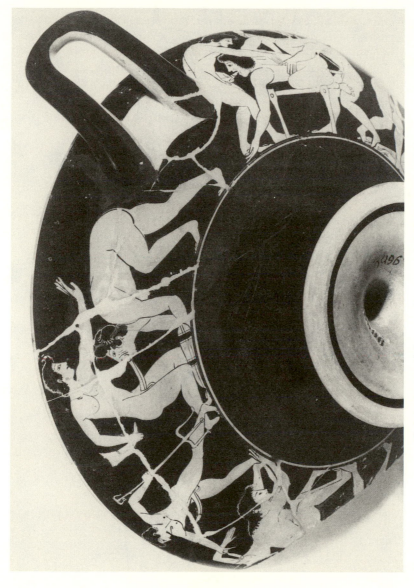

Pl. VII. Attic red-figure cylix, around 510 B.C. (see n. 11).

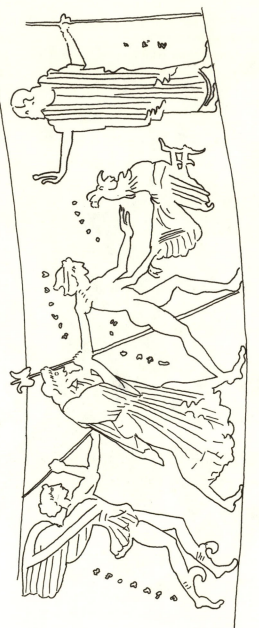

Pl. VIII. Black-figure white alabaster, early fifth century B.C. (see n. 14; copied by F. Lissarrague).

Pl. IX. Attic red-figure column crater, around 485 B.C. (see n. 15).

Pl. X. Attic red-figure column crater, around 485 B.C. (see n. 15).

have it — an attempt to provide a graphic reproduction and imitation of the literary satire that characterized iambics and comedy.[17]

Let us now consider these images of erotic overtures and couplings from the spatial point of view. The various objects that are depicted in them locate them within the framework of either the gymnasium, or the banquet, or the kind of procession (kômos) that would follow the latter. The sexual exploits of the satyrs, for their part, are also regularly accompanied by indications of the consumption of wine. But that is not all. Once it is noticed that the ceramic vases that carry these figurative representations are themselves all utensils that are indispensable for the mixing and serving of wine, the inquiry into the function of the scene depicted can be shifted to the object on which that scene is displayed.[18] Seen from this angle, a cantharos, crater, or cylix that is used for wine is found to bear a remarkable resemblance to an erotic poem: a poem that tells of love while at the same time being itself, as a poem, a tool of seduction, a poem that is, furthermore, very likely to be presented, as a sign of adoration, to the girl or boy who is the object of the poet's love.

The link established between erotic iconography and love poetry by their common practical efficacy prompts a further three, complementary, comparisons. It will be remembered that, according to the poetics of the late archaic period, painting and literature differ only in their respective modes of expression. Apart from the matter of poetry being given a spoken form, seen from this ancient Greek point of view, drawing and poetry appear interchangeable. There was, at any rate, an equivalence between the two upon which, according to Plutarch, Simonides had certainly commented. Even more significant is the archaic idea that assimilated poetic creation to a craftsmanlike "know-how" (sophia), so that a poem produced by a poet-artisan who marked it with his signature could be considered homologous to a vase modeled and illustrated by an artist who then stamped it with his seal.[19]

That first homology between the product created by a poet and the object fashioned by a painter can be developed further in two additional directions. From the point of view of the scenes that vases and poems

---

[17] The hypotheses cited here have been formulated in that order by Reinsberg 1989, 91ff.; Keuls 1985, 160ff.; Brendel 1970, 26ff.; and Dover 1978, 152ff.

[18] The connection that existed up until the beginning of the classical period between erotic scenes and the Dionysiac use of the objects upon which they appeared is touched upon by Brendel 1970, 29ff., who on page 19 comments upon the generally symposiac context of such scenes themselves. The advancement of sexual excitement seems to have led from the symposium into the kômos: see Peschel 1987, 27ff. and 89ff.

[19] Simon. in Plut. Glor. Ath. 346f. and Poet. 17f. (in particular). On this representation of archaic poetics, which saw the poem as a craftsman's product, see the reflections of Detienne 1967, 106ff., and Gentili 1984, 7 and 210ff. (who stresses the economic implications of this assimilation).

presented for their public to see or to hear, the iconographical distinction that I thought it possible to make between, on the one hand, ritualized love (in the scenes of courtship, pursuit, or touching) and, on the other, unbridled copulation (imitating satyr sexuality) seems to coincide with a fundamental dichotomy that marks archaic poetry and was discerned by Aristotle. There seems to be a correspondence between the representation of the beautiful bodies of gods, heroes, and young people, whose nudity is in many cases discreetly veiled, and the eulogistic poetry that expresses respect for all that is noble and tends to imitate "fine actions, executed by men all of identical quality." In contrast, the representations of copulations by artists whose imaginations, liberated by the consumption of wine, were inspired by the ithyphallic bestiality of satyrs could be likened to the poetry that apportions blame, in which "vulgar authors imitate the actions of the wicked." What might appear to us to be obscenity could thus in truth be derision, always supposing that it is legitimate to attribute to symposiac iconography a function of social criticism and derision analogous to that of iambic poetry (a question upon which only the iconologists are qualified to pronounce judgment).[20]

We are thus presented, by very different semiotic means, with a heroizing celebration of the beauty of men, who, possibly amid seemly conviviality, behave themselves in a godlike manner, and satire and caricature that censures the kind of sexual behavior that, under the influence of drink, reduces men to the level of the most bestial of animals. The tragic poet Chaeremon compared a good mixture of wine to a good use of Eros: in moderation, Eros is welcome; in excess, he is disruptive in the most harmful ways.[21]

But what was the purpose of this dichotomy between the beautiful and the ugly in the scenes depicted on vases and in the sung words of poetry, a dichotomy that, through praise and blame, is reinforced by a value judgment? At this point it should be remembered that — in the late archaic period, precisely — vases themselves could speak. The power of speech conferred upon them by the inscriptions that were frequently

---

[20] Aristotle, *Poet.* 4.1448b24ff. Pindar, already, in *Pyth.* 2.54ff., opposes the poetry of praise (*epainos, egkômion*) to that of blame (*psogos*): see Gentili 1984, 141ff., who shows that each of these types of poetry corresponds to a particular poetic genre; see also Detienne 1967, 25ff., who traces the origins of this opposition and reduces it to a contradictory polarity between truth and oblivion; see the comments of Nagy 1979, 222ff., and Vernant 1990, 67ff. An indication of the comic mockery prevalent in the iconography of satyrs is detectable in the scene depicted on the Attic red-figure cylix (mentioned above in n. 10), in which an ithyphallic satyr has a go at the Sphinx, which, on the edge of the painting, is supposed to be part of the frame scenery!

[21] Cheremon frag. 787 Nauck², cited in particular by Ath. 13.562e.

integrated into their images could be used to perform a variety of roles: to identify the protagonists in the scene represented on them, to make a brief commentary, which in some cases would issue from the lips of an actor in the scene, or to serve purely as a graphic ornamentation to complement the drawn composition. But some of these inscriptions are not enuncive, but enunciative; that is to say they do not relate to what the figurative representation (the "story" told by the image) conveys, but rather to the object, the vase itself, and the process of its fabrication (or enunciation!) and eventual use: signatures, remarks addressed to the drinker, or even marks of ownership (the latter generally being of a secondary nature in that they were incised after the pot's firing). Of all this collection of inscriptions (which is as yet by no means fully classified), the most distinctive type includes all those that proclaim the beauty of some young man; the proper name that appears in these does not refer to any of the actors in the scene represented on the vase, but to some external figure. The vase itself and the scenes that it displays thus function as a message of praise, addressed to an adolescent whose written name is probably generic. The laudatory impact of these statements is no doubt increased by the fact that, to judge from the collections of vases on which they appear, they tend to be attached to scenes showing civilizing heroes fighting monsters, Homeric heroic combat, exercises in the palaestra, or guests at a symposium, if not to scenes of homophile courtship.[22]

These "pederastic acclamations" bring us to the third of the perspectives and comparisons mentioned above, and this time the function of the object is involved. To whom could such an acclamation be addressed if not to one or another of the participants in the celebration in

---

[22] A catalog of these inscriptions of pederastic praise has been drawn up by Robinson and Fluck 1937, 66ff., and by J. D. Beazley, *Attic Black-Figure Vase-Painters* (Oxford 1956), 664ff.; *Red-Figure Vase-Painters* (Oxford [3]1963), 1559ff. and 1698ff.; and *Paralipomena* (Oxford [2]1971), 317ff. and 505ff. A first attempt at a classification of iconic inscriptions may be found in F. Lissarrague, "Paroles d'images," in A. M. Christinat (ed.), *Ecritures* II (Paris 1985), 71–89. In "Apprendre à boire, apprendre à manger," *La part de l'oeil* 5 (1989), 45–53, I tried to demonstrate the process of an object's fruition by its receiver, as it is brought about by an image and its inscriptions. For the relationship of those inscriptions with the production of *kleos*, see now N. W. Slater, "The Vase as Ventriloquist: *Kalos*-Inscriptions and the Culture of Fame," in A. Mackay (ed.), forthcoming. According to Buffière 1980, 143, who examines the collection of these "pederastic" inscriptions, they are intended to be amorous invitations; but see E. D. Francis and M. Vickers, "Leagros Kalos," *Proc. Cambr. Philol. Soc.* 207 (1981): 98–136. It is worth noting that in a few rare cases such statements of homophile praise appear in scenes depicting satyrs or maenads. Possibly these are intended to convey the same kind of ironic criticism that is expressed directly in the few graffiti that accuse the young man of being buggered! (see below ch. VII, §1.1, n. 15).

which the object is being used; in other words, in the symposium phase of the banquet? And it was, precisely, during the symposium that the archaic poets' verses of amorous desire were designed to be sung. These inscriptions of acclaim seem to turn the ceramic object into a seductive gift analogous to that constituted by the erotic poem.

In all likelihood Pindar's ardent eulogy of the beauty of young Theoxenus of Tenedos was classified by the Alexandrians in the book of *Egkômia*, or songs of praise. It is clear from the contents of these poems that this was the category in which poems intended for symposia were collected. Such songs of praise, also known as *skolia*, were from time to time sung in the course of the symposiac celebrations. According to Dicearchus, at first each of the guests, in turn, would sing a song of his own, after which the most talented of them would proceed, one by one, in a less regular, more winding order (*skolion*), to sing a song accompanied by a lyre, a *skolion* in the strictest sense of the term. This song, composed of interlinked sequences, would — just like the cup of wine — circulate among those present.[23] The elegiac couplets attributed to Theognis are known to have been designed to be recited before the symposium guests, as were many of Anacreon's short compositions. However, a symposium was not an occasion reserved solely for the performance of erotic poems or ethical exhortations.[24] Poets such as Archilochus and Hipponax took over the elegiac and above all the iambic forms and, in polar contrast to the glorifying eulogy and by dint of derision or caricature, used them to criticize the political and sexual behavior of their fellow citizens.

A few fragments of a poem by Alcaeus, in this vein, allow us to glimpse the political implications of a handsome youth's likely rejection of his erotic contract with the poet. The invective, which mentions the

[23] Pind. frag. 123 Maehler: see above ch. I, §2. The *Skolia* of Pindar are studied by B. A. Van Groningen, *Pindare au banquet* (Leiden 1960), 11ff. and 51ff., and Vetta 1983, xxviff. Dicaearchus, frag. 88 Wehrli; cf. also Aristox. frag. 125 Wehrli, who adds that the *skolia*, whose circulation "in the round" was determined by the placing of the tables and couches, were also sung at marriage feasts and included both gnomic and erotic themes. The links between the love of boys, poetry, and banquets are also described in the anecdotes about Sophocles recounted by Ath. 13.603f.: Soph. test. 75 Radt, and Buffière 1980, 149ff.

[24] E. L. Bowie, "Early Greek Elegy, Symposium, and Public Festival," *Journ. Hell. Stud.* 106 (1986): 13–35, has shown that a short elegy, whatever its content, could hardly have been sung in any context except that of a symposium; see also G. Tedeschi, "Solone e lo spazio della communicazione elegiaca," *Quad. Urb. Cult. Class.* 39 (1982): 33–46; following that article, R. Pretagostini, "Anacr. 33 Gent. = 356 P.," ibid., 47–55, pointed out the two opposed aspects of a symposium, the measured and the frenetic. On the relation of Anacreon's poetry to the banquet, see F. Lasserre, "Les *erôtiká* d'Anacréon," in R. Pretagostini (ed.), *Tradizione e innovazione nella cultura greca da Omero all' età ellenistica* I (Rome 1993), 365–75.

symposium context, goes on to associate the betrayal by the *pais* with a false accusation. But the most striking polarity is to be found in Anacreon's poetry, most of which was designed to be sung at symposia. If the text in question is indeed a single poem, the young girl with pretty cheeks who is mentioned at the beginning, and who rejects the poet a few lines farther on, becomes Herotime, "frequented by the people" — a description used for prostitutes, we are told by the ancient commentators. In the best vein of insulting mockery characteristic of the Iambic tradition, the poet's addressee is accused, in a series of scornful metaphors, of drunkenness, spitting, and nymphomania: she is "an unfenced garden, available to all."[25]

If a homology did, by and large, exist between a poem and an image, and both circulated among those present at a symposium, acting as the instruments of either erotic praise or erotic criticism, what could have been the function of those poetic and iconic statements? Extending the analogy, we could perhaps attribute to images that glorify the loved one and that are accompanied by pederastic acclamations the same role of courtship and amorous praise as that intended for erotic poetry — poetry that, it will be remembered, was intended to win over the young beloveds and persuade them to enter into the *philia* proposed by the adult poet, thereby affording a at least partial satisfaction to an erotic desire that was doomed to asymmetry. Some of the scenes displayed on drinking cups represent the ritual preliminaries to legendary or asymmetrical erotic relations; others depict sexual intercourse where Eros is absent. Thus they truly do seem either to seek to establish a contractual link of *philotês*, such as is suggested by the proferred gifts of amorous courtship, or possibly by an exchange of glances, or else to be designed to pour sexual derision upon symposium drinkers who gradually succumbed to the power of alcohol and would in consequence soon be reduced to the bestial state of satyrs. In that precise case, the sexual relationship seems to coincide with a power relationship in which the male has the upper hand.[26] But if we decide to attribute to the ceramic object and its historiated ornamentation (sometimes reinforced by an

---

[25] On the context of the execution of the poems of Archilochus, see Gentili 1984, 249ff., and Vetta 1983, xviff. With regard to Alcaeus, see frag. 306A.b Voigt, with commentary by M. Vetta, "Il P. Oxy. 2506 fr. 77 e la poesia pederotica di Alceo," *Quad. Urb. Cult. Class.* 39 (1982): 7–20, and also W. Rösler, *Dichtung und Gruppe* (Munich 1980), 37ff., 94ff., and 240ff. See Anacr. frags. 346.1.3 and 13 (see above ch. I, §3.1), 455, 480, and 446 Page: other examples and commentary are in E. Degani, "La donna nella lirica greca," in R. Uglione (ed.), *La donna nel mondo antico* (Turin 1989), 73–91.

[26] On the commitment represented by scenes of "pederastic" gifts, see Koch-Harnack 1983, 66ff., and Reinsberg 1989, 174ff. For E. Pellizer, "Outlines of a Morphology of Sympotic Entertainment," in Murray 1990, 178–84, the symposium was itself the place where passions were expressed and desires were regulated.

inscription) the same performative function as a poem, we need to go further. We need to investigate the institutional foundations of the symposium of the late archaic period, bearing in mind that a symposium meeting was as much an arena of civic debate as a place of education. And this matter of the symposium's institutional foundations leads to another question: that of the social role played by Eros and Aphrodite.

# PART THREE

## EROS IN SOCIAL INSTITUTIONS

# Chapter V

## EROS IN THE MASCULINE: THE *POLIS*

TO ADDRESS THE question of Eros' institutional role, we need to broaden the semantic viewpoint that we have so far adopted. We must now examine the function of this institutionalized Eros. The erotic practices of the symposium have introduced us to a form of social conditioning that was essentially masculine. But the flight of winged Eros leads us on farther, into a ritualized ceremony centered first and foremost on a woman. Although the texts and images that make it possible for us to reconstruct how a marriage unfolded were produced by men, the principal protagonist was the young wife. However, we must beware of presenting it as the direct homologue of the men's symposiac gatherings. Whereas the latter were continuously repeated, the marriage ceremony took place only once. Marriage was a rite of passage for girls, whereas for boys symposia constituted no more than a preparation for that transition. But what exactly was the transition that was involved in these complementary institutions?

The ethical image of the institutions of the Greek *polis* has varied over the years and from one place to another; it has recently been the subject of both an internal and an external reassessment.[1] The idealized representation of a homogeneous social body subject to a distributive and egalitarian form of justice stands in sharp contrast to the dissensions and rivalries of *stasis*, or internal strife; and on the level of poetry the polarity between praise and blame provides a dialectic reflection of those forms of civic life. Equally, the extension of the group of men who could take part in the management of political power by promoting community values may be contrasted to the apparent emergence of innovative individuals such as legislators, poets, and painters: these used a traditional language that made it possible for the members of the group collectively to take over their individual inventive creations or even to identify with them. The fluctuating construction of social relations between different aristocratic groups in the *polis* may be regarded either as symbolic of a distributive cohesion or as evidence of dialectical decision making. But whichever view one takes, it implies a reorientation, if not a metamorphosis, of many institutions and the creation of other,

---

[1] Cf. N. Loraux, "Repolitiser la cité," *L'Homme* 97/98 (1986): 239–54, and S. Scully, *Homer and the Sacred City* (Ithaca and London 1990), 6f.

new ones.[2] If that was true of the distribution of hierarchized monarchical power into new structures, the expansion of the production and the circulation of goods thanks to technical innovations, and the conversion of religious practices into poliad or Panhellenic cults, it also affected institutions related to the passage of future citizens from childhood to adulthood.

When examined from an institutional point of view, the relations between adults and adolescents — whether or not eroticized — refer us to educational practices and, as social anthropology has taught us, any society that has no educational system to provide for the transition into adulthood of the future members of the community develops ritualized processes for the purpose. The common features that these share from one community to another have led to the definition of the abstract anthropological concept of the rite of tribal initiation. Of course, in the absence of any documentary evidence, the existence of such rites of tribal initiation in the communities of prepolitical Greece can only be hypothetical: a hypothesis formulated on the basis of modern anthropology's postulate that such an institution is universal. This means that in any analysis of the educative institutions of the emerging *polis*, the notion of tribal initiation rites based on a tripartite division (segregation, marginality, and aggregation), which is a category of modern anthropological thought, can be used only as a strictly formal and operational tool. Any traces that might suggest such a pattern will not be interpreted in historical terms, as survivals, but instead will be considered in the anthropological perspective of a social function, whose form and content varied from one city to another, from one period to another, and from one gender to the other.[3]

More specifically, it is worth noting that when examined from the point of view of their institutional aspects, the love relations of melic poetry, along with its practical function, lead us not only toward certain institutional forms of education but also into particular well-defined spaces: the space of banquets, certainly, but also that of the palaestra (or wrestling ring), and eventually that of marriage. A brief overview of the iconographical scenes of erotic courtship, which are often more explicit than the declarations of the poets as to where they take place, reveals

---

[2] See in this connection the remarks of A. Snodgrass, *Archaic Greece* (London and Melbourne 1980), 84ff., and those of I. M. Morris, *Burial and Ancient Society* (Cambridge 1987), 171ff., with the essays of O. Murray, "Cities of Reason," and C. Sourvinou-Inwood, "What Is Polis Religion?," in O. Murray and S. Price (eds), *The Greek City from Homer to Alexander* (Oxford 1990), 1–25 and 295–322.

[3] The concept of tribal initiation, elaborated on the basis of the work of A. van Gennep in *Les rites de passage* (Paris 1909), is explained in particular by Brelich 1969, 14ff., who presents a critique of the notion of survival (49ff.).

distinctive signs, some of which refer us to the symposium, others to the spaces designed for physical exercise, the palaestra and the gymnasium.[4]

## 1. THE PROPAEDEUTIC PRACTICES OF THE SYMPOSIUM

Let us first return to the banquet. I should point out that up until now I have prudently used either this generic term or else the word *symposium* (Greek: *sumposion*), which more precisely designates the drinking party that would lead on from the actual meal. The discussion that follows will be limited to the convivial gatherings in which the poems of Alcaeus, Anacreon, Theognis, and Solon, cited above, would be sung. It will focus upon the little cities that were developing during the sixth century, such as Mytilene, Megara, and Athens, and it will leave aside the great ritual gatherings such as the syssities (common messes) that were held in, for example, Sparta. The Greeks appear to have drawn a clear distinction between the various ritualized forms of the banquet, in particular the *daïs* and the *sumposion*. The term *daïs* designates the feasts of the gods and also the meals of mortal men in which the meat from sacrifices was shared and consumed. *Sumposion*, on the other hand, denotes the gatherings in which cups of wine circulated, in ritual fashion. According to the iconic representations of these convivial gatherings, the lyre—implying music and poetry—would be a feature of a sacrificial meal, whereas at a symposium the flute would be preferred.[5] It would clearly be tempting to complement this distinction by the opposition that the Greeks drew between poetry of praise and poetry of blame, which was sometimes reflected in vase paintings, and to suggest that eulogies were characteristic of the *daïs*, criticism of the symposium.

However, the scant literary evidence that exists on this matter must deter us from doing so. While it is true that in his elegiac poem on fair distribution Solon represents the *daïs* as the model of a celebration enjoyed in a seemly fashion, what he contrasts this to is the unjust behavior of those who transgress the proper limits and thereby destroy the city. Similarly, in Xenophanes' famous elegy, the rules of the symposium

---

[4] See Reinsberg 1989, 174ff.; it is unlikely that it is possible to confirm, following Bremmer 1990, 145, that the palaestra was chronologically substituted for the banquet as the framework of such scenes of courtship. See also the corpus assembled by Schnapp 1984 and now in *Le chasseur et la cité. Chasse et érotique dans la Grèce ancienne* (Paris 1997), 345ff. On the spatial and architectural distinctions between the palaestra and the gymnasium, see below n. 33.

[5] See in this connection the dossier and study presented by P. Schmitt-Pantel in "Sacrificial Meal and Symposion," in Murray 1990, 14–33, and *La Cité au banquet* (Rome 1992), 4ff. and 59ff. On the relations between music and the division of meats at a *daïs*, see Nagy, quoted above, ch. I, §5, n. 50.

and the state of shared purity that those rules foster include hymns
addressed to the gods, which are couched in pious formulae and tell of
seemly behavior; but the respect of those rules is shattered when those
songs of praise addressed to the gods are superseded by legends that
portray monstrous, violent beings such as the Titans, the Giants, and
the Centaurs and that tell, to no good effect, of internecine conflicts.
Furthermore, if Solon's model sacrificial meal may indeed be interpreted
as representing a microcosm of the perfect city, it is also possible to
detect in it an allusion to the enunciative and polemical circumstances
in which Athens' legislator's elegiac verses were sung.[6]

## 1.1. Erotic Modes of Behavior and Civic Commitment

Sacrificial meals possibly, and symposiac gatherings certainly, were occasions for reciting poems that, using examples drawn from legend or
direct eulogies of the ethical values upon which community life in the
*polis* was founded, were presented as exhortations. Let us consider the
urgent appeal that the author of the following Theognidean distiches
addressed to his chosen listener (who may have been either simply generic or a particular individual):

> 'tis with good intent to thee that I shall give thee the counsels
> which I learnt [*emathon*] from good men in my own childhood.
> Consort not with the bad, but ever cleave unto the good,
> and at their tables eat and drink, and with them sit,
> and please them for their power is great.
> Of good men shalt thou learn [*matheseai*] good. . . .
> Consort therefore with the good
> and someday thou'lt say that I counsel my friends [*philoisin*] aright.[7]

A banquet, probably as a meal but above all as a symposium, was certainly a place for learning; learning by example, but also learning
through poetry, from the praise of aristocratic values or the narration of

---

[6] Sol. frag. 3.5f. Gentili-Prato, with the two interpretations, which I consider to be
complementary, by W. J. Slater, "Peace, the Symposium and the Poet," *Ill. Class. Stud.* 6
(1981): 205–14, and by Tedeschi, quoted above, ch. IV, §2, n. 24. Xenoph. frag. 1 Gentili-Prato, with the commentary by P. Giannini, "Senofane fr. 2 Gent.-Pr. e la funzione
dell'intellettuale nella Grecia arcaica," *Quad. Urb. Cult. Class.* 39 (1982): 57–70, and by
G. Cerri, *Platone sociologico della comunicazione* (Milan 1991), 39ff.; D. B. Levine,
"Symposium and the Polis," in Figueira and Nagy 1985, 176–96, has shown how the
linguistic and semantic wordplay in the poetry of Theognis turn the polis into a symposium.

[7] Thgn. 27ff., in J. M. Edmonds (trans.), *Elegy and Iambics* I (Loeb 1931). On the basis
of other texts, too, Bremmer 1990, 137ff., has recently confirmed the didactic aspects of
symposiac poetry; see also Vetta 1983, xxxvff. In general, see J. Latacz, "Die Funktion des
Symposions für die entstehende Literatur," in W. Kullmann and M. Reichel (eds), *Der
Übergang von der Mündlichkeit zur Literatur bei den Griechen* (Tübingen 1990), 227–64.

exemplary tales, and probably also from contemplating the fine bodies and heroic scenes depicted on the utensils used to serve the wine. For a poet such as Pindar, the only difference between the *(ep-)ainein* of praise and the *parainein* of a precept was that indicated by the prefix *epi-*, which conveyed an invitation. But, still according to Pindar, whoever expressed *epainos* (praise) could also express *mômos* (blame): praise would be complemented by derision conveyed through speech or image, derision of the bestial deformities and excesses that led to *hubris*.[8]

The values praised in song, displayed and thus taught at the banquets of little sixth-century cities, were founded upon the bonds of *philia*, the bonds of the mutual attachment and trust that gathered citizens together in the same place, there to share meat and wine. But not every citizen, for the social and moral qualities required of a *philos hetairos* (a dear companion or fellow) excluded from such a circle of friends the *kakos*, the evil man, who was to be avoided as an unsafe harbor is. The solidity of *philia* was measured, above and beyond shifting words, according to the yardstick of brotherly love. As it paid homage to the gods and defined common values, such a group of *hetairoi* gathered together as *philoi* at a banquet considered itself to represent the ideal civic community.[9] So the relationship of *philotês* that a narrator of symposiac poetry tried to establish with his young addressee was bound to prefigure the political bond of trust that united all the members of a *hetaireia* (fellowship).

When the poetry of a Theognis or an Anacreon shifted from the mode of moral exhortation into that of erotic invitation, it resorted to the seductive ploys of Aphrodite to turn the future citizen into a *philos*. And once a narrator of erotic Theognidean poetry became the *philos* of a youth, he considered himself to be his *hetairos pistos*, his faithful companion. However, if the boy abandoned the *philotês* of the poet and disgraced it by joining a different group, the praise would turn into blame and — as we have seen — the young man would be cursed by the

[8] Compare Pind. *Nem.* 7.61 (when the object of the *ainein* is a *philos*) and *Ol.* 6.12 to *Pyth.* 6.23 and *Isthm.* 6.68, together with the commentary by Nagy 1979, 238ff., and 1990, 147ff. and 196ff.; see also Pind. frag. 181 Maehler.

[9] Thgn. 113ff. and 97ff. The numerous Theognidean distiches that praise the *philia* that is the basis of a *hetaireia* have been analyzed by W. Donlan, "*Pistos philos hetairos*," in Figueira and Nagy 1985, 223–44, and Konstan 1997, 48ff. The constitution and composition of the *hetaireia* in sixth-century Athens are studied by F. Sartori, *Le eterie nella vita politica ateniense del VI e V secolo A.C.* (Rome 1967), 53ff., who, however, underestimates the importance of their political role; their arrival and their various political functions in a number of archaic cities are stressed by Schmitt-Pantel, quoted above, n. 5, 59ff., who underlines the symposium's importance as an education leading to citizenship (70ff. and 76ff.). See also O. Murray, "The Symposion as Social Organization," in R. Hägg (ed.), *The Greek Renaissance of the Eighth Century B.C.* (Stockholm 1983), 195–99.

poet, who would condemn him to never again arouse (with his gaze, *eisorôn*) the "love" (*philein*) of any man. When it was a matter of integrating future citizens into the social fabric of the fellowship, the affective methods of *philia*, which corresponded in particular to the erotic gaze, were adopted; and the lesson for the youth was conveyed through the dialectics of praise and blame.[10]

In the light of the political and affective nature of the bonds that united *hetairoi* in the symposiac celebration, the relations of homophilia postulated by archaic erotic poetry could be seen by the boys that it addressed as a propaedeutic introduction to the relations that obtained between adult citizens. The very inversion of the signs of sexuality that those relations of homophilia involved set the seal upon their initiatory function. The reformulation of the rites of tribal initiation within the framework of a civic institution, in which the modern categories of "private" and "public" were confused, no doubt makes it no more possible for us to distinguish the first ritual phase, namely that of rupture. However, according to the canonical schema of the anthropologists, this ought to precede the period of initiatory marginality that is characterized by a series of inversions of the rules that are applied to the adult community, particularly in the sexual domain. Even if these homophile love affairs, with their propaedeutic function, were essentially fleeting (quite literally, transitory), the anthropological comparison suggests that we should not be in the least doubt about the reality of the feelings and practices that they involved.[11]

Even though "the (Greek) love of boys" certainly sought to transform itself into a permanent relationship of *philia*, with all the mutual obligations that this implied, it made use of the inversion and asymmetry characteristic of rites of passage to create that bond, with the aid of Eros. So-called "Greek homosexuality" must be understood as a

---

[10] Thgn. 1311ff.; see also 1241ff. or 1377ff. and above ch. I, §3.1; on the relation between *philia* and distinction (*timê*), see Vetta 1980, 49ff. and 95. While G. Nagy, "Theognis of Megara: A Poet's Vision of His City," and L. Edmunds, "The Genre of Theognidean Poetry," in Figueira and Nagy 1985, 22–81 and 96–111, emphasize the political aspects of the exhortations in Theognis' symposiac poetry, Bremmer 1990 underlines the educative role of the "pederastic" practices of the banquet; on the pedagogic importance of *paidophilein* claimed by Theognis, see Lewis 1985, 216ff., but also W. Jaeger, *Paideia* I (Paris 1964), 236ff. (English translation: *Paideia: The Ideals of Greek Culture* I [New York ²1945]). As we are reminded by F. Frontisi-Ducroux, "La bomolochia," *Recherches sur les cultes grecs et l'Occident* 2, 1984, 29–50, the young Spartans were invited to attend syssities to hear political talk and to become accustomed to teasing and sarcasms without growing angry, in a place where indecent talk and gestures were not tolerated; see Plut. *Lyc.* 12.6.

[11] To mention just Papua New Guinea, see the comparative studies of G. Bleibtreu-Ehrenberg, *Mannbarkeitsriten* (Frankfurt am Main and Vienna 1980), and those of G. H. Herdt (ed.), *Ritualized Homosexuality in Melanesia* (Berkeley 1984).

practice that was part and parcel of educational procedures that still stemmed largely from the rites of tribal initiation.[12]

Between the mix-sixth and the early-fifth centuries there is a striking coincidence between the erotic poetic activity of poets such as Ibycus, Theognis, and Anacreon, the profusion of citizen groups (*hetaireiai*), and the diffusion of scenes of homophile love.[13] These manifestations of altogether different symbolic and semiotic kinds all stemmed from the still very aristocratic ideology upon which the earliest forms of political life in the city were founded. The educational system designed to reproduce those forms seems to have included many practices of an initiatory type. One of the most important seems to have been that of (initiatory) homophilia.

Many commentaries have been devoted to the Cretan custom according to which, even as last as the classical period, a well-born youth would be brought up in the *andreia* (masculine group) of his *erastês* before entering a period of solitary hunting, which prepared the boy for reintegration into the *polis*; so we need not dwell on the details here. Upon his return from the "forest," and thus at the end of the period of his existence on the margins of society, the young man would be presented with a set of military equipment that turned him into a soldier, while the gift of an ox enabled him to offer up a sacrifice to Zeus and that of a drinking cup marked his integration into the symposiac celebrations of a group of adult men. With its triadic structure and its characteristic functions, such a rite of passage would appear to be the very epitome of the canon of tribal initiation.[14] Particularly noteworthy is the fact that while the *erômenos* (the beloved one) who benefited from this initiation process received a title (*kleinos*, the glorious one) to mark his privileged selection, the name of *philêtor*, granted to an adult *erastês*

---

[12] Foucault's analysis, 1984, 237ff., which is essentially based on the philosophical texts of Xenophon and Plato, very much underestimates this aspect of an initiatory ritualization in the love felt by adult citizens for adolescents who were the sons of citizens; on this subject, see the excellent remarks of L. Edmunds, "Foucault and Theognis," *Class. Mod. Lit.* 8 (1988): 79–91; see also Cohen 1991, 192ff.

[13] By concentrating exclusively upon images of "pederastic" courtship, attestations of which go back to about 560 B.C., H. A. Shapiro, "Courtship Scenes in Attic Vase-Painting," *Am. Journ. Arch.* 85 (1981): 133–43, restricts such manifestations to Athens and to the "aristocratic" policies promoted by the Pisistratids.

[14] Eph. *FGrHist.* 70 F 149.21, cited by Strab. 10.4.21; see the by now classic observations of H. Jeanmaire, *Couroi et Courètes* (Lille 1939), 450ff., and Brelich 1969, 197ff., following Bethe 1907, 438ff., and also the comparative parallels collected by Sergent 1984, 15ff. and 84ff.; see now W. Armstrong Percy III, *Pederasty and Pedagogy in Archaic Greece* (Urbana and Chicago 1996), 15ff. and 95ff. On the role of the game in scenes of erotic seduction in the classical iconography, see now Schnapp, quoted above n. 4, 318ff.

(the lover), for its part acknowledged the relationship of *philotês* established by the love that he felt for the young man.

## 1.2 Sexual Roles and Social Relations

A few lines by Sappho show us that the mutual bond of trust established by the asymmetrical relationship of love between adults and adolescents was not limited to men. The poetic words that Sappho addresses to her *philai* (her friends) or her *hetairai* (her companions) should probably be read bearing in mind the relationship of *philotês* evoked by Aphrodite herself, in the poet's *Hymn* to her mentioned earlier; we should also remember the imbalance that resulted when such a relationship of trust was repudiated. Athenaeus, using his usual method of juxtaposing an assortment of quotations, presents the friendship between Leto and Niobe as a model of such relationships: Sappho herself calls the goddess and the heroine *philai hetairai* (companions dear to each other). Citing the poet Sappho from Lesbos, Athenaeus tries to distinguish between, on the one hand, the trivial meaning acquired by the term *hetairai* and, on the other, the sense of a relationship founded on *philia*; that is to say a sincere loyalty placed under the protection of Aphrodite, a kind of intimacy that could be experienced not only by men but also by free women and girls.[15] When the female narrator of one of Sappho's poems, if not Sappho herself, describes herself as a "trustworthy friend" (*philia ekhura*, an expression that is echoed by the verbal form *philêsô* that is then used), she confirms that aspect of trust, also noted by Athenaeus. Athenaeus is equally aware of the erotic aspect of the relationship of *philia*, but he tends to regard this as mutual. Rereading Sappho's opus with the eye of a historian, the poet's biographer recognizes among the names of the girls mentioned in her poems quite a number of *hetairai kai philai*.[16]

---

[15] Sappho frags. 43 (possibly in a marriage song), 160, and 142 Voigt; the latter two are cited by Ath. 13.571cd. The distinction between these two meanings of *hetaira* (see below ch. VI, §1, n. 3) is, furthermore, at the origin of the entire biographical tradition that, by distinguishing Sappho the poetess from Sappho the *hetaira*, has attempted to whitewash Sappho in the face of the accusation of *aiskhra philia*: see Ael., *Var. Hist.* 12.19 = Sappho test. 4 Campbell, *Anth. Pal.* 5.246, etc.; see Lardinois 1989, 21ff.

[16] Sappho frags. 88a.17 and 24, and 126 Voigt; see also frag. 94.34 Voigt. *Sud.* s.v. *Sappho* (S 107 Adler) = test. 2 Voigt. In addition to these relational terms, *sunzux* (frag. 213 Voigt), the meaning of which I tried to use in 1977, I, 370ff. and 428 ff; for "communal interaction" inside Sappho's "circle," see now Hatherly Wilson 1996, 117ff. However, Stehle 1997, 31ff. and 252ff., denies to Alcman's and Sappho's poems any educative value, despite their dependence on the culture of the song and dance performance. The relationship of *philia* established by a feminine homoerotic relationship may be represented in the iconography in scenes where two women shelter together under a cloak that

As among men, a relationship of *philia* between an adult woman and a girl developed within a group (*hetaireia*); and, also as among men, this relationship instigated by Eros was combined with a pedagogical function that justified Sappho's biographer identifying some of the young addresses of her poems as her *mathêtriai* (pupils). However, the "circle" of girls groups around Sappho and her poetry was not a pure mirror image, in early-sixth-century Mytilene, of the *hetaireia* to which Alcaeus addressed his verses. A modern anthropologist alert to differentiation between the social roles of the two sexes would not be disappointed here. For while these educational structures were similar in form and functions and all, regardless of gender, deployed the same erotic language, they were distinguishable by virtue of their content. The great debate opened by women's studies on the specifically feminine aspects of Sappho's poetry has been centered above all on the erotic sensibility and the particular sexuality of its author. The gendered dimension of Sappho's poems in truth depends rather on the social and pedagogical function of the poems sung and danced on ritual and communal occasions. This had a decisive influence not so much on linguistic forms but rather on the performance settings and the meaning of words used in poems sung by young girls or women. Allusions to politics, and to the civic and social qualities of the *agathoi*, and ethical maxims on fidelity, justice, and wealth were replaced, where women were singing, by evocations of beauty enhanced by ornamentation and apparel, appeals to the charm and elegance of feminine maturity, and invitations to enter into intimacy with Aphrodite. Furthermore, songs celebrating the memory of the erotic charms of girls who had subsequently progressed to adulthood were not to be heard at symposia. These were sung either at the sites of cults where the coming of the goddess of love was expected, or else in "the house of the servants of the Muses"; that is to say within the spatial and ritual framework of the "circle" that was believed to have surrounded the poetess.[17]

---

is also that of matrimonial initiation: images in Koch-Harnack 1989, 143ff., see below ch. VI, §2.2, n. 19, but also above ch. IV, §1.2, n. 8, for representations of men under a *khlaina*.

[17] See in particular Sappho frags. 2 and 150 Voigt, and below ch. IX, §2, n. 6. The question of Sappho's circle in relation to the amorous and musical education that was dispensed within it and the places where this occurred is studied in detail by Burnett 1983, 209ff.; see also Lanata 1966, 65ff., and Calame 1977, I, 367ff. and 427ff., together with the excellent remarks of Lardinois 1989, 25ff.; H. N. Parker's attempt, in "Sappho Schoolmistress," *Trans. Am. Philol. Assoc.* 123 (1993): 309–51, to assimilate Sappho's group to a simple *hetaireia* did not convince me: see the response of A. Lardinois, "Subject and Circumstance in Sappho's Poetry," *Trans. Am. Philol. Assoc.* 124 (1994): 57–84, and Hatherly Wilson 1996, 103ff; on the question of the erotic language of Sappho, see above ch. III, §1.2, n. 6.

The transitory *philia* established by an asymmetrical feminine erotic relationship of an initiatory type probably did, as in a male community, tend to establish a stable relationship of *philotês*. However, for women, it constituted the basis of not a political group, but a conjugal union.

Seen from the point of view of their propaedeutic function, however, which is manifested in the inversion typical of initiation, ancient Greek preclassical homophile relations present an asymmetry that should not be interpreted in terms of a passive role (for the adolescent) and an active role (for the adult). Neither the active transformation demanded of the boy or girl, nor even the physical position adopted by adolescent boys in sexual contacts with mature men, justify such an interpretation. As we shall see, for the Greeks of the classical period, passivity and the distate that it provoked were associated with the ongoing homosexuality of effeminate men. Furthermore, even if the roles assigned to the adults of the two sexes were clearly distinguishable and peculiar to their respective genders, the homology between the processes that — autonomously — led up to those roles rules out ascribing the essential asymmetry of those processes to any difference between the sexes: the educational asymmetry of the love relationship between adolescent and adult is fundamental for the construction of both genders. This provides an illustration of another prejudice of the contemporary anthropology of sexism; even if quite recently, in scholarship inspired by women's studies, it has been possible to show that Sappho's poems present the signs of a specifically feminine control of sex roles and erotic desire. It is only at the point when a conflict arises between these distinct and differentiated roles that the male camp, on the strength of its own particular right to public speech, is in a position to depreciate the (active) functions that are reserved for women.[18]

Just as the process of initiatory education through love assigned to adult women a space bounded by the *oikos* and the local cult sites, it situated men in a space bounded by banquet halls and the agora. Mean-

---

[18] Greek homophilia has been interpreted in terms of an active/passive polarity in sexual roles both by scholars inspired by ancient philosophers, such as Dover 1978, 81ff. and 100ff., and Foucault 1984, 246ff., who speaks rather of an "avoidance," but see also 55ff., or L. Brisson, *Le Sexe incertain* (Paris 1997), 41ff., and by scholars influenced by the feminist movement, such as Keuls 1985, 274ff., or E. Cantarella, "L'omosessualità maschile nel diritto ateniese," in P. Dimakis (ed.), *Eros et droit en Grèce classique* (Paris 1988), 13–41, with the references given in 1988, 76ff.: as a passive partner, the boy would assume the same role as the woman (see Halperin 1990, 30ff.: above ch. III, §1). For the expression of feminine desire in Sappho, see duBois 1995, 127ff., with her critique of Foucault, and for the feminine control of sexuality, see A. Carson, "Putting Her in Her Place: Woman, Dirt and Desire," in Halperin, Winkler, and Zeitlin (eds.) 1990, 135–70, and Hatherly Wilson 1996, 87ff.

while, for adolescents, the spatial equivalent of the agora was the pa-laestra.

## 2. Erotic Practices of the Palaestra

From Plato down to Athenaeus, there can be no doubt that philosophi-cal reflection on the role of Eros located homophile contacts between adults and adolescents in the gymnasia or, as Plato's Phaedrus prudently adds, "other meeting places."

### 2.1 Eros in the Gymnasium

The most striking evidence of the place reserved for Eros in spaces de-signed for exercise and physical education is the altar raised to the god of amorous desire at the entrance to the gymnasium of Athens; it was included in the very sanctuary of Athena, to whom this prestigious place of athletic and musical emulation was dedicated. A distich adorn-ing the altar recalled the legend of the founding of this establishment and directly linked homophilia with the cult of Eros-of-the-many-wiles. According to that legend, the altar had been set up by the polemarch Charmos, famous for having been the *erastês* of Hippias, the son of Pisistratus. That was a propaedeutic affair if ever there was one, for the legend adds that Hippias later married Charmos' daughter![19] It was in the gardens surrounding the gymnasium of the Academy that Plato founded his school, within a perimeter apparently reserved for the in-stallation of scholarly establishments. Legend has it that during the night before his meeting with Plato, Socrates saw a young swan fly off from near the statue of Eros that stood in front of the Academy. As soon as he made contact for the first time with the philosopher, he real-ized that the swan in his dream must have been the young man.[20]

The small town of Elis, near Olympia, is astonishing to travelers, for is has no fewer than three gymnasia. In the most ancient of them, which was reserved for training for the Olympic Games, altars were dedicated to Heracles of Ida, to Demeter and her daughter, to Eros, and to An-teros. In the "soft-floored" gymnasium, chiefly for the use of ephebes,

[19] Plato, *Phaedr.* 255bc, Ath. 13.561de and 609d = *PA* 15520, who draws his informa-tion from an *Atthis*, possibly that by Cleidemos (*FGrHist.* 323 F 15), Paus. 1.30.1; cf. also Plut. *Sol.* 1.7 who makes Charmos the lover of Pisistratus and in this connection mentions a statue of Eros: see N. Robertson, "The Origin of the Panathenaea," *Rhein. Mus.* 128 (1985): 231–95 (258f.).

[20] See Travlos 1971, 42ff.; the legend, including the detail of the statue of Eros, is told by Apul. *Plat.* 1.1 and Hermias in Plat. *Phaedr.* 7: see F. Lasserre, "Le chant du cygne," *Et. Lettres* 3 (1986): 49–66.

there stood a bust of Heracles; and in one of its palaestras there was a sculpted relief depicting Eros and Anteros fighting over a palm leaf. The title of Helper (*Parastatês*), under which Heracles was venerated in the old gymnasium of Elis, is reminiscent of the name given to the *erômenoi* honored in the Cretan customs reported by Ephorus: *parastathentes*. Furthermore, thanks to the proximity of Artemis' sanctuary to the third of these gymnasia, this goddess was given the title "Faithful to the young" (*Philomeirax*).[21]

The presence of an anti-Eros opposite Eros does not, in truth, undermine the asymmetrical nature of the homophilia consecrated by the religious practices of the gymnasium. For far from embodying reciprocated love, as is all too often and ideally claimed, Anteros is the figure who stands for the erotic rivalry that this bas-relief of Elis represents. The famous anecdote that serves as the founding myth behind the cult that the metics (resident aliens) of Athens paid to Anteros presents this god not as the personification of the feeling with which an *erômenos* responded to an *erastês*, but rather as the *daimôn* who avenged despairing lovers. Eros was to be found at the side of the *erastês* Timagoras the metic; and even if the gesture of his *erômenos*, who also ended up by committing suicide, implies a measure of reciprocity, the aetiological account tells first and foremost of a case of (amorous) antagonism between an adult metic and a free youth. And even for Plato, when a distortion of the traditional physiology of love makes it possible to suggest a response of reciprocity on the part of the *erômenos*, and a mirror image of *erôs* seems worthy to be called *anterôs*, the *erômenos*, for his part, regards this not so much as an effect of *erôs*, but rather as a consequence of *philia*. As we shall see, asymmetry imposes certain constraints, even in philosophy.[22]

## 2.2. Homophilia in the Gymnasium

The link between the practices of the gymnasium and the love of boys is confirmed by one of the laws of Solon, which takes us back to the sixth

---

[21] Paus. 6.23.1f.; see Strab. 10.4.21. On the masculine loves of Heracles, see Buffière 1980, 375ff.; on Eros in the gymnasium, see also Fasce 1977, 39ff. and 175ff.

[22] Paus. 1.30.2; Plat. *Phaedr.* 255de. Various interpretations of the figure of Anteros as representing reciprocity are cited by Fasce 1977, 41, n. 128: see on this subject, below ch. X, §3, with n. 15. While it is true that the verb *anteraô* may denote a "loving" exchange, it only does so in the domain of the nonerotic love of one's country (Aesch. *Ag.* 544f.), or else when it designates mutual love between a man and a woman (Xen. *Symp.* 8.3). The term *anterastês*, for its part, can only designate a rival in love: see Aristoph. *Eq.* 733ff., and also Plato himself, *Resp.* 521b, and also Plut. *Amator.* 761c; see also the term *anterômenos* used by Eupol. frag. 428 Kassel-Austin; see Dover 1978, 52ff., and the useful comments provided by Halperin 1986, 66, n. 14. The idea of amorous reciprocity is still

century B.C. In the fourth century B.C., Aeschines himself cited this law, which forbade slaves to exercise in a gymnasium and there establish amorous relations (*paiderastein* or *erân*) with youths of free status. According to one anecdote, the tyrant Polycrates of Samos had the palaestras destroyed in order to put an end to such erotic relations and the consequent *philiai* that were formed there. While it may seem paradoxical to anyone who has read Ibycus, it is an anecdote that reflects preoccupations similar to Solon's.[23] As for metics, men who were free but not citizens, they had a rival Eros of their own to worship.

It is clearly with the perspective provided by this institutional reference that we should interpret the many legends about the premature disappearance of loved adolescents, *erômenoi*, accidentally killed or abducted by their respective *erastai* (lovers) while exercising in the gymnasium: young Hyacinth felled by the discus thrown by Apollo, his *erastês*; Chrysippus, the son of Pelops, abducted by Laius, who fell in love with the youth while teaching him how to drive a chariot; and — much later — Antheus, the young Trojan loved by Paris and killed by his lover in the course of gymnastic games. The deaths or abductions of all these youths, which should be regarded simply as stories rather than as references to rituals of initiation, focus the attention on the combination of relations of homophilia with education dispensed through the teaching of gymnastic skills.[24] This is also the point at which to recall the figure of Iolaus, the young Theban who assisted Heracles and was loved by him. He was revered in Thebes, where a festival of athletics was held in his honor and where his tomb was to be found: this *mnêma* was situated beyond the Proetid Gate, close to the stadium and to a gymnasium that was named after Iolaus. Aristotle records that this was where *erastai* and *erômenoi* would go to swear their oaths of fidelity (*pisteis*).[25]

---

present through the study of F. Frontisi-Ducroux and J.-P. Vernant, *Dans l'oeil du miroir* (Paris 1997).

[23] In addition to Aesch. 1.138f., this law (frag. 74 Ruschenbusch), is paraphrased by Plut. *Sol.* 1.6, *Amator.* 751b, etc.: see M. Manfredini and L. Piccirilli, *Plutarco. La vita di Solone* (Milan 1977), 113ff., who analyze the many passages attesting to the love that Solon himself felt for adolescents; Ath. 13.602d. It is worth noting that in the second century still, a Macedonian law affecting gymnasiarchs (*SEG* XXVII.261 and XXXII.634) prohibited access to the gymnasium not only for slaves, freedmen, the mentally defective, and drunkards, but also for male prostitutes (*hetaireukôs*)! See L. Moretti, "Sulla legge ginnasiarchica di Berea," *Riv. Filol. Istr. Class.* 110 (1982): 45–53, and Cantarella 1988, 48ff., together with the critical remarks of P. Gauthier and M. B. Hatropoulos, *La loi gymnasiarchique de Beria* (Athens 1993), 84ff. On the problem of fixed homosexuality, see below ch. VII, §1.

[24] See essentially Eur. *Hel.* 1465ff., Ath. 13.602f ff., and Apoll. 3.5.5, Tzetz. *ad Lyc. Alex.* 1342, with the commentary by Sergent 1984, 97ff., 84ff., and 280ff., and also the elegiac poem given by the *P. Oxy.* 3723.

[25] Aristotle frags. 44 and 1008 Gigon, cited by Plut. *Pel.* 18.4 and *Amator.* 761de; Paus.

The iconography of the late archaic and early classical periods, with its clear representations of gymnasium activities, uses distinctive signs to mark out this second most popular space (after the banquet hall) for scenes of courtship and homophile love. They generally incorporate an animal, either from the farmyard or from the wild, but tamed. Such an animal would be a gift from the adult to the *erômenos* and appears to have been a material sign of the contract of *philia* offered to the young man who, like the animal, had also been tamed. The giving of such an animal appears to be the iconic equivalent of a metaphor frequently used in the texts, the metaphor of the yoke that the *erastês* imposes upon the *erômenos*, to tame or domesticate him. The artists of the archaic period seem to have delighted above all in painting pictures showing the hunting of the animals that, once tamed, would then make their appearance in courtship scenes. So they certainly seem to have been well aware of this phase that preceded the sealing of an erotic contract between a youth and an adult. However, the very fact that these panthers or hares are hunted and subsequently tamed not by the adolescents but by the adults should deter us from giving these images the directly initiatory interpretation that they might appear to warrant.[26] If any initiation *was* involved here, it took place not during the hunt, but in the gymnasium or nearby.

Over and above the satirical distance that they assume where homoerotic practices are concerned (a subject to which we shall be returning), the texts of Aristophanes himself attest the degree to which gymnasium activities influenced the development of homophile relations. Clearly, the decency inculcated by good old-fashioned education demanded that the bodies of adolescents should leave upon the palaestra sand no traces of a kind to arouse the desire of their *erastai*. However, in the Utopian city imagined by Pisthetairos in the *Birds*, to abstain from using sweet words and enticing caresses to seduce a child emerging in all his finery from the gymnasium would be to deserve the sharpest of reproaches. On two occasions, Aristophanes, expressing himself either through the chorus leader or through the *parabasis*, congratulates himself on steering clear of palaestras so as to avoid the temptation of corrupting boys there. Cicero, when pondering upon the origins of the love of handsome

---

9.23.1; see already Pind. *Ol.* 9.98ff.; on this heroic polymorphous figure, see Calame 1977, I, 423ff., and Sergent 1984, 171ff.; on the festival of the Ioaleia, see the historicist hypothesis of A. Schachter, *Cults of Boiotia* II, *Bull. Inst. Class. Stud. Suppl.* 38.2 (London 1986), 17ff. and 64ff. Pindar, *Ol.* 1.25ff., imagines a similar relationship between Pelops and Poseidon: see E. Krummen, *Pyrsos Hymnon* (Berlin and New York 1990), 184ff.

[26] See the corpus put together and analyzed by Schnapp 1984, 67ff., who, in his historical perspective, tends to project scenes of homophile courtship into the domain of wild nature.

youths, quite naturally traced them to the gymnasia of the Greeks *in quibus isti liberi et concessi sunt amores.*[27]

## 2.3. Graffiti and "Pederastic Acclamations"

Even more direct evidence relating to Eros and the gymnasium is available to us. Who in the scholarly world today does not know of the famous sixty-century "pederastic" graffiti of Thera? The most explicit of these calls upon Apollo Delphinios to witness that on this very spot Crimon made love with the son of Bathycles. The verb *oiphein*, which elsewhere designates the most regular form of coitus, sometimes with a satirical connotation, is in one inscription (on Santorini) replaced by *erasthai*. The structure of these inscribed statements suggests that the anthroponymous subject of these verbs corresponds to the name of an adult male. Alongside these inscriptions relating to sexual performances is another series of graffiti in which proper names are accompanied by adjectives such as *agathos* or *aristos*, which in some cases refer to the activity of dancing.[28] A parallel to this second type of "pederastic" inscriptions has recently been found on the island of Thasos, where graffiti of a later period (the mid-fourth century) have been deciphered: these statements are similar to those of Santorini, but praise not so much the moral and social virtues of the boys but rather their physical qualities. Aetes, for example, is declared to be not only handsome (*kalos*) but also, in another inscription, in the flower of youth (*hôraios*), comely (*euprosôpos*), gentle (*hêdus*), and charming (*eukharis*). Elsewhere, he is said to have a beautiful (*eurhuthmos*) face and an "urbane"

---

[27] Aristoph. *Nub.* 973ff., *Av.* 137ff., *Pax* 762ff., and *Vesp.* 1023ff.; Cic. *Tusc.* 4.70; for other references, see Henderson 1991, 216ff. Dover 1978, 54ff. and 154ff., points out that in the dialogues of Plato, the gymnasium is generally the place where Socrates' young friends would meet the boys whom they desired; see in particular the *Charmides* (154a ff.) and the *Lysis* (206e ff.).

[28] *IG* XII.3.537a = *SGDI* 4788, which may also be translated as follows: "C. copulated at this spot with a boy, the brother of Bathycles"; see also 538 = 1411; 542; for inscriptions with *agathos*, see 540 = 1413, 541, 543 = 1414: see Bethe 1907, 460ff.; on the problem of the dating of these epigraphs, see Cantarella 1988, 22 n. 12; on their form, see B. B. Powell, *Homer and the Origin of the Greek Alphabet* (Cambridge 1991), 171ff. It seems that at least two of these inscriptions (536 and 552) were the object, *a posteriori*, of unappreciative commentaries in which the *erastês* was called *pornos*! By translating it as "to sodomize," Buffière 1980, 58, overinterprets the sense of the verb *oiphein*: see Theocr. 4.62ff. with sch. *ad loc.* (152 Wendel), who translates this verb as *sunousiazein*, and also Plut. *Pyrrh.* 28.6, who records the recommendation of a Spartan in which the act designated by *oiphein* resulted in the generation of fine children for the city! See D. Bain, "Sex Greek Verbs of Sexual Congress," *Class. Quart.* 41 (1991): 51–77, and below ch. VII, §1.2, n. 15.

expression (*asteoprosôpos*).[29] And at Nemea itself, the location of the Panhellenic games celebrated by Pindar, a graffiti of the same type is flanked by a commentary in a second hand that declares that the handsome Acrotatos is the (beloved) of the person who inscribed the inscription. This pederastic utterance is thus provided with its utterer: the *erastês* of Acrotatos.[30]

By using the deictic and local adverb of place, the graffiti of Thera show that their location is also where the act to which they refer took place. The localizing sense of this *hic* is by no means unimportant, for these homophile inscriptions are carved on the rocks flanking the great terrace constructed at the same date in front of the temple dedicated to Apollo, a terrace that was later to be converted into a gymnasium. Whether this Apollo of Thera was revered as Delphinios or as Carneios, as appears to be suggested by later inscriptions, both the terrace and the epithets refer us to the ritual gymnastic practices of adolescence.[31] It comes as no surprise, then, to find the graffiti located in the tunnel that led to the stadium. As for the inscriptions of Kalami, on the island of Thasos, their location on the seashore, on the rocks of a small cove close to the remains of a fort, has suggested to their editors that they were carved by the lovers of ephebes stationed in this garrison on the island's "frontier." Certainly, in Thera and Nemea it is a remarkable coincidence that the graffiti consecrating the practice of homophilia should be located close to the places set aside for gymnastic exercises, just as the speech inscribed on the altar of Eros, close to the Academy of Athens, suggests (through the use of a deictic) that this monument was likewise situated on "the shady fringes of the gymnasium."[32]

Asymmetric erotic desire, which was a consequence of the practices of the gymnasium and the palaestra, thus found fulfillment on the

[29] SEG XXXII.847; all these adjectives are intelligently discussed by the publishers of these descriptions, Y. Garlan and O. Masson, "Les acclamations pédérastiques de Kalami," *Bull. Corr. Hell.* 106 (1982): 3–22. The confinement of the ephebes' exercises to frontier regions is well described by Vidal-Naquet 1983, 151ff. Other "pederastic" inscriptions, from Thasos, have been reprinted in SEG XXXI.763–72: the first of them, of later date, combines praises for the beauty of both girls and boys.

[30] SEG XXIX.349; graffiti published by S. G. Miller, "Excavations at Nemea, 1978," *Hesperia* 48 (1979): 73–103 (100ff.).

[31] For the situation of the temple and the terrace: see F. Hiller von Gaertringen, "Thera," *Realenc. Alt.-Wiss.* V A, Stuttgart 1934, coll. 2260–302 (coll. 2289ff.). The few bits of information that we possess about the Carneia of Sparta, the metropolis of Thera, enabled Brelich 1969, 148ff. and 179ff., to detect in this festival a celebration of the integration of neoinitiates into the Spartan political community; in Sparta, the temple of Apollo Carneios was situated close to the Dromos where the races of the *neoi* took place: Calame 1977, I, 351ff. The relations of Apollo Delphinios to the ephebes are studied by F. Graf, "Apollon Delphinios," *Mus. Helv.* 36 (1979): 2–22.

[32] Inscription cited by Ath. 13.609d (see above n. 19).

fringes of those places, but in their immediate neighbourhood — not out in wild ground, as might be supposed from a strict projection of the ritual pattern of tribal initiation. Gymnasia of the archaic period would frequently be situated near the ramparts surrounding the town, yet would still be included within the city perimeter. This spatial relationship to the *polis* was all the closer given that these were — and for a long time remained — the places where the traditional Greek education, based on the teaching of music and gymnastics, unfolded.[33] In Greece, the ritual inversion to be expected in an educative process of an initiatory type was essentially realized at the sexual level. However, it is again noticeable that, from a social and spatial point of view, the system, which was semantically adjusted to fit in with the idea of the developing city structures, did not completely overturn the values to which the adolescent would subscribe once he became an adult citizen.

These eloquent and meaningful rocks are somewhat reminiscent of the illustrated and inscribed objects that would be passed around at a banquet. A number of scholars have already made that comparison; however, they paid scant attention to the fact that the declarations that those objects carried are always made by an *erastês*.[34] In consequence, they underestimated the essentially pedagogical nature of inscriptions that tend, by very virtue of being written down, to turn the scene depicted (or indeed the cup itself), or even the place where a couple come together, into a "monument" to the erotic and educative relationship that was formed either at a banquet or in the gymnasium. It follows that, as performative words or assertions that consecrated some performance, these epigraphical statements were also part of the dialectic of *epainos* and *mômos*, praise and reproach. That is borne out by the fact that the acclamations at Kalami, on the island of Thasos, may sometimes take on a critical tone. Although the handsome Myiscus is so charming and sweet that he is worthy of having the locutor (who is probably the enunciator) consider him his very own (*emos*), in one instance at least he becomes a savage, uncouth evil (*agreos/agreios*). The

[33] The generally outlying situation of gymnasia, as distinct from the more confined spaces of the palaestras, is described by S. L. Glass, "The Greek Gymnasium," in W. J. Raschke (ed.), *The Archaeology of the Olympics* (Madison and London 1988), 155–73; see also the classic study by J. Delorme, *Gymnasion* (Paris 1960), 51ff. and 253ff. On the foundations of traditional Athenian education, see H. I. Marrou, *Histoire de l'éducation dans l'Antiquité* (Paris ⁶1964), 69ff. (English translation: G. Lamb, *A History of Education in Antiquity* [New York 1956]).

[34] See in particular Dover 1978, 114ff.: although he rejects the interpretation according to which these objects are offerings from the *erastês* to the *erômenos*, Dover provides no coherent explanation of his own. On the "pederastic acclamations" inscribed on vases, see the references given above ch. IV, §1.2, n. 22; Robinson and Fluck 1937, 21ff., link these declarations with the inscriptions of Thera.

boy's very name, a nickname in the diminutive, might well be an allusion to the excessive sexuality that the Greeks attributed to the mouse (*mus*).[35]

Caught up in the dialectic of praise and criticism that was characteristic of this culture in which a citizen's status depended upon his reputation, a fleeing liaison between an adult and an adolescent sometimes transgressed the bounds of convention that were considered appropriate for Greek homophilia. If it did so, it was condemned as aberrant and pilloried by the mockery of comedy (to which we shall soon be turning). For the moment, suffice it to repeat that it was precisely in the domain of sexuality that the educative system set up in the cities of archaic, and no doubt also classical, Greece conformed most closely with the canon of tribal initiation rites, as defined by cultural and social anthropology. There is, thus, not the slightest reason to doubt the initiatory function of the sexual aspect of Greek homophilia.[36]

In conclusion, as evidence of the key place allotted to Eros in the process of Greek initiatory education, let us consider some anonymous lines of poetry that were sung in Chalcis. They set the seal of approval upon one of the many anecdotes that held up as an example for the young *erômenos* of the death in battle of his adult *erastês*, who was loved (*philêtheis*) by the youth and whose desire for the latter drove him to perform such model exploits:

> You boys who possess the Graces (*kharites*) and noble fathers,
> do not grudge your youthful beauty
> in converse with good men (*agathoi*);
> for together with bravery (*andreia*) Love, loosener of limbs (*lusimelês*),
> flourishes in the cities of the Chalcidians.[37]

---

[35] This, at any rate, is the hypothesis suggested by J. Taillardat, "MUIKKOS, AGREIOS or AGRIOS?," *Bull. Corr. Hell.* 107 (1983): 189–90; elsewhere he gives *agreos*, interpreted as *agrios*, a positive sense of "passionate," "determined"; the name of the *eromenos* should in that case be compared to that of the beloved boy to whom Meleager addresses some of his epigrams: Myiscus, as ardent for pleasure "as a mouse," see above ch. III, §2.1, with n. 9.

[36] I make this point briefly to counter both the objections raised by H. Patzer, *Die griechische Knabeliebe* (Wiesbaden 1982), 43ff. and 125ff., against the sexual nature of the initiatory institutions of the Greeks, and also the thesis advanced by K. J. Dover, "Greek Homosexuality and Initiation," in *The Greeks and Their Legacy* II (Oxford 1988), 115–34, concerning the superimposed nature of the pedagogic relationship with regard to the amorous relations between *erastês* and *erômenos*. One could even ascribe an initiatory significance to the nudity of the handsome bodies of the adolescents exercising in the gymnasium and thereby prompting the admiration of vase painters: see L. Bonfante, "Nudity as a Costume in Classical Art," *Am. Journ. Arch.* 93 (1989): 543–70.

[37] *Carm. pop.* 873 Page, an archaic song for the cithara probably intended to be sung at banquets, in D. A. Campbell (trans.), *Greek Lyric* V (Loeb 1993); G. Tedeschi, "Lo

As an aetiological tale, this account testifies not only to the function fulfilled by the Eros that develops along with "manliness" (*andreia*), but also to the esteem (*etimêsan*) that surrounded a *paiderastein* that had initially been a target of criticism (*en psogôi*). According to this Chalcidian legend, it was thanks to an amorous and trusting relationship with an older man that a youth turned into a soldier and a citizen in the course of the practices of the banquet or the gymnasium. In either case, poetry sanctioned the propaedeutic role of *erôs* for the *philia* that had to reign among the citizens in the *polis*.

---

*skólion* per gli *erômenoi* calcidesi," in K. Fabian (ed.), *Oinera teukhe* (Alessandria 1992), 85–94. The anecdote is recounted by Plutarch, *Amator.* 760e ff., who attributes it to Aristotle, frag. 44 Gigon (possibly confused with the Chalcidian historian of the same name); see also Ath. 13.601e. Other frequently cited anecdotes similarly represent homophile love as motivating exemplary virtues: see Buffière 1980, 366ff., and Sergent 1984, 199ff.; they are mirrored at a social level by the warrior practices attributed to certain cities: see Dover 1978, 190ff.

The homophile relationship (Plat. *Symp.* 182c) between the tyrannicides Aristogiton (*erôs*) and Harmodius (*philia*) shows that propaedeutic "pederasty" was not restricted to the Dorian domain, nor, probably, to the Indo-European: see Dover 1978, 194ff., and J. Bremmer, "An Enigmatic Indo-European Rite: Paederasty," *Arethusa* 13 (1980): 279–98.

# Chapter VI

## EROS IN THE FEMININE: THE *OIKOS*

WHAT HAPPENED to the love life of these boys and girls educated through Eros, once they reached adulthood? To tackle this question we shall have to adopt a different perspective, since among adults the victims of Aphrodite and Eros were usually women. Furthermore, if we are to remain with Athens, a slight chronological shift will be necessary: the lack of documentation forces us to move from the late archaic period to the heart of the classical period, when the extension of the democratic system was in full swing. It must be admitted that there are no traces of the existence at this date of any initiatory type of education system for girls comparable to what it is possible to reconstruct for late-seventh-century Sparta and Mytilene. There are, however, signs that point to a sequence of age groups, and the fact that in Athens young or adolescent girls participated in religious celebrations such as the Brauronia and the Arrhephoria suggests that these did involve rites of tribal initiation. In particular, the ritual established for girls participating in the Arrhephoria manifests a strong link if not with homophilia, at least with sexuality generally. We shall be returning to examine this in connection with the spaces that were reserved for Eros.[1]

Once she reached adulthood, a daughter of an Athenian citizen — whatever the form of her education — was destined for marriage. However, in fifth-century Athens the bond of matrimony, which was founded upon cohabitation, was flexible enough for other women, too, to be integrated into the kinship of the *oikos*, or household. For example, a noncitizen woman could find a place there as a concubine. Within the confines of the present work it is not possible to address the legal and affective aspects of this remarkable status for women.[2] But the condition of a *hetaira*, which frequently led into it, is also very interesting,

---

[1] See in this connection the evidence carefully reviewed by Brulé 1987, 79ff. and 240ff.; on the *arrhephoroi* in particular, see below ch. IX, §3, n. 10.

[2] On this subject see A.R.W. Harrison, *The Law of Athens* (Oxford 1968), 1ff., and the many references given by E. Cantarella, *L'ambiguo malanno* (Rome ²1985), 68ff.; L. Gallo, "La donna greca e la marginalità," *Quad. Urb. Cult. Class.* 47 (1984): 7–51 (together with the earlier bibliography), W. Schuller, *Frauen in der griechischen Geschichte* (Constance 1985), 44ff., and Cohen 1991, 149ff., correcting the by now traditional image of the seclusion of Athenian women in their own quarters: see for example S. B. Pomeroy, *Goddesses, Whores, Wives and Slaves* (New York 1975), 79ff.

particularly as it reflects aspects of the intermediate kind of status experienced by Sappho's young pupils even as, both sexually and socially, they were moving toward men.

## 1. AN INTERMEDIATE STATUS: THE *HETAIRA* AT THE BANQUET

Classical sources present a complex image of courtesans. It oscillates between the portrait of the likes of Aspasia, whose beauty and intelligence won her the place of Pericles' legitimate wife, and that of a flute player, whose sexual services could be hired whenever the need arose. The very word *hetaira* has a wide semantic field bounded by two poles that are neatly summed up in a gloss by Hesychius: a *hetaira* could be either a dear friend (*philê*) or a prostitute (*pornê*). A similar distinction was made for male prostitution. The law took a hand in regulating the *hetairêsis*, prostitution, but in the invective of the orator Aeschines, *hetairekôs*, a companion, became *peporneumenos*, a prostitute: it all depended upon how many clients the prostitute served.[3]

The frequently analyzed speech attributed to Demosthenes that accuses Neaera of usurping the status of a wife provides a perfect illustration of the social advancement that was possible for a courtesan, who might climb from the status of a slave prostitute to that of the wife of a citizen. The position of a *hetaira*, which was characterized by the relative freedom accorded to a freedwoman or the daughter of a metic, was situated midway between the above two polar conditions. But quite apart from her fluctuating social status, which could undergo remarkable variations depending upon the circumstances, the distinguishing mark of a *hetaira* of classical Athens was that she took part in banquets for men, as is attested by the same speech. On that basis, archaeologists who interpret pictorial representations tend — probably mistakenly — to lump together in the single category of *hetairai* all the young women, whether richly clothed or naked, who were to be found alongside men — either ephebes or adults — on the symposium couches.[4]

However that may be, a *hetaira* certainly was a woman who took part in banquets and whose status corresponded to a certain social representation. Phrynion bought the young Neaera from her pimping

---

[3] Hsch. s.v. *hetaira* (*E* 6480 Latte); Athenaeus, 13.571b ff., makes the same distinction, on the basis of Anaxilas, frag. 21 Kassel-Austin. On the various aspects of the status of a *hetaira*, see C. Mossé, *La femme dans la Grèce antique* (Paris 1983), 62ff., and Reinsberg 1989, 80ff.; for the distinction between *hetaira* and *pornê*, see now Kurke 1997, 108ff.; on male prostitutes, see below ch. VII, §1.2.

[4] Ps. Dem. 59.18ff. See the corpus of images collected by Peschel 1987, who contents herself (19ff. and 25) with too general a definition of a *hetaira*; and Reinsberg 1989, 91ff., who makes the same mistake: see now the good commentary by Kurke 1997, 133ff.

mother in Corinth and gave her her freedom; then he took her with him
to Athens, where she became famous, and benefited from a certain social image, thanks to Demosthenes' speech about her. From that time on
she took part in all the Bacchic revelries of this debauched citizen and
was at his side in every symposium and every *kômos* that he attended.
In his speech, Demosthenes claimed that the very fact that the girl took
part in banquets proved that she was a courtesan.[5] However, even if the
roles played by a *hetaira* in these citizen gatherings were those of a
subordinate, they cannot be reduced to the passive behavior of a mere
sexual object. To be sure, when she got up on to a *klinê* (couch) to take
her place beside an adult symposiast, hers was always the subordinate
position; but in addition to the undeniable sexual favors that were expected of her, there was also her flute playing and her dancing. Whether
played by a man or by a woman, the *aulos* not only dominated the
symposium and the procession that followed it, but was also the instrument that generally accompanied elegies: these, as a number of sources
testify, were usually sung at banquets.[6] This means that even before the
flute music, in combination with the wine, exerted its orgiastic power
upon the symposiasts, leading them on to erotic excesses, the woman
who played the *aulos* had been called upon to play her part in the
educative singing of poetry and in the dancing that were also features of
these convivial gatherings.

Another point to note, from the spatial point of view, is that for a
woman to take part in symposia meant moving outside the gynaeceum
(where, however, Athenian women were not as closely confined as is
sometimes suggested). The speech against Neaera makes this one of its
most telling points. When Lysias — probably Lysias the logographer —
brought to Athens a very young courtesan along with her mistress and
another of the latter's young charges in order that the third of these
women could be initiated into the Mysteries of Eleusis, he was careful
not to invite them to his own house. Out of deference to his wife and
his mother, he installed them in the home of one of his young bachelor
friends who lived in the deme of Colonus! It is true that the archaeologists tell us that every Athenian home of any distinction contained one

---

[5] Ps. Dem. 59.33; see also 24, 25, 34 etc.; on the career of Neaera and the various
statuses she usurped, see Calame 1989, 105.

[6] See Mimn. test. 5 Gentili-Prato or Thgn. 939ff., 943ff. and 1041ff.; for bibliographical references, see above, ch. IV, n. 24, and also, on the *hetaira* who played the flute, the
study by C. G. Starr, "An Evening with the Flute-Girls," *Par. Pass.* 33 (1978): 401–10;
iconography in Peschel 1987 *passim*. We should remember that, on account of its orgiastic character, Aristotle, *Pol.* 8.1341a 17ff., denied that the playing of the *aulos* had any
educative value, although acknowledging that both before and after the Persian Wars the
Athenians encouraged the learning of this skill: see Aristoph. frag. 232 Kassel-Austin.

room that was specifically reserved for men (the *andrôn*); but the fact
that direct access to it would be arranged from the front door or from
the street shows that it was of a semipublic nature. In similar fashion, in
all buildings ranging from the public Prytanaeum to the banqueting
halls attached to sanctuaries, spaces for eating or for drinking would be
positioned on the border between the inside and the outside. It is also
worth remembering that the drunken *kômos* that followed a symposium would move from inside the house out to the open space of the
streets.[7]

The liminal space in which *hetairai* exercised their skills was complemented by the status that was assigned to them, which was also of an
intermediate character, as is attested by at least two sources of evidence.
The first is the famous banquet song in which Pindar praises the fifty
courtesans presented to Aphrodite by Xenophon of Corinth out of gratitude for his double victory at the Olympic Games — a civic act if ever
there was one, and one that that was totally unrelated to any form of
sacred prostitution, which was forbidden by the religious laws of the
Greeks. Now, the praises showered upon the *hetairai* from Corinth assimilate them to girls who have not yet reached the status of adulthood
that is conferred by marriage.[8] It is as unmarried girls, whose condition
coincided with the relative indeterminacy of a *hetaira*'s status, that these
courtesans were admitted to the men's banquets.

The second source of evidence here is iconography, from which we
learn that a *hetaira* could herself take the place of a symposiast, in all
probability in a parody of his role. Draped in a man's *himation* (over-
coat), if not naked, a *hetaira* is frequently to be found at the head of a
bed, facing one of her companions, with whom she is playing the customary symposium games. The written statements that accompany such
scenes specify what these games are, for they take the form of invitations to partake of wine or to play at *kottabos*. Moreover, the names of

---

[7] Ps. Dem. 59.21ff. On the location of spaces reserved for banquets, see, for the *oikos*,
Keuls 1985, 210ff., with the references provided by Gould 1980, 48, and also M. Jame-
son, "Private Space and the Greek City," in Murray and Price (eds.), above ch. V, n. 2,
171–95; on sanctuaries, see C. Börker, *Festbankett und griechische Architektur* (Constance 1983), and B. Berquist, "Sympotic Space," in Murray 1990, 37–65. As for representations of the *kômos*, see Peschel 1987, 21ff. The Attic iconography of the late archaic
period frequently depicts girls and young women outside the house, in particular in scenes
of seduction modeled on homophile courtship: see F. Lissarrague, "Un regard athénien,"
in Schmitt-Pantel 1991, 179–240 (217ff.).

[8] Pind. frag. 122 Maehler, with the commentary that I attempted for that poem in 1989,
104ff., and the critical remarks formulated by L. Kurke, "Pindar and the Prostitutes, or
Reading Ancient 'Pornography,'" *Arion* III, 4.2 (1996): 49–75; on the rule of sexual
purity to be respected when entering a sanctuary and on the ban against coitus within the
precinct, see also Parker 1983, 74ff.

those to whom these invitations to play the game of *kottabos* (heel taps game) are addressed — Leagros, or the handsome Euthymides — are masculine![9] So far as can be seen, although it is sometimes hard to tell exactly, the written words are addressed to a courtesan who is represented in the masculine position. In view of the loving praises that tend to be showered upon Leagros and Euthymides in other iconographic inscriptions, the short speech addressed to the courtesan makes her an *erômenos* rather than an *erastês*. The intermediate status of the *hetaira* no doubt facilitated this double reversal of sociosexual roles.

The nature of any status linked with transition is relatively indefinite, and this is probably why it is a courtesan, with just such a status, who tends to be the principal protagonist in many scenes of sexual excess. As we have seen, obscene iconography, which to us looks like pornography, regularly links various forms of such excess with the consumption of wine, in the context of either a symposium or the procession that followed it.[10] All of them constitute expressions of an inventive sexuality from which, however, Eros is absent since desire has by then been consummated. Even more than the youthful sons of citizens, *hetairai*, by exciting desire, brought into being relationships in which sexual impulses could be satisfied but which were essentially fleeting. Furthermore, in contrast to the relationships that adults sought to establish with their *erômenoi* or with the daughters of citizens, these amorous relations in principle remained unproductive. Nevertheless, over and above the simple satisfaction of pleasure, *philia* offered a basis upon which to develop relations of mutual trust not only between a citizen and a courtesan but even between two courtesans. There are so many possible meanings for the term *hetaira* that it is always difficult to be sure of the correct interpretation. However, two funerary inscriptions from Athens may illuminate such relationships in one particular respect. In the first, a "companion" (*hetaira*) dedicates a funerary stele to a young woman who has died in the flower of her youth, as testimony to their loving relationship (*philotês*), based upon fidelity and affection (*pistê, hêdeia*):

> In gratitude for sweet and loyal friendship,
> > Euthylla, your companion, has erected this stele on your tomb,

[9] See in particular, on invitations to drink, the Oltos cup, Madrid Nat. Mus. 11267 (*ARV*[2] 58, 53) and, on the game of *kottabos*, the psykter of Leningrad Hermitage B 644 (*ARV*[2] 16.15 and 1619) and the hydria of Munich Antikenslg. 2421 (*ARV*[2] 23.7 and 1620): these pieces date from the late sixth century B.C. Corpus collected and illustrated by Peschel 1987, 70ff. and 110ff.; see also Reinsberg 1989, 112ff. As for the possible civic identity of Leagros, see Robinson and Fluck 1937, 132ff.

[10] Corpus of images in Keuls 1986, 161ff.; Peschel 1987, 57ff. and 115ff.; and Reinsberg 1989, 96ff.

Biote; she weeps for the eternally mourned memory
  of your youth now gone forever.

On the second stele, a number of *hetairoi* declare—as a group!—that
they are laying a wreath upon the funerary monument of a certain Anthemis, to celebrate the memory of her virtue (*aretê*) and her fidelity
(*philia*):

> This is the tomb of Anthemis; her companions surround it, to crown it,
>   in memory of her virtue and faithful companionship.[11]

It would appear that Anthemis, a *hetaira*, had succeeded in establishing
between herself and her companions mutual relations of trust that were
the basis of their fellowship. Two parallel inscriptions testify to the existence of an equivalent ritual for men: the consecration of a funerary
monument to a *hetairos* by his fellows. The parallelism shows that the
closest status to that of a *hetaira* was definitely that of a symposiast,
integrated into his particular group of loyal companions.

That is certainly an assimilation suggested—at a later date, admittedly—by Apollodorus of Athens, the historian of religion, when he
attempts to explain the function of the cult that the Athenians devoted
to Aphrodite Hetaira: in the worship of the goddess who went by this
name, no distinction was made between *hetairoi* and *hetairai*. The latter
thus became *philai*. In support of the explanation suggested by Apollodorus, Athenaeus cites precisely the verses by Sappho to which we
have already drawn attention, in which the poet uses both those terms
to describe the girls who were her pupils! His citation itself testifies to
the indeterminate status of a *hetaira*, a status that oscillated between the
feminine and the masculine. In the same way—to return to the fifth
century B.C.—the young courtesan in Aristophanes' *Women at the Assembly* uses the expression *mou hetairos*, my companion, to refer to the
man who, later in the comedy, takes the place of an *erastês*. But here, as
with Aphrodite Hetaira, we are certainly back in the domain of erotic
love since both the girl and the young man declare themselves to be
possessed by Eros and Cypris.[12]

These transitory amorous relations between girls who are *hetairai*
and men who are still young appear in certain respects simply to consti-

[11] *CEG* I.97 and 92 Hansen; two women were indeed represented and named in the
painting adorning the (lost) stele of the second inscription: Herophile and Anthemis, who
dedicated the tomb. See also *CEG* I.139 and 171 Hansen.

[12] Apollod. *FGrHist.* 144 F 112, cited by Ath. 571c ff. (see above n. 3), who also
mentions Sappho frags. 160 and 142 Voigt (see above ch. V, §1.2, n. 15) and Menander,
frag. 323 Koerte, who demanded that a distinction should be made between the *hetairai*
and the *hetairoi* who praised their charms! Aristoph. *Eccl.* 912, 994, 954ff.: see below ch.
VII, §1, n. 6. On the cult of Aphrodite Hetaira, see my references in 1989, 109, n. 6.

tute preludes to the consummation of love since, for women even more than for men, the deployment of the gifts of Aphrodite was consecrated by marriage, an institution all too often claimed to have excluded the satisfaction of desire and sexuality generally, in classical Greece.

## 2. THE TRANSITION TO MATURITY: THE YOUNG WIFE

Notwithstanding the diverse nature of the documents that make it possible to reconstruct the ancient Greek marriage ceremony, anthropologists of ancient Greece are by now in agreement as to the sequence of the rites that constituted the procedure. The principal stages of the classical ritual of marriage are now known to us: the offering of locks shorn from the adolescent's head, followed by the ritual bathing of both the betrothed; the wedding feast in the house of the father of the bride, followed by her unveiling; the nocturnal torch-lit procession, followed by the welcome offered, in the bridegroom's house, by his mother; the eating of a quince that symbolized the *consummatio matrimonii*, followed by a song to awaken the young married couple and the presentation of the dowry gifts for the new wife.[13]

### 2.1. A Rite of Passage into Civilization

There can be no doubt that the ceremony as a whole represented a rite of passage. Materially, that is to say spatially, that passage was made by its main protagonist, the young bride, and it was thought through and symbolically reformulated at two levels in the ritual ceremony. On the one hand, from the point of view of the actors in the ritual, it is clear that the bride left her father and his house to move to a new hearth, to live there alongside her future husband's mother. Furthermore, at the wedding feast the men and the women ate in separate groups, the bride being surrounded by the *numpheutria* (assistant to the bride) and the girls who were her friends; then, in the wedding procession, the bride was seated in a chariot next to a male relative or a friend of the groom, but during this intermediate journey to the house of her future husband she was still attended by her mother, while a mixed chorus accompanied the wedding procession, singing *hymenaean* songs. It was only once the bridegroom's mother had made the bride welcome that husband and

---

[13] For a reconstruction based on the texts, see Calame 1983b, XVIff., and A. Avagianou, *Sacred Marriage in the Rituals of Greek Religion* (Berne and Vienna 1991), 1ff.; and for a reconstruction based on the iconography, see Reinsberg 1989, 49ff., and J. H. Oakley and R. H. Sinos, *The Wedding in Ancient Athens* (Madison and London 1993), 22ff. A bibliography on this subject may be found in Contiades-Tsitsoni 1990, 33ff.

wife came together in the *thalamos*, on the nuptial bed, and there ate the quince. While respecting the rule of virilocality, Greek marriage eased the way to it through the mediation of women or, to be more precise, through a progression of stages that led from the separation of the two sexes to their intermingling.

On the other hand, some of the acts of this ritual occasion used the dietary level to express the transition of the bride from being the daughter of her father to being a woman, the wife of her husband, for food was always of central importance in the Greeks' representations of the sequence of stages that led to feminine maturity and human reproduction. A young child crowned with acanthus leaves and acorns ran about during the wedding banquet, repeatedly declaring that the bride and groom had "escaped from an evil to find something good" and offering the guests bread from the winnowing basket that he carried. In this way, the foodstuffs of the wild life that the girl was leaving were set in opposition to this product of cereal cultivation, which symbolized not only the advent of civilization but also the maturity of the adult woman. The ceremony proceeded as an expression of civilization, which was given material represention by the barley grill carried by the bride during the *numephagôgia* and by the instruments of seduction presented to her at the end of the ceremonies of transition.[14] Where the woman was concerned, Greek marriage was certainly conceived (mainly by the men) as a passage from "nature" to culture, mediated by the union of the sexes.

## 2.2. The Role of Eros and Sexuality

After the bride, the next most prominent protagonist in the matrimonial ritual was Eros. Admittedly, his presence at the heart of marriage is attested by only one classical text, which does so by evoking the paradigmatic wedding of Hera and Zeus. This mythical reference occurs in the marriage hymn that the chorus of Aristophanes' *Birds* sings at the end of the comedy, to celebrate the happy marriage between Royalty (Basilinna) and Faithful Companion (Pisthetairos). In the joyous nuptial procession that takes place, it is the child with golden wings himself who assumes the role of attendant to the future wife. On the other

---

[14] The carrying of a barley grill and the consumption of a quince by the bride are prescriptions attributed to Solon: frags. 71b and 127 Ruschenbusch; on the meaning of the *epaulia*, see below n. 26. The metaphorical relation established by the Greeks between production through agricultural labor and the fecundity of marriage was celebrated in Athens at the festival of the Thesmophoria; see L. Bruit-Zaidman, "Les filles de Pandore," in Schmitt-Pantel 1991, 363–403. Other documents that are helpful in any reconstruction of the unfolding of the marriage ceremony are mentioned in the studies cited in n. 13. On the erotic qualities attributed to the quince, see below ch. VIII, §3, n. 15.

hand, the artists of classical Athens frequently represent the adolescent, winged incarnation of amorous desire, integrating him into every phase in the marriage ceremony. In scenes depicting the procession bringing water for the prenuptial bath, the dressing of the bride, the unveiling, the nuptial procession, and the reception of the future wife, Eros is regularly to be seen at the side of the heroine of the ritual, assisting her. But behind young Eros there always lurks the unseen power of Aphrodite, and in many (admittedly later) documents she too seems to enter the wedding chamber to preside, along with her assistant, over the ritual of the wedding night.[15] Moreover, the presence of the divine powers of love is not limited to that nuptial ceremony, which the painters are prone to depict in a "paradisiacal" setting. Eros has no qualms about entering even the women's quarters, where he is to be found bringing clothing to a woman engaged in adorning herself, or helping another who is busy at her wool work.[16]

It is clearly impossible to know exactly how a young woman would have felt about her marriage and conjugal union. However, a number of complementary representations of the marriage ceremony itself, albeit mostly by male writers, do help us to envisage the ritual from a native vantage point.

Returning briefly to the archaic period, we find that the vocabulary used in the marriage hymns that punctuated each stage of the wedding ceremony provides us with added insight into the role played here by amorous desire.[17] We know that the Alexandrian editors of Sappho classified Book VIII of her opus as *Epithalamia*, or marriage songs. Other poems, also composed for nuptial ceremonies, were for metrical reasons classified in other books of the work of the poet from Lesbos. But,

[15] Aristoph. *Av.* 1728ff. with sch. *ad* 1737 (300 White). For the iconography, see the documentary evidence presented by Hermary 1986, 905ff., and by Reinsberg 1989, 51ff. In the tragic texts, Aphrodite reigns supreme over marriage: see Aesch. *Eum.* 214ff. and *Suppl.* 1035ff.; also Eur. *Phaeth.* 227ff. (see below n. 18).

Other deities, such as Hera and Artemis, also play a part in marriage: see M. Detienne, "Puissances du mariage," in Y. Bonnefoy (ed.), *Dictionnaire des mythologies* II (Paris 1981), 65–73, and Redfield 1982, 194ff.

[16] Hydria Vienna Kunsthist. Mus. IV 386 (*ARV²* 1131.157; the woman is sometimes identified as Aphrodite); lekythos New York MMA 06.1021.90 (*ARV²* 682.102). These scenes cannot possibly correspond to wedding preparations, as Hermary claims, 1986, 906ff., adding other documentary evidence. On the divinization of marriage scenes, see C. Bérard, "L'ordre des femmes," in *La cité des images* (Paris and Lausanne 1984), 85–104.

[17] From the point of view of practical genre, *humenaion* is the general concept that is expressed in all the (ideally choral) singing that accompanied the wedding ceremony, in particular the epithalamium, sung outside the nuptial chamber, and the *diegertikon*, sung to awaken the couple; the classic study is R. Muth, "'Hymenaios' und 'Epithalamion,'" *Wien. Stud.* 67 (1954): 5–45, which is by no means superseded by Contiades-Tsitsoni 1990, 30ff.

leaving those aside, most of the few fragments of specifically matrimo
nial poems that we possess are devoted to praising the beauty of the
*numphê*, or young wife. They do so using the very same terms that we
have already encountered in erotic poetry. Not only do these extremely
fragmentary verses praise the elegant gait, the graceful beauty, the sweet
gaze, and the magnificent appearance of the young woman, but they do
not hesitate to evoke the *erôs* that beams from her face and kindles
desire. The new wife is thus credited with the gifts of Aphrodite herself.
Furthermore, in one of Sappho's marriage hymns paraphrased in the
*Epithalamium to Severus* by Himerius, the goddess described by the
poet enters the marriage chamber herself, riding in the chariot of the
Graces and accompanied by a chorus of infant Loves bearing torches.
And in Euripides' *Phaethon*, the dramatic marriage hymn sung for the
hero by the complementary chorus composed of maidens (*parthenoi*)
begins in the manner of a veritable hymn to Aphrodite: Aphrodite, who
is the mistress of the infant Loves and the most beautiful of the goddesses, Aphrodite who guides girls into marriage and is the mother of
Hymenaeus, a foal newly subjected to the yoke of marriage.[18]

Just as the words used for marriage are the same as those used for
courtship, so too are the gestures. Thus, to take one example, the cloak
(*khlainêi*) with which Archilochus covers the girl whom he has just seduced in order to satisfy his desire reappears as the *gamikê khlanis* that
Faithul Companion brings with him to celebrate her marriage with
Royalty, in the above-mentioned scene from Aristophanes' *Birds*.

Returning to legend, but in literature of a later date, on the marriage
coverlet presented to Habrocomes and Antheia, in the novel by Xenophon of Ephesus, Ares is portrayed wrapped in a *khlanis* and guided by
Eros as he approaches Aphrodite. In this novel, the instrument of nuptial union itself thus carries a mythical representation of its own symbolism. Similarly, in the *Idyll* converted into an epithalamium by Theocritus, Menelaus receives Helen under the single cloak (*mia khlaina*)
that is to enfold the nuptial embraces of this utterly paradigmatic
couple.

Elsewhere, other couples are depicted enfolded in a similar cloak.

---

[18] Sappho frags. 103.1, 103B, 108, 112, and 194 Voigt; I have not included frags. 27,
30, 31, and 44 Voigt in the present study. The problem of the epithalamia in Sappho has
been most recently mentioned by Lasserre 1989, 36ff., 62ff., and 81ff., who is often more
thorough, even if more adventurous, than Contiades-Tsitsoni 1990, 68ff., who tries to
identify marriage fragments in other melic poets, too. The paraphrase of Himerius is the
subject of a commentary by J. D. Meerwaldt, "Epithalamica I," *Mnemosyne* IV.7 (1954):
19–38. Eur. *Phaeth.* 227ff., reconstructed and commented upon by J. Diggle, *Euripides,
Phaethon* (Cambridge 1970), 148ff.: we know that in one of the versions of the legend,
Hymenaeus dies on the very day of his marriage (see the frag. of Pindar cited below in n.
23). On the role played by Aphrodite in marriage, see Pirenne-Delforge 1994, 421ff.

Whatever their sexes, the two partners united in this fashion are generally positioned face to face. Over and above the image of texture (woven material) that it seems to suggest, this cloak of amorous and nuptial "initiation" could thus constitute a symbolic representation of the mutual relationship of *philotês*. In the light of all this, to speak of the "sexual surrender" of the bride in a classical marriage seems somewhat far-fetched.[19]

## 2.3. Shared Love, Violence, and Reproduction

The expression "sexual surrender" is all the more inappropriate given that, whatever the effective asymmetry between the respective social positions of women and men in Greek conjugal cohabitation, from Homer right down to Xenophon the texts are unanimous in suggesting that, in Greek marriage, the relationship of *philotês*, through the fulfillment of amorous desire, which represents the matrimonial union, was based upon sexuality. The obvious social distinctions of gender seem to have been wiped out, at least for the duration of the wedding night. Marriage was a relationship of mutual trust that was analogous to that which, ideally, would be established by the propaedeutic love of a boy, and it was directly established by Eros.

There is no need to return to the conjugal loves of the Homeric gods and heroes, but it is worth noting that in Semonides' invective against women, the bee woman was distinguished from her fellow sisters in that in old age she was still dear (*philê*) to her husband, who returned her love for him (*phileonti*). Remaining with the elegiac genre, we should also note the words Theognis has the Muses and the Charites sing in celebration of Cadmus and Harmonia, herself the daughter produced from the union of Ares and Aphrodite: "a beautiful thing inspires attachment" (*hotti kalon philon esti*). Proclaimed here on the occasion of a marriage ceremony, the old proverb on the affection that one feels for moral beauty becomes charged with the eroticism that is evoked by the beauty of Aphrodite's daughter and that underpins the bond of *philotês*

---

[19] Archil. frag. 196a.42ff. West (see above ch. IV, §1.2, and below ch. IX, §1, n. 1); Aristoph. *Av.* 1693 and 1758; Xen. Eph. 1.8.3; Theocr. 18.18ff. These passages are considered alongside the corresponding iconographical representations by Arrigoni 1983, 41ff., who gives them an initiatory interpretation, and more prudently by Koch-Harnack 1989, 136ff.; Scheid and Svenbro 1994, 61ff., have recently shown the metaphorical significance of the *khlaina*, seen as a product of nuptial intermeshing or "weaving," but also as a representation of the fabric of politics. It is therefore impossible to maintain along with Keuls 1985, 41ff., that in classical Athens "the combination of marriage and sexual desire is improper and scandalous." Foucault 1984, 164ff., is much more circumspect in this respect.

established by marriage.[20] This bond of mutual affection is also evident not only in the exchange, exacerbated by the neglect of their love, between the husband and wife in Aristophanes' *Lysistrata*, but also in the scene of comic parody that concludes Xenophon's philosophical *Symposium* on a symposiac note: in this dramatized representation intended to entertain the guests, an erotic encounter between the handsome Dionysus and the charming Ariadne leads, with the use of the verb *philein*, to an oath of mutual love. The embrace shared by the girl dressed as a newly wed bride and the seducer-god is so convincing that the married men among the symposiasts can think of nothing but rejoining their respective wives in bed, while the bachelors are left with but one desire, to get married![21]

Returning to iconography, to reflect upon the scenes in which homophile couples and heterosexual couples all partake together in the same pleasure, under similar cloaks, one is led to suspect that the *khlaina* specifically symbolizes the relationship of *philotês*, a relationship prepared for as much by the initiatory bonds of education through Eros as by the bonds established in marriage based on love. In the light of this homology, one can fully appreciate the irony of the scene evoked in the epilogue to Plato's *Symposium*: when Socrates is embraced by Alcibiades, who has slipped under his cloak, he rejects the young man's beauty. All that Socrates wants from the love of boys is a relationship of *philia*, so he treats the impassioned Alcibiades as he would a son of his or a younger brother.[22]

The emphatic presence of Eros and Aphrodite throughout the rite of passage that turned a girl into a spouse adorned with all the seductions of love should not obscure the fact that, except in the matrimonial customs of Sparta, the violence done to the future wife was, at least as a form of prelude, always a factor in the legendary representations of marriage. Violence was one of the motivating forces of narrative action, particularly in the legend of Hymenaeus, the hero who was commemorated at every turn in the nuptial ritual. Take, for instance, the Athenian

---

[20] Sem. frag. 7.83f. West; see E. Pellizer and G. Tedeschi, *Semonides* (Rome 1990), 143ff.; Thgn. 15ff. repeating the proverb cited in particular by Eur. *Bacch.* 881 and 901, and by Plat. *Lys.* 216c; see also Rocchi 1989, 117ff., who points out all the links between this exemplary marriage and music.

[21] Aristoph. *Lys.* 870ff., where the verb *philein* is endlessly repeated; Xen. *Symp.* 9.2.ff. On a legal level, these relations of mutual trust belong essentially to domestic space: see Gould 1980, 46ff. From a purely physiological point of view, Greek doctors and anatomists considered that the woman's pleasure was no less than that of the man's: Hippoc. *Gener.* 4, Aristot. *Gen. An.* 20.727b32ff., etc.: see Halperin 1990, 201 n. 126.

[22] Images collected by Koch-Harnack 1989, 109ff.; see above n. 19; Plat. *Symp.* 219a ff., together with the commentary by Scheid and Svenbro 1994, 78ff.

version of this hero's life, in which all the narrative and genealogical elements are highly significant: in a number of texts, Hymenaeus is represented as the liberator of a group of Athenian girls who had been abducted by Pelasgian pirates. While on a visit to Athens, the young man, a native of Argos, learned of the abduction and took action to save the girls from being violated by the foreigners from inland Greece, thereby making it possible for them to be married in a perfectly legal fashion when they returned to Athens. Taking the form of an *aition*, the legend explained that this was why, from that time on, Athenian girls always invoked the heroized Hymenaeus when the time came for them to be married.[23]

This tradition of pursuit, rape, and violence may illuminate the brutal attacks to which both goddesses and mortal women are subjected by gods seized by a desire that eventually leads to a bed on which the couple is united *en philotêti*. In the scenes of pursuit evoked in accounts of the love affairs of the gods, the deity pursuing his victim has himself frequently been the target of Eros' arrows: for example, Poseidon who seizes hold of Amymone (with Aphrodite looking on), Zeus who pursues Ganymedes (under the influence of an adolescent Eros whose feelings toward Zeus reflect Zeus' toward his future cupbearer), and Dionysus who snatches the hand of the consenting Ariadne while Eros presents him with the headband of love and Aphrodite greets the couple, holding a marriage crown in readiness.[24]

Not only are some of these pictorial representations of amorous pursuits painted on vases designed to be used at the marriage ceremony or by women generally, but the force to which the god subjects the girl who is in thrall to Eros may be regarded as an iconographic metaphor for the taming effect with which marriage is credited in the Greek discursive texts. One could, indeed, go farther and establish an analogy

---

[23] See in particular sch. A. Hom. *Il.* 18.493 (II.173 Dindorf), Procl. *ap.* Phot. *Bibl.* 321a 22ff. and Serv. *in* Verg. *Aen.* 1.651 (II.276 Harvard); for us, the legend goes back to Pind. frag. 128c.7ff. Maehler; it is also recounted by Hdt. 6.137.3 (the daughters of Athenians importuned as they go to draw water at the Enneakrounos, and "women" abducted while celebrating Artemis at Brauron; see also Hecat. *FGrHist.* 1 F 127) and Pherec. *FGrHist.* 328 F 110ff. (little Athenian girls "impersonating bears" for Artemis at the Brauronia), but with no mention of Hymenaeus' rescue of the Athenians: see Calame 1983b, XXXIff. According to Plutarch, *Lyc.* 15.4ff, in Sparta a bride would be abducted and placed in the hands of the *numpheutria*, who disguised her as a man; the wedding night was thus preceded by a brief period of segregation: see Vidal-Naquet 1983, 205ff., and A. Paradiso, "Osservazioni sulla cerimonia nuziale spartana," *Quad. Stor.* 24 (1986): 137–53.

[24] Pelike Rome Villa Giulia 20486 (*ARV*² 494.2), black-figured alabaster, Berlin F 2032 (pl. VI), oinochoe Paris Cab. Méd. 460 (*ARV*² 606.83); see on this subject Kaempf-Dimitriadou 1979, 27ff. (pl. 18, 6), 8f. (fig. 1) and 31f. (pl. 22, 3–5).

between the power that Eros exerts over the deity smitten by desire and the yoke that that deity is himself seeking to impose upon the object of his love. And when it is Eros himself who pursues a woman, the terms of that analogy become fused.[25] The imposition of the yoke of love through *erôs* thus corresponds to a girl's domestication through legitimate marriage. As in erotic poetry, the subduer only subdues because he himself is subdued.

We should therefore not take these powerful iconic and linguistic metaphors too literally nor ascribe to them a sociologizing psychology of conjugal oppression. The sophistic arguments of Gorgias' *Encomium of Helen* show that the will of the gods, the violence of rape, the effect of bewitching words, and the interventions of Eros are all by and large equivalent. Each of the motives imagined for Helen involves her being subjected to a constraint; so whatever the explanation given for her behavior, she should be declared innocent of willfully abandoning her home for Troy. From this point of view, the erotic verses of archaic poetry may be seen as a seductive linguistic equivalent to the violent pursuits and abductions of myth.

There is also another metaphor closely associated with Greek marriage that it is possible to analyze, in particular by elucidating the symbolic meaning that it conveys through the ritual. Several phases of the marriage ceremony feature an extra protagonist who should not be overlooked: a *pais amphithalês*, a child "who flourishes with his father and mother clustering round him," according to the etymological explanation suggested by ancients commentators. It seems that this actor in the ritual was to be found leading the *loutrophoria* procession (the carrying of the nuptial washing vessels); and, as noted above, he also played an active part in the wedding feast and in some vase paintings is present at the *numphagôgia*, if not at the presentation of extra gifts known as the *apaulia*.[26] Whatever his role, this little boy, whose ritual

---

[25] The relation between scenes of abduction and vessels offered to a married woman has been pointed out by Kaempf-Dimitriadou 1979, 48. The analogous relation suggested here can be traced starting from the studies of F. Zeitlin, "Configuration of Rape in Greek Myth," in S. Tomaselli and R. Porter (eds.), *Rape* (Oxford 1986), 122–51, and C. Sourvinou-Inwood, "A Series of Erotic Pursuits," *Journ. Hell. Stud.* 107 (1987): 131–53. Eros in pursuit of a woman: hydria The Hague Mus. Meerm.-Westr. 634 ($ARV^2$ 1209.58). In connection with marriage seen as a domestication and taming, see the references provided by Calame 1977, I, 411ff., and Seaford 1987, 111.

[26] See Reinsberg 1989, 52ff.; on the *epaulia*, see Poll. 3.39 and *Sud.* s.v. (*E* 1990 Adler) with Redfield 1982, 192ff.; the expression *pais amphithalês*, used for the child who took part in a number of Athenian rituals, conveys a metaphor of growth: see A. Oepke, "Amphithaleîs im griechischen und hellenistischen Kult," *Arch. Rel.-Wiss.* 31 (1934): 42–56, and L. Robert, "*Amphithales*," *Harv. Stud. Class. Philol.* Suppl. 1 (1940): 509–19.

Note that the words denoting young men and girls (*koroi, korai*) mentioned in the

description draws upon the metaphor of a human branch that grows thanks to the harmony between its parents, could well, throughout the marriage ceremony, represent the function of reproduction that is, quite rightly, frequently ascribed to the institution of marriage. Certainly, the union between two lovers, whether it be conjugal or not, more often than not leads to the birth of a child. Limiting ourselves to texts already mentioned, we may for instance refer to the *Iliad*'s list of Zeus' mistresses to whom the ardent god compares Hera, the most desirable of them all. These women whom he has — explicitly or implicitly — loved are all mentioned in connection with the offspring who resulted from their embraces with the king of the gods. In Semonides, the bee woman, bound to her husband in a relationship of mutual and enduring love, gives birth to a fine and illustrious line of descendants. And even in Theocritus' purely literary and etiological *Epithalamion*, Helen, led by Menalaus to lie with him beneath the matrimonial cloak, is immediately celebrated as a potential mother who can give birth to offspring who resemble her.

> Happy groom, some good man sneezed for thy success,
> when with the other princes thou camest to Sparta,
> and of all heroes thou alone shalt have Zeus, son of Cronos, as father of thy bride.
> His daughter has come beneath the one coverlet with thee,
> an Achaean maiden such as who none other walks the earth,
> and wondrous shall be the child she bears if it be like its mother.[27]

In the classical Greek representation of conjugal union, the — in effect essential — function of reproduction thus depends directly upon the intervention of Eros and the fullfilment of love on a shared bed, the purpose of which thus becomes twofold.

Clearly, this provides an added reason for centering marriage upon the woman. In one version of the Athenian legend of Hymenaeus, the hero is presented as an adolescent who is in love with a young and noble Athenian girl. According to this myth, his beauty was so exquisite

---

refrain of the *diegertikon* also convey the idea of a young child: see Aesch. frag. 43 Radt, *carm. pop.* 881 Page, and P. Chantraine, *Dictionnaire étymologique de la langue grecque* (Paris 1968), 567ff.; see also G. Lambin, "Trois refrains nuptiaux et le fr. 124 Mette d'Eschyle," *Ant. Class.* 55 (1986): 66–85.

[27] Theocr. 18.16ff. in A.S.F. Gow (trans.), *Theocritus I* (Cambridge 1950); Hom. *Il.* 14.313ff.; Sem. frag. 7.83ff. West. The matrimonial function of reproduction in the strict sense of the term is dramatized in Hesiod's great narratives, *Theog.* 602ff. (the "myth" of Pandora) and *Op.* 182ff. (the "myth" of the races). And it was particularly as mothers that Athenian women were respected and feared by their citizen husbands: see Gould 1980, 57, and A.-M. Vérilhac, "L'image de la femme dans les épigrammes funéraires grecques," in Vérilhac 1985, 85–112.

that he could pass himself off as a girl, just as Achilles did on Syros. While mingling with the Athenian girls taking part in the cult of Demeter at Eleusis, he was carried off, along with them, by pirates and taken far away beyond the sea to a deserted region. But while the pirates slept, he slew them all. As a reward for liberating his beloved's companions in misfortune, he won her hand in marriage. It was clearly on the strength of this fine tale that it became customary for marriage ceremonies in Athens to be punctuated by invocations to this young hero. The hero of marriage went one better than Theseus in that in his case the initiatory process followed a virtually perfect sequence.[28] The unmarried adolescent youth became a (married) adult as a consequence of inverting the signs of sexuality, moving to a far-distant and deserted place, and successfully performing a heroic feat by resorting to a cunning ploy. In contrast, the girl whom he loved, despite passing through this same sequence of legendary events, remained an adolescent. For her, the rite of passage could only be completed by the marriage ceremony.

## 2.4. The Status of the Young Bride

Our study of the role played by Eros has enabled us to establish a connection between the education received by Athenian boys in the late archaic period and the institution of tribal initiation. But for girls the crucial moment of transition, controlled by Aphrodite and her young companion, was clearly that of marriage.[29] For a girl, one feature of this was her accession to a new legal status, while another was the exchange of gifts and her moving in to live with a new "master" or "guardian" (*kurios*), namely her husband, an Athenian citizen. While the legal position of an adult woman in Athens in the classical period has been comprehensively studied,[30] the same cannot be said of her moral position or her social status.

---

[28] Serv. in Verg. *Aen.* 4.99 (III.286 Harvard); on Achilles, see Dowden 1989, 49ff. The excesses in the initiatory interpretation of Theseus' Cretan exploit are criticized in my study of 1996, 432ff.

[29] This does not mean that girls were deprived of all education before marriage in Athens. The study by Brulé 1987 shows, following others, that the education system for adolescent girls was linked to a number of religious institutions: see below ch. IX, §3. On marriage as a rite of passage, see already V. Magnien, "Le mariage chez les Grecs anciens: L'initiation nuptiale," *Ant. Class.* 5 (1936): 115–36, and the references provided by Redfield 1982, 189ff.

[30] Legally, an Athenian woman was considered a minor: see D. M. MacDowell, *The Law in Classical Athens* (London 1978), 84ff., and R. Just, *Women in Athenian Law and Life* (London and New York 1989), 40ff., together with the clear synthesis by Gould 1980, 43ff. See, too, the studies by H. S. Versnel, "Wife and Helpmate," in J. Blok and P. Mason (eds.), *Sexual Asymmetry* (Amsterdam 1987), 59–86; by C. B. Patterson, "Marriage and the Married Woman in Athenian Law," in S. B. Pomeroy (ed.), *Women's His-*

She would accede to that social status by passing through three principal stages, the second of which was that of a *numphê*: in all marriage hymns, from Sappho all the way to Theocritus, this is the word used to denote the young affianced bride. In one hymn, the girl now described as a *numphê* thinks back to her condition as a maiden (*parthenia*), now a thing of the past (although it should be noted that the term *parthenia* has nothing to do with the modern concept of virginity). In another poem, the young adolescent girls (*parthenikai*) performing the "epithalamium" distinguish carefully between their own condition and that to which the *numphê* Helen has acceded through her marriage to her betrothed (*gambros*), Menelaus.[31]

The chronological and social limits of the specific status of a *numphê* are defined for us most clearly in another mythical account. In Apollonius Rhodius' version of the legend of Cyrene, the young woman after whom the the Greek colony in Africa was named, a shepherdess grazing her flocks on the banks of the Peneus river, is, like Atalanta, anxious to preserve her bed and her status as a young girl (*parthenie*). But when Apollo carries her off to the future site of the Greek colony in Libya, she becomes a nymph among the Nymphs (the wordplay here was very much to the Alexandrian taste). The transition is effected thanks to the loving commitment (*philotês*) of the god. It is as a *numphê* that Cyrene then gives birth to Aristaeus.[32] She was a *parthenos* (a young girl) in the days when she was a shepherdess; then, when she was united with Apollo, she became a *numphê* (a bride); not until she gave birth to a child did she become a *gunê* (a woman). If we translate the legend to the social level, we thus find that the status of a *numphê* extended from the moment of sexual union consecrated by marriage up to its realization through the birth of the woman's first child.

---

*tory and Ancient History* (Chapel Hill and London 1991), 48–72; by Des Bouvrie 1990, 39ff.; and by C. Schnurr-Redford, *Frauen im klassischen Athen* (Berlin 1996), 260ff. The position of the Greek married woman in kinship relations has recently been skillfully redefined by C. Leduc, "Comment la donner en mariage," in Schmitt-Pantel 1991, 246–314.

[31] Sappho frags. 103.5, 103B, 116, but also 30.2ff. and 114 Voigt, and Praxilla frag. 754.2 Page; the context of the citation of that last fragment (Dem. Phal. *Styl.* 140) has the *numphê* explicitly bid farewell to her "virginity"; Theocr. 18.2 and 50. The bride is called a *numphê* in the descriptions of the *numphagôgia* by Hom. *Il.* 18.492ff. and by Ps. Hes. *Scut.* 273ff., and also in that of the probable awakening ceremony by Sappho frag. 30.4ff. Voigt: on this poem see Lasserre 1989, 37ff., and Contiades-Tsitsoni 1990, 100ff.

Without noting the particular state of a *numphê*, G. Sissa, *Le Corps virginal* (Paris 1987), 110ff. (English translation: *Greek Virginity* [Cambridge and New York 1990]), shows that in classical Greece the state of a *parthenos* had nothing to do with anatomical virginity; on the absence of an ideal of virginity in Greece, see also Parker 1983, 92ff.

[32] Ap. Rhod. 2.500ff. (on Cyrene, see also below ch. VIII, §2).

It is Hera, better than anyone, who, as the goddess who represents the fulfillment of women in marriage, most effectively defines the condition of a *numphê*. In a fragment from Aeschylus' *Xantriai*, the chorus expresses its fears concerning the unfortunate marriage of Semele, fears that august wife of Zeus allays by invoking the Nymphs. The Nymphs are present at all the celebrations of mortals, in particular marriage ceremonies. It is they who guide girls to the marriage bed, they who watch benignly over young brides, imparting modesty to their shining eyes, and they who eventually make their dreams of healthy offspring come true, by helping them through their confinements. The Nymphs of legend thus act as the protectors of *numphai* throughout all the stages that determine their social status.[33]

Just as particular social categories were often associated with the names of particular deities, the biographical tradition attributed to Pythagoras the invention of words. In particular, the philosopher was said to have derived from the names of various deities the words used to designate the various feminine age groups, thereby honoring the legendary piety of women. Persephone's title of *korê* was thus applied to unmarried girls; from the Nymphs came *numphê*, which was applied to recently married women, and from Demeter (*mêtêr*) came the word used to designate a wife who had already borne a child or children. The author of the gloss reported by Photius in his lexicon correctly defined *numphai* as newly wed girls (*hai neogamoi korai*). The same dictionary, in agreement with medical observations, also ascribes to this term the meaning of "clitoris" (on the basis of what metaphor is not clear).[34] The condition of a *numphê* is thus associated with physical gratification. That is no doubt precisely what the classical writers themselves intended to indicate when they placed young brides under the direct influence of Eros and Aphrodite.

[33] Aesch. frag. 162 Radt, with the commentary by F. Lasserre, *Nouveaux chapitres de littérature grecque* (Geneva 1989), 69ff.

[34] Tim. *FGrHist.* 566 F 17 and Iambl. *Vit. Pyth.* 11.56; Phot. *Lex.* s.v. *Numphai* (I.451 Naber); the famous religious ruling of Cyrene (115B.73f. Suppl. Sokolowski), which dates from the fourth century B.C., made a clear distinction between a *parthenos* (adolescent girl), a *numphê* (newly married woman who had not yet produced a child), and a *guna* (adult woman), where sacrifices to Artemis were concerned. The specific status of the *numphê* was eventually recognized by M. Detienne, "Orphée au miel," in J. Le Goff and P. Nora (eds.), *Faire de l'histoire* III (Paris 1974), 56–75 (as opposed to the *korê* and the *mêtêr*); see also Brulé 1987, 319ff., Dowden 1989, 104ff. and 201, on the basis of the study by P. Chantraine, "Les noms du mari et de la femme, du père et de la mère en grec," *Rev. Et. Gr.* 59/60 (1946/47): 219–50, and, with some confusions, V. Andó, "Nymphe: La sposa e le ninfe," *Quad. Urb. Cult. Class.* 81 (1996): 47–79. In literature, Ariadne embodies the very model of a *numphê*: see Calame 1996, 198ff. and 244ff.; on derivative meanings of *numphê*, see Winkler 1990, 181ff. (in a study published earlier with more extensive notes in Foley 1981, 63–89).

The love inspired by Cypris led not only to union, but also to fecundity. The few references that shed light on the role played in marriage by the Nymphs, as deities, certainly suggest that it was a complementary one that led to the fulfillment of the union. An Alexandrian commentator on Pindar declares "without the Nymphs, there can be no fulfillment in marriage." Meanwhile, in classical Athenian tragedy, we find Euripides' Orestes wondering whether the sacrifice that Aegisthus is preparing to offer up to the Nymphs, close to the grazing land reserved for horses, following his union with Clytemnestra, is destined to bring about the birth of a male child. And, in the *Life of Plato*, we are told that, following the philosopher's birth, his parents immediately took the newborn babe to Mount Hymettus, there to make sacrifices to Pan, the Nymphs, and Apollo the Shepherd. Turning from legend to ritual practice, it is furthermore worth noting that relatively recent excavations in Athens have revealed the remains of a sanctuary consecrated to *Numphê*, the Nymph or Young Bride. The large number of *loutrophoi* (urns used for carrying water) found there suggest that the figure of the deified *numphê* was offered a ritual sacrifice to mark either the day of the bride's bath or the completion of the marriage ceremony.[35]

The bed on which deities, mythical heroes, and young Athenian married couples were united in love, spurred on by Eros, would thus also be the bed of childbirth. The *akoitis* spouse, she who shared the bed, that is to say the loving and legitimate wife, was also *alokhos*, she who was attached to the bed, a fecund woman who produced legitimate descendants. A study of etymology reveals the affinities that the Greeks discerned between the young wife's bed of love and the childbearing woman's bed of pain.[36] The multiple significances that were attributed to the conjugal bed help us to understand how marriage related to the metaphorical field of agricultural labor throughout the various phases in the production of the fruits of the earth. To cite only *loci classici* chosen from the texts of fifth-century Attic drama, when Aeschylus' Oedipus sows his seed in the plowed field from which he himself sprang, what grows there, as *numphios*, is a "bloody stock"; Sophocles' Oedipus meanwhile reflects that his wife (*gunê*), who is not his wife, is the maternal field in which both he himself and his own children have all first seen the light of day.[37] For the Greeks, the agricultural cycle,

---

[35] Sch. Pind. *Pyth.* 4.104; Eur. *El.* 623ff.; Olymp. *Vit. Plat.* 1. For a description of the sanctuary consecrated to the Nymph, see Travlos 1971, 361ff.

[36] See Loraux 1989, 32ff.; for the etymology and use of the two Homeric terms for a legitimate wife, see *LfgrE*, s.vv. *akoitis* and *alokhos*; see also above ch. II, §1, n. 2.

[37] Aesch. *Sept.* 753ff. and Soph. *Oed. Tyr.* 1251ff.; the affinities between agricultural labor and marriage are discussed by M. Detienne and J.-P. Vernant, *La cuisine du sacrifice en pays grec* (Paris 1979), 42 and 114ff. (English translation: *The Cuisine of Sacrifice*

from the plowing and the sowing of the seed through to the harvesting of the grain, corresponded exactly to the stages that, through the intermediary status of the *numphê*, turned a girl (*parthenos*) into an adult woman (*gunê*).

But there is no classical text that conveys the mutual interaction of Love, marriage, and agricultural reproduction better than the words that Aphrodite herself pronounces in the last tragedy in Aeschylus' trilogy devoted to the destiny of the Danaids, who were being forced into marriage:

> The holy heaven yearns to wound the earth,
> and yearning layeth hold on the earth to join in wedlock;
> the rain, fallen from the amorous heaven,
> impregnates the earth, and it bringeth forth for mankind
> the food of flocks and herds and Demeter's gifts;
> and from that moist marriage-rite the woods put on their bloom.
> Of all these things I am the cause.[38]

---

*among the Greeks* [Chicago 1989]); see also P. du Bois, *Sowing the Body* (Chicago and London 1988), 39ff.

[38] Aesch. frag. 44 Radt, see also Eur. frags. 484 and 898 Nauck²; on Aeschylus' treatment of the tragic destiny of the Danaids, see below ch. VII, §2.1, n. 29. The place and function of the declaration by Aphrodite have been the subject of numerous hypotheses outlined in A. F. Garvie, *Aeschylus' Supplices* (Cambridge 1969), 204ff.; on its meaning, see Zeitlin 1992, 230ff. According to Proclus, in Plat. *Tim.* 40e (III.176 Diehl), at the mysteries of Eleusis that Athenian priests looked up to the sky and asked for rain (*huê*) and down at the earth, begging it to conceive or grow fecund (*kuê*); see also Paus. 1.24.3.

# Chapter VII

## DIONYSIAC CHALLENGES TO LOVE

WHENEVER IT IS a matter of educating future citizens or of introducing their wives into their roles as fully developed women, Aphrodite and Eros take a hand in the institutions designed to facilitate the passage to adult life, in order to produce a sexuality that is at once controlled and productive. Despite the apparent reversal of the norms of heterosexual interchange that homophile relations effected, they were in truth designed to promote integration.

However, for men at least and in particular in fifth-century Athens, there were plenty of instances of sexual deviance. To judge from the iconography, these were generally placed under the sign of Dionysus. It comes as no surprise to find that this god of transitions to other states also encouraged sexual transgressions: under the influence of too much wine, symposium participants became satyrs who behaved like animals or maenads seized by Bacchic madness. But the interpreters of iconography insist that it was not until the end of the fifth century that Eros made his appearance in the Dionysiac *thiasos*. An explanation for this paradox has already been suggested, but at this point it is worth spelling it out: in the classical iconography of the symposium and the *kômos*, the erect phalluses of the guests and the compliant demeanors of their female companions suggest that, emulating the ithyphallism of satyrs, the protagonists in these Dionysiac scenes have doubly overstepped the bounds of civilized behavior; they have become possessed by the most bestial aspects of their libido. They are no longer themselves, no longer human beings, so they have no need of any further encouragement from Eros and Aphrodite.

Yet even thus spelled out, the explanation is somewhat cursory. To be sure, already in the *Iliad*, Dionysus is the god of *mania*, the god who transmits to his followers both male and female the orgiastic frenzy by which he himself is possessed; he is the god who himself is as mad about women as Paris, and who then maddens them in their turn, as in the case of the Proetides.[1] Now, in the *Odyssey*, Dionysus collaborates with Artemis to punish Ariadne for copulating with Theseus on an island supposed to be consecrated to himself; in Hesiod's *Theogony*,

---

[1] Hom. *Il.* 6.132: see sch. *ad loc.* (II.153 Erbse); *Hhom. Dion.* 17 (see Hom. *Il.* 3.39 and 13.769) and Hes. frag. 131 Merkelbach-West; see G. A. Privitera, *Dioniso in Omero e nella poesia greca arcaica* (Rome 1970), 153ff.

however, Dionysus is given Minos' fair-haired daughter as his wife
(*akoitis*). The *Theogony* then proceeds to include the marriage between
this heroine (who is so close to Aphrodite) and the god of wine in a
brief list of unions that all led to immortality.[2] The Dionysus of legend
thus contributes to the civilizing effect of marriage by giving Ariadne
sons whose names evoke his own divine attributes. With his power to
transport mortals beyond the limits assigned to men, he also enables
them to cross another important boundary, that which separates the
world of men from the world of the gods.

This ambivalent ability both to cross boundaries and also to act as a
force for integration is reflected in the cult of Dionysus. It is particularly
noticeable in Athens where, on the occasion of the festival of the An-
thesteria, the god was brought not merely into the city, to his temple in
the neighborhood of the Marshes, but right into the residence of the
king-archon. There — it is worth remembering — he was united in a marriage ceremony, which was possibly parodic, with the wife of the town's
chief magistrate. This was, of course, an adulterous relationship; nevertheless, it took place at the civic heart of the State and in the context
of a celebration of the year's new wine, which was consumed initially
with moderation but eventually in excess. Similar rituals were performed in Patras where, in even more emphatic fashion, Dionysus allowed his servants to overstep the bounds set along the path to political
life. In the course of celebrations designed to honor the local hero associated with the suppression of human sacrifices, first youths, then
women, began by honoring Artemis on the banks of the river of
Meilichios (calm); then, on their way back to the city, they proceeded to
celebrate Dionysus the Magistrate, performing rituals that commemorated the region's political past.[3]

It was this Dionysus, in all his ambiguity, who would be present at a
symposium attended by Greek citizens, first while they consumed wine
in moderation, thereby reinforcing the bonds that united them as *philoi*,

---

[2] Hom. *Od.* 11.321ff., Hes. *Theog.* 947ff.; see also the relationship of *philotês* established between the heroine and the god according to Xen. *Symp.* 9.5ff.: above ch. VI,
§1.2. On the various versions of Ariadne's sojourn on Naxos and her marriage to Dionysus, see my study of 1996, 105ff. and 199ff.; see also M. Daraki, *Dionysos* (Paris
1985), 92ff.

[3] The marriage of Dionysus and the *basilinna* is attested in texts dating from the fourth
century: Ps. Dem. 59.72f. and Ps. Aristot. *Ath. Pol.* 3.5; other references to the An-
thesteria can be found in Calame 1996, 249ff. and 327ff. The cult devoted to Dionysus
Aisymnetes in Patras is known to us from Paus. 7.18.1ff.; following others, J. Redfield,
"From Sex to Politics," in Halperin, Winkler, and Zeitlin 1990, 115–34, has pointed out
the integrating role of this politician Dionysus. On this civilizing god, see also M. Detienne, *Dionysos à ciel ouvert* (Paris 1986), 59ff. (English translation: *Dionysus at Large*
[Cambridge, Mass., and London 1989]).

and later amid the drunkenness in which they were no longer themselves. As we have seen, when subjected to the madness of love, Anacreon, after wrestling with Eros, turns to wine mixed with water,
seeking liberation from the intolerable bonds imposed upon him by
Aphrodite. But in another poem, Dionysus, the playfellow of Eros, the
Nymphs, and Aphrodite, is called upon to intercede as an adviser to the
young Cleobulus, the object of Anacreon's ardent desire. Thus Dionysus—who is probably also involved in the first of these two
poems—is capable not only of arousing love but also of curing those
stricken by it.[4]

It is accordingly not surprising that in classical Athens resistance to
the implacable forces of amorous desire and sexuality should find expression in speeches delivered in the course of the ritual dramas performed in honor of Dionysus. Sometimes such resistance was expressed
within the horizontal dimension of the world of mortals. What were
discussed there were the institutional and moral limits set upon the
urges that drive human beings closer to the animals: clearly, the examples that most spring to mind come from comic drama, with its suggestive costumes and masks and all its deliberately obscene talk. But it also
found expression in the vertical dimension, for tragedy questioned not
only the boundaries that separated the state of amorous desire from the
state of death but also the relations between desirous lovers and the
gods upon whom they depended: in tragedy, a wedding was more likely
than not to turn into a funeral, thereby transforming a horizontal transition into a vertical one that led down to the underworld. In confor-
mity with Aristotle's theory of the derivation of the different genres,
drama thus reproduced the polarity of *mômos* (blame) and *epainos*
(praise).[5] The criticism expressed in iambic poetry was made more trenchant by the constant satirical references of comedy, while in tragedy,
epic eulogy developed into a challenge that was directed—through the
masks of Dionysus—against the power of the gods and the legendary
and ethical values upon which life in the city was founded.

---

[4] In connection with the brief frag. 428 Page (commented on above in ch. I, §1), see
Anacr. frags. 346.4 and 357 Page. For a reconstruction of the invocation to Dionysus in
frag. 346.4, see the commentary by Gentili 1958, 204ff. Privitera, above n. 1, 115ff., has
shown that there is no more than an apparent contradiction between the two requests
made to the god of wine.

[5] Aristot. *Poet.* 4.1448b21ff.; the ritual origins and aspects of these *kômoi* for Dionysus
are discussed by A. W. Pickard-Cambridge, *Dithyramb, Tragedy and Comedy* (Oxford
[2]1962), 132ff.; as for the celebrations for the god of wine in the Great Dionysia, see still
the study by the same scholar in *The Dramatic Festivals of Athens* (Oxford [2]1968), 57ff.
The generic links between poetry of blame, iambics, and comedy are traced by Nagy
1979, 243ff., and by R. M. Rosen, *Old Comedy and the Iambographic Tradition* (Atlanta
1988), 9ff.

## 1. The Institution of Comedy

When in love, the actors in the comedies of Aristophanes appear to refer to the same concept of love as do the archaic poets: they certainly make use of exactly the same erotic vocabulary. In the famous scene of *The Women in the Assembly* in which the young man tries to escape from the old women whom the newly instituted communist regime has ordered him to satisfy, the hasty conversation that he snatches with the girl he loves is full of expressions that could well come straight from a poem by Sappho. This amorous girl is wracked by desire (*erôs me donei*), caught in the grip of a strange and disturbing passion (*atopos pothos*); and she prays to Eros to draw the young man to a bed (*eunê*) that has the same metaphorical significance as it would have in erotic poetry. The young man, for his part, attributes to Cypris the mad passion (*ekmaineis*) that he feels for the young beauty. Extolling his love with tender words, he too draws upon the vocabulary of erotic poetry. Expressions such as "my sole concern, inscribed in gold," "the sweet branch of Cypris," and "the Muses' bee" are reminiscent of Alcman and Ibycus. But when their repetition becomes excessive, and when the sweet words of love degenerate into the more emphatic mode of a more vulgar rhetoric ("creature of the Charites," "the very face of sensuality"), his speech takes on a note of comic exaggeration. Symmetry presides over the relationship between this young man and this girl, characterized as it is by repeated appeals to Eros and a desire to share a bed together, and strengthened by the mutual trust that it inspires; and the use of a lyrical rhythm reminiscent of Bacchylides, the melic poet, imbues it with a heroic solemnity. Nevertheless, if the girl maintains a certain restraint as she declares her longing to fondle her beloved's curly locks, her lover, for his part, declares himself to be seized by the far more crude desire to "fit the fair one's rump."[6]

All this mutual desire and immediate gratification and all these sexual metaphors lead us away from melic poetry and plunge us instead into

---

[6] Aristoph. *Eccl.* 952ff. In his commentary on this passage, M. Vetta, *Aristofane. Le donne all'assemblea* (Milan 1989), 248ff., notes a number of coincidences between these expressions and archaic erotic poetry: Sappho frag. 130 Voigt (*donei*), Alcm. frag. 3.68 Page (*ernos*), Ibyc. frag. 288 Page (*Kharitôn tholos, meledêma*), and also, for example, Anacr. frag. 428 Page (*mainomai*) and Alcm. frag. 3.74 Page (*melêma*). Despite its use in *Anth. Pal.* 7.600.2, *thremma* generally refers to the animal kingdom and *truphê* designates the softness of luxury that is mocked by the comic poets; on 1.964ff., see Henderson 1991, 140ff.

In general, the protagonists of Ancient Comedy, like the archaic poets, are consumed by love: references can be found in A. M. Komornicka, "Sur le langage érotique de l'ancienne comédie attique," *Quad. Urb. Cult. Class.* 38 (1981): 55–83.

the world of certain iconographical representations, where love is con-summated there and then, on a bed or off it. Whatever its ritual origins, comedy derives its sexual exhibitionism and also no doubt the obscenity of its speech from the cult of Dionysus and from the practices of drunk-enness. Not content with presenting on the stage the kind of phallic processions from which Aristotle claims it to be derived, the ritual of comedy required its actors to sport satyr masks and bulging, false but-tocks and genital appendages, the flaunting of which underlined the sex-ual and obscene nature of the whole drama.[7] Illuminating though it may be to compare classical comedy to the manifestations of carnival, con-siderable qualifications of Bakhtin's well-known theory are called for.[8] Attic comedy did not so much present a reversal of the existing social norms, but rather used the ritual means of extravagant costumes and risqué language to produce a critical and satirical exaggeration of the circumstances in which a citizen could break the rules of normal behav-ior. So what was represented was not really sexual license, but rather a satirical parody of transgressions that were more or less tolerated in social life, a parody conveyed by a series of travesties of the sexual roles adopted in social life. In Aristophanes' comedies, the obscene sexual references, along with the masks and the costumes, were simply a means of satirizing and criticizing civic life.

## 1.1. Satires of Passive Homosexuality

Lack of space precludes the inclusion of more than a single example, but it is a typical one: that of the amorous relations between two people of the same sex. Subsequently, in the course of a brief examination of tragedy, we shall, in the interests of symmetry, consider a problem con-cerning heterosexual relations. The comedies of Aristophanes certainly do not question the idea of erotic relations with boys: such homophile relationships, which developed in the context of the educational prac-tices of the gymnasium are an essential element in the Utopia elaborated in the *Birds*. Likewise, for Phales, who, in the phallophoria of the *Acharnians*, strides as an erect phallus around the border regions to which Dionysus gives one access, it is as normal to love boys as it is to

---

[7] Aristoph. *Ach.* 241f.; Aristot. *Poet.* 4.1449a 2ff. The question of the ritual phallic origin of comedy is well explored by H. Herter, *Vom dionysischen Tanz zum komischen Spiel* (Iserlohn 1947), 15ff.; on the attributes of comic costume, see the references given in "Démasquer par le masque," *Rev. Hist. Rel.* 206 (1989): 357–76. On the iconography, see Brendel 1970, 15ff.

[8] For a good critique on what is sometimes taken as a unilateral comparison, see S. Goldhill, *The Poet's Voice* (Cambridge 1991), 176ff.; see also W. Rösler and B. Zimmer-mann, *Carnevale e utopia nella Grecia antica* (Bari 1991), 15ff.

cheat on one's wife by pouncing on a little Thracian slave girl on the outskirts of a wood. Without a doubt, if the "little young man" educated by the sophists, in the *Clouds*, wants to abide by the rules of seemliness that Right Logic endeavors to teach him, he has to give up banquets and other forms of symposiac celebrations as well as women and young boys.[9]

The satire directed at homophilia is only slightly tinged with irony. In contrast, where effeminate men are concerned, no quip is deemed too crude. Consider the mockery aimed at Agathon, the tragic poet who appears on stage adorned in finery fit for the beautiful Cyrene. Agathon is the only person in a position to lend Euripides' older kinsman the feminine attire that will enable him to gain admission to the Thesmophoria, normally reserved for women. Even before the great tragic poet, Agathon, makes his appearance on stage, the mention of his very name provokes unequivocal sexual allusions: he is a man who welcomes the embraces of anyone he chances to meet, a poet in whose behind anyone can stick his member, a musician whose feminine singing voice profoundly stirs Euripides' kinsman, and an author of satirical dramas that can be inspired by anyone standing behind him with an erection; he is — and here comes the word, at last — "buggered" (*katapugôn*), a term that is immediately glossed by another of Aristophanes' favorite insults. He is one of those "wide arseholes" (*europrôktos*), always quivering with "passion" (*pathêmata*).[10] Agathon is so effeminate that Euripides prefers to get his kinsman to take his place and dress up in Agathon's clothes to gain access to the Thesmophoria, from which men are excluded! There can be no doubt that it is the effeminate, adult homosexual, and passive to boot, who is the target of Aristophanes' lewd mockery here.

When, in the *Frogs*, Dionysus announces that his heart has been assailed by a passionate desire (*pothos, himeros*), Heracles at first assumes this to be love for a woman, next that it is love for a boy; eventually it occurs to him that Euripides might have in mind love for an adult man, such as Cleisthenes. Only, this last hypothesis is interpreted by Dionysus as a sick joke. For Aristophanes ridicules active homosexuality as much as he does the passive variety: the politician Cleon is repeatedly accused of sodomizing his victims. Any homosexual relationship that involves

---

[9] Aristoph. *Av.* 137ff.: see above ch. V, §2.2, with n. 27; Aristoph. *Ach.* 263ff. and *Nub.* 1071ff.; see Buffière 1980, 180ff.

[10] Aristoph. *Thesm.* 35, 50, 59ff., 133, 157ff., and 199ff. Only in comedy could an effeminate homosexual (played by a man!) be dressed up as a woman: see F. I. Zeitlin, "Travesties of Gender and Genre in Aristophanes' *Thesmophoriazousae*," in Foley 1981, 169–217 (= 1996, 375–416), and L. K. Taaffe, *Aristophanes and Women* (London 1993), 79ff.

two adults is severely criticized.[11] Similarly, in one satyr play, the marginal space represented and the energy of the chorus of satyrs have the effect of converting the relationship between a banqueter and his young cupbearer into a homosexual relationship between two adults: to be more specific, when intoxicated by drinking wine that he has failed to mix with water, Polyphemus mistakes a bearded Silenus for the fresh-cheeked Ganymedes, whom he claims to prefer even to the Charites:

> Calloo, callay! How close I was to drowning in it! This is pleasure unalloyed. I think I see the heaven and the earth swimming around together. I see Zeus's throne and the whole revered company of the gods. Shall I not kiss them? The Graces are trying to seduce me. No more! With this Ganymede here I shall go oft to bed with greater glory than with the Graces. And somehow I take more pleasure in boys than in women.[12]

As one peruses the list of the forty or more figures who are accused of passive homosexuality in Attic comedy, and as one notices how frequently the comic authors of the classical period refer to sodomy, it seems reasonable to wonder whether the accusation might not be of a purely formal nature and whether the terms used do not correspond simply to general insults. A scene such as the one in the *Clouds* in which all the citizens of Athens, right across the spectrum from its magistrates, through its tragic authors and orators, to the spectators of the play themselves, are accused of being "big arseholes" might certainly be thought to support such a hypothesis.[13] However, to reach such a conclusion would be to forget that this stream of invectives begins with a most precise description of the practices in which sodomites indulge. It would also be to disregard the noun that Aristophanes forges from the adjective *katapugôn*, turning the insult into an abstract concept.[14] Above all, it would be to forget that the adjective *katapugôn* (bugger) was already being used in graffiti back in the archaic period.

---

[11] Aristoph. *Ran.* 52ff., *Eq.* 261ff., and *Vesp.* 1284ff. For Aristophanes, the love of women and homophilia were on the same level, as opposed to a fixed homosexuality, whether passive or active: see Henderson 1991, 215ff.

[12] Eur. *Cycl.* 576ff., in D. Kovaks (trans.), *Euripides* I (Loeb 1994): see the study (entitled misleadingly) by W. Poole, "Male Homosexuality in Euripides," in Powell 1990, 108–50.

[13] The list is given and analyzed by Henderson 1991, 205ff.; see also Cantarella 1988, 69ff.; see Aristoph. *Nub.* 1083ff. The important point is not the correspondence between the accusation of sodomy and the reality of the sexual practices of those accused (as assumed by Dover 1978, 139ff., who reviews the various uses of these insulting words), but rather the extremely negative judgment passed on homosexuality between adults.

[14] The term *katapugosunê* is used by Aristophanes, *Nub.* 1022ff. and frag. 128 Kassel-Austin, and also by Cratinus frag. 58 Kassel-Austin; see S. Beta, "Il linguaggio erotico di Cratino," *Quad. Urb. Cult. Class.* 69 (1992): 95–108.

Between the end of the seventh century and the beginning of the fourth, in parallel to the "pederastic acclamations" carved on rocks situated in the vicinity of gymnasia and to the inscriptions painted on the drinking cups that circulated at symposia, a number of graffiti on shards applied the very same kind of description to some young man. They replaced terms of eulogy that praised the youth's beauty by insults that suggested that he was a homosexual who submitted to sodomy. The contrast between these two types of written declarations is all the more striking in that the accusation of sodomy is sometimes likewise leveled at women. Two such graffiti pillory a girl who is mocked because she allows herself to be penetrated anally by her masculine partner, who is on that account dubbed an *oiphotês*, or "bugger."[15] The insulting nature of these inscriptions is emphasized by the fact that they took the form of fleeting incidental graffiti, in contrast to the eulogistic declarations that were deliberately painted on vases depicting erotic scenes, which were possibly intended as gifts for the beloved.

## 1.2. From Unnatural Vice to Political Insults

There can thus be no doubt about it: the target of such insulting expressions was in truth not the homosexual nature of the implied relationship, but rather the passivity of the partner, whether a man or a woman, who submitted to anal coitus. As has already been noted, in archaic and classical Greece, it was not passivity that constituted the essential characteristic of the asymmetry that obtained in a homophile relationship between an adult and an adolescent, nor indeed of the gender difference between the sexual roles of men and women. However, when associated with anal penetration, passivity did become one of the targets of the jibes of comedy, which, like iambic poetry, was very prone to focus its sarcasm on the organs of feeding, defecation, or sexuality. Hipponax already had expressed a wish that one of his enemies should be given a "stretched arsehole."[16] For a fifth-century Athenian, there was nothing

---

[15] A (provisional) corpus of these graffiti has been collected with a commentary by M. Lombardo, "Nuovi documenti su Pisticci in età arcaica II," *Par. Pass.* 40 (1985): 284–306. On the basis of *katapugôn*, one of the authors of these graffiti even invented a feminine form, *katapugaina*: see ibid., 300ff., and Dover 1978, 113ff. The verb *oiphein*, from which *oipholês* is derived and which is a general term for coitus (cf. Hsch. s.v. *oipholês* and *oipholis*; O 434 and 435 Latte), does not refer specifically to sodomy: see above ch. V, §2.3, n. 28, and the frag. 251 West of Archilochus who, in a ritual context and an iambic poem, seems to have attributed to Dionysus himself the title of *Oipholios*, the Fucker.

[16] The scatological field of satirical and comic obscenity has been well defined by J.-C. Carrière, *Le Carnaval et la politique* (Besançon and Paris 1979), 135ff. See Hippon. frag. 133 Degani, with the short commentary by Henderson 1991, 22; among other insults in

abnormal about a relationship with a boy: abnormality was, instead, associated with adult men and women who allowed themselves to be penetrated anally. Adolescents who abandoned the *diamerismos*, expected in homophile relationships in favor of anal passivity incurred as much disapproval as adults who became effeminate as a result of neglecting their proper "active" role. Only the latter would have been included in the modern category of homosexuality — not the ephemeral type associated with educative practices, but the lasting kind of inversion that is centered on passivity and sodomy.

Two particularly telling texts testifying to the remarkable axiology of the relationships between partners of the same sex have come down to us. The first attempts to provide a physiological explanation for homosexuality of the lasting kind. One of the *Problemata* attributed to Aristotle ponders the reasons for the sexual pleasure that some men derive from passive relations. It quickly decides that such individuals suffer from a congenital defect in their sexual organs: because these are atrophied, the sperm, which cannot escape, becomes concentrated in the region of the anus, as it does in women; and this concentration leads to a desire for the pleasure of passive relationships. However, although the origin of anal passivity (*paskhein, to pathos*) is physiological in beings who suffer from such an "unnatural" (*para phusin*) defect, it may in some cases result from habits contracted in puberty. In the course of a process frequently mentioned in the classical period, habit then becomes second nature and the memory of the pleasure experienced in adolescence leads the adult to continue to desire anal coitus.[17]

The second document does not offer any physiological explanation but draws our attention to the legal sanctions incurred by this particular

---

iambic poetry, it is worth remembering *katômokhanes* (Hippon. frag. 39.1 Degani). In these circumstances, it seems risky to proceed to make the triple assimilation "buggered = *erômenos* (insulted) = reader (passive) of a written and insulting inscription," as J. Svenbro suggests, in *Phrasikleia* (Paris 1988), 210ff. (English translation: *Phrasikleia* [Ithaca and London 1993]); the more so since, in the inscriptions cited in support of this hypothesis, the "writer-bugger" (*ho grapsas*) speaks orally (*phêsin*), as does Hecataeus at the beginning of his work: *FGrHist*. 1 F 1a!

[17] Aristot. *Probl.* 4.879a 36ff.; see also Aristot. *EN* 7.1148b 29ff., with commentary by Halperin 1990, 133ff. One could deduce from this passage that in the fourth century B.C., the homophile "between the thighs" relationship was replaced, for boys, by an anal sexual relationship; this anatomical theory of homosexuality continued to be entertained right down to Caecilius Aurelianus, translator of Soranus in the fifth century A.D.: see P. H. Schrijvers, *Eine medizinische Erklärung der männlichen Homosexualität aus der Antike* (Amsterdam 1985), 8ff. The physiological idea of a woman's sexual enjoyment with respect to the emission of sperm elaborated in classical Greek medicine has been well explored: see in particular G.E.R. Lloyd, *Science, Folklore and Ideology* (Cambridge 1983), 86ff., and A. E. Hanson, "The Medical Writers' Woman," in Halperin, Winkler, and Zeitlin 1990, 309–38.

form of homosexuality: the Greeks condemned it because they judged it to be degrading and unnatural. Modern scholarship has produced a number of long commentaries on the diatribe in which, following the peace negociated with Philip in 346, Aeschines attacked Timarchus. As the reader may refer to these for further information, let us consider this speech without more ado. The charge leveled against this ally of Demosthenes, who, like the latter, belonged to the anti-Macedonian party, criticizes the private life of the politician, whom it accuses of, among other things, having prostituted himself (*hetairêsis*) in his youth. Aeschines' paraphrase of the law relating to such behavior first shows that it excluded from all public responsibilities any man who, having reached adulthood, prostituted himself (*ho hetairêkôs*) and that it also deprived him of his rights as a citizen. But Timarchus' abuse of his own body went even farther. Not content with living with an older man, the handsome young man (*eusarkos, neos, meirakion*) had then fallen in love with a series of singers and flute players and had taken new partners, uncouth men (*agrioi*) to whom he had rented out his body. According to Aeschines, having behaved in such an excessively outrageous fashion, Timarchus was not simply a young man who had had a liaison with an adult man (*hetairêkôs*), but was furthermore a vulgar prostitute who had sold himself to the highest bidder (*peporneumenos*). Even though the law seems to have made no provision for this distinctive behavior, Aeschines makes the most of it to show that Timarchus has carried depravity (*anaideia*) to its very limits. Those who succumb to love (*erômenoi*) in accordance with the laws of restraint (*sôphrosunê*) — such as Aristogeiton in his partnership with Harmodius, or Patroclus in his friendship with Achilles (*philia di'erôta*) — are set in absolute opposition to those who prostitute themselves (*peporneumenoi*) for money. In cases of the latter type, the *erôs* of *homophilia*, with all its propaedeutic value, is reduced to the level of pleasures that are degrading (*aiskhrai hêdonai*).[18]

Does this mean that Timarchus was assimilated to a woman, as is suggested by the denunciation, pronounced in the course of a full public assembly, of the strange masculine couples composed of a "man" (*anêr*), and a "wife" (*gunê*)? No, it does not, for although the behavior of an adulterous woman, censured by the law, did serve as a term of comparison for the crime committed by Timarchus, the woman transgressed in accordance with nature (*kata phusin*), whereas the man who

[18] Aeschin. *Tim.* 18ff., 41ff., 51ff., 159ff., and 132ff.; see these passionate passages along with the commentary by Dover 1978, 19ff. and 106ff., who ponders upon the sanctions that might affect the clients of the prostitute, and adds a number of other examples of accusations of masculine prostitution; but it was certainly a practice that was tolerated on the part of nonfree men.

abused his own body acted against nature (*para phusin*).[19] Thus, in the eyes of the law, what was shocking about relationships into which a young man entered with other men outside the context of homophilia of the fleeting kind was not so much the passivity of his anal sexual behavior (which is implied throughout the speech) but rather the fact — in the case of a free, adult citizen — that he had sold his own body.

Whether the emphasis was laid on its physiological aspect (anal) or its moral implications (its lack of propriety), in Greece masculine homosexuality between adults was regarded as a practice that was contrary to nature. To lend oneself to sodomy was tantamount to doubly rejecting one's condition as a man: it was to live as a nonfree being (not as a woman); and it was also to bypass the ethical code of the assymmetrical homophile love that turned adolescents into good citizens. So it comes as no surprise to find that, in Old Comedy, scatological and insulting accusations of sodomy were frequently leveled at politicians such as Cleon or Alcibiades. Aeschines' libelous charges against his opponent Demosthenes fall into the same category. Recalling the nickname that Demosthenes' nurse had given him and adapting its spelling (*Bat(t)alos*), Aeschines denigrates his enemy as a stammerer and a "little arsehole," and immediately goes on to associate such a description with the lack or virility (*anandria*) and debauchery (*kinaidia*) of this man who dressed in women's clothing.[20]

From Archilochus down to Plato, to allege that a man led the life of *kinaidoi*, which meant that he indulged in practices akin to masculine prostitution, was not so much to describe him as to pass moral judgment on him. In Plato's *Gorgias*, Socrates insists on the importance of distinguishing between pleasure and well-being: the abominable, degrading, and wretched nature of the way of life of debauchees made it imperative to draw a clear distinction between pleasures that were good and those that were bad.[21] What was at stake here was not one's oppo-

---

[19] Aeschin. *Tim.* 111 and 185; the interpretation suggested by Cantarella 1988, 77ff., is too hasty.

[20] On politicians accused of passive homosexuality, see above n. 13; Alcibiades and Cleon, in particular, were also accused of active practices: the references can be found in Henderson 1991, 218ff. On the critique aimed at Demosthenes, see Aeschin. *Tim.* 126 and 131 and also *Amb.* 99. Plato's condemnation of masculine homosexuality (*Leg.* 836b ff. and 841d; see also 636c and Xen. *Mem.* 2.1.30) concerns sexual relations between grown men, not between adolescents and adults; the reason why they are "against nature" (*para phusin*) is that they involve the same sex (*arrhenes*); hesitation on this subject on the parts of Foucault 1984, 243ff., and Cohen 1991, 183ff.

[21] Archil. frag. 294 West, Plat. *Gorg.* 494d ff.; the various imputations of "debauchery" in the classical texts are carefully analyzed by J. J. Winkler, "Laying Down the Law," in Halperin, Winkler, and Zeitlin (eds.) 1990, 171–209 (republished in Winkler 1990, 45–70); see also Dover 1978, 73ff. and 106, and Parker 1983, 98 (in particular on the similar

nent's real sexual life, but his moral behavior, which could be be smirched by the kind of insulting accusations of anal and passive behavior that were a particular feature of iambic poetry of invective. But at the same time, such an accusation certainly reflected the disapproval that was prompted in classical Greece by homosexuality of the lasting kind, which ran contrary both to the condition of a free man and to nature.

## 2. The Institution of Tragedy

Tragedy leads the reader away from masculine love and back to the Eros who assails women. From the point of view of the physiology of love, the great tragic texts have nothing particularly new to offer. The vehicle of "the flower of desire that bites into the heart," as an arrow of love would, is still the gaze, particularly the gaze of Helen as she arrives in Troy. Medea is assailed in her *thumos* by desire for Jason, and Io the virgin, having inflamed Zeus himself with the arrow of desire (*himeros*), is in her turn pursued by the sting of the gadfly that penetrates her heart.[22] The erotic poems of the archaic period have already familiarized us with this physiological concept of amorous desire that is at once spellbinding and stinging.

### 2.1. Metaphorical Play with Marriage

Where feminine sexuality is concerned, it is — or seems to be — the domain of the institution of marriage that the Greek tragedies performed during the festival of Dionysus most powerfully mount their challenge. It has been suggested, not without reason, that in ancient Greece "marriage was to sexual consummation what sacrifice was to the consumption of food in the form of meat." If that is so, then tragedy undertakes to superimpose the terms of that fine homology one upon the other in

judgment passed on cunnilingus). In the treatise on *Physiognomy* attributed to Aristotle (808a 12ff.), the *kinaidos* represents a particular type, characterized by specific physical traits.

[22] Aesch. *Ag.* 737ff.; see also 416ff.; Eur. *Med.* 8, but also 556; Aesch. *Prom.* 649ff. and 593ff. in particular. See other parallels to this physiology of love in the study by S. Durup, "L'espressione tragica del desiderio amoroso," in Calame 1983b, 143–57; the author nevertheless concludes too hastily in favor of a reversible amorous gaze and hence of a reciprocity of sentiment that is simultaneously felt. This concept of Eros is still present in Fischer 1973, 49ff., and above all in the useful comparison with melic poetry undertaken by Müller 1980, 238ff. M. Weissenberger, "Liebeserfahrung in den Gedichten Sapphos," *Rhein. Mus.* 134 (1991): 209–37, is thus tilting at windmills when he shows that the idea of a love conceived as an external force should be understood to be the mark of archaic thought. For the contemporary arts, see I. Rizzini, *L'occhio parlante* (Venice 1998), 144ff.

the themes it chooses. It is not that tragedy turns the institution of marriage into a sacrificial practice exactly, but rather that the tragic poets are prone to represent the destinies of girls who fail to achieve their projected marriages.[23] They are fated instead to a premature death, so that in their cases the transition to adulthood is replaced by a passage that leads to Hades, a passage often effected through a sacrifice, either real or metaphorical. In some cases it is the transition itself that turns into a disaster.

Thus, the reception with which Zeus the Host (*Xenios*) greets Helen upon her arrival in Troy turns into the metaphorical *numphagôgia* of an Erinys who brings bad luck and grief to the entire family of her young fiancé. It is true that this ill-fated wedding was not the first for the young woman and that it involved the betrayal of Menelaus, her legitimate husband. All the same, when, in the *Agamemnon*, Aeschylus set the contrary forces of Eros and the Erinys in opposition, he was not alone in choosing the theme of girls fated to be sacrificed before reaching maturity, or that of beautiful wives whose second marriages lead them to a tragic end. Certainly, the repertory of mythical stories offered tragedy a wide choice for those two particular scenarios, a choice that perhaps seemed all the more attractive given that the premature demise of adolescent girls appears to have been of concern in daily social life as well as in legend. An epigram attributed to Sappho celebrates the memory of a girl whose premature death metaphorically assigned her to the nuptial chamber of Persephone. It suggests that that deathly marriage, so favored as a tragic theme, was the origin of the rite in which a deceased girl's companions offered up locks of hair before their marriages. In this way, the death of an adolescent girl that probably occurred in real life was transformed through ritual into an event that certain modern scholars have interpreted as an initiatory death.[24]

As many studies have already been devoted to the tragic treatment of the death of girls before they ever accede to the married state, let us briefly consider just two of those figures: namely Iphigenia and Anti-

---

[23] This famous formula comes from Vernant 1974, 149. In Sophocles' *Women of Trachis*, for example, after a series of reversals, sacrifice and marriage remain complementary: see C. Segal, "Mariage et sacrifice dans les *Trachiniennes* de Sophocle," *Ant. Class.* 44 (1975): 30–53, and *Tragedy and Civilization* (Cambridge, Mass., and London 1981), 61ff. and 74ff.

[24] Aesch. *Ag.* 744ff.: see P. Judet de La Combe, *Agamemnon 2* (Lille and Paris 1982), 86ff.; Sappho *Epigram* 2 Page; a list of girl victims of an "initiatory" death, before they accede to the maturity of marriage, is provided by Dowden 1989. On the prematrimonial offering of locks of hair, see ibid., 2ff. and 66, but also, for boys, see Vidal-Naquet [2]1983, 147ff. Both the legend of Hymenaeus (see above ch. VI, §2.2, n. 18) and the funerary epitaphs for girls who died prematurely associate marriage with death: examples in Seaford 1987, 111ff.

gone. The fate suffered by Agamemnon's daughter seems the very model of the mythical theme that par excellence confirms the homology suggested between marriage and sacrifice. Clearly, the legend itself tells only of the sacrifice of Iphigenia. However, in *Iphigenia at Aulis*, Euripides uses the false pretext of the girl's marriage to Achilles to establish a series of ironical metaphorical connections between that lie and the real reason for Iphigenia's presence at Aulis. Clytemnestra herself claims to be the *numphagôgos* of a girl destined for the most brilliant of marriages; but the very last words uttered by Iphigenia before her disappearance evoke the other life that awaits her in lieu of a torch-lit marriage ceremony. At the same time, by consenting to be sacrificed, Iphigenia rejects the *oikos* in favor of the *polis*; on the tragic stage, women tend to be even less confined to the women's quarters than they were in reality in the institutional life of the classical period.[25] The marriage ceremony thus becomes often a metaphor for the procedure of ritual sacrifice; and it is by dint of making it a metaphor for a ritual of death that tragedy appears to challenge the institution of marriage.

As for our other "spouse of Hades," Sophocles' Antigone, the only marriage chamber that she is ever to know is the tomb into which, like a young bride, she is forced by the will of Creon, there to kill herself by her own hand. It is there, in the dark abode of Hades, that Haimon's suicide over the girl's lifeless body transforms their last embrace into a marriage (*numphika*) marked by bloodshed. Antigone was thus condemned to death even before her passage into Hades became a metaphorical marriage with death.[26] Sacrifice and suicide are two modes of violent death; and — through a metaphorical echo rather then a homology — when such a death strikes down a girl destined for marriage, the effect is to emphasize the dangerous, even fatal, aspects of the rite of passage that marriage represents. When tragedy compared a girl's death to a marriage in Hades, it tended to focus not so much on the loss of the "virginity" that was, to be sure, lamented in the archaic ritual of marriage, but rather on the violence that was inherent in the passage

[25] Eur. *IA* 609f. (see 458ff. and 732) and 1505ff.; see in this connection the analysis by Seaford 1987, 108ff., and by Lyons 1997, 67ff., with the subtle study by H. P. Foley, *Ritual Irony* (Ithaca and London 1985), 67ff. On the role of the tragic woman in the *polis*, see, by the same author, "The Conception of Woman in Athenian Drama," in Foley 1981, 127–68.

[26] Eur. *IA* 461; Soph. *Ant.* 804, 816, and 1205; see also 891, 946ff., and 1240ff. The equation "tomb = nuptial chamber" is to be found in some epitaphs: see J. C. Kamerbeek, *The Plays of Sophocles* III. *Antigone* (Leiden 1978), 146ff. On the death of Antigone, see the new interpretation suggested by C. Sourvinou-Inwood, "Sophocles' Antigone as a 'Bad Woman'," in F. Dieterlen and E. Klock (eds.), *Writing Women into History* (Amsterdam 1990), 11–38; see also R. Rehm, *Marriage to Death* (Princeton 1994), 59ff.

that led toward a woman's maturity and her submission to a new "master."[27]

The brutal constraint that was an essential element of marriage seen from the woman's point of view is an integral feature of the legend of the Danaids. The daughters of Danaus, having sought refuge in Argos, were ready to take up arms in order to elude the violence with which the sons of their uncle Aegyptus threatened them by seeking to force them into legitimate marriage.[28] Aeschylus adapted this epic material to make his *Suppliant Maidens* a tragedy about girls in flight from marriage and the constraints that it imposed. Clinging to their freedom, they beg the ever-indomitable Artemis to help them escape sharing the bed of a male. The Danaids strive to elude the *hubris* and violence (*bia*) of the sons of Aegyptus. Right up to the last lines of the tragedy, they hope that Zeus will come to their aid by exercising the same "benevolent violence" that he manifested toward their ancestress, Io. They pray that they will be spared an "ill marriage and a bad husband." However, the servants of these daughters of Danaus who are rebelling against the violent aspects of marriage rebuke the obstinacy of the young women from Egypt, telling them that no woman should ever forget Aphrodite. They launch into a veritable hymn to the goddess, in which they describe her surrounded by Pothos, desire, Peithô, spellbinding persuasion, Concord, and a throng of infant Loves, who come and go whispering together:

> Yet there is no disdain of Cypris in this our friendly hymn;
> for she, together with Hera, hath power most near to Zeus,
> and for her august rites
> the goddess of varied wiles is held in honour.
>   And in the train of their mother are Desire
> and she to whom nothing is denied, even winning Persuasion;
> and to Harmonia hath been given a share of Aphrodite,
> and to the whispering dalliances of the Loves.

---

[27] The loss of the status of adolescence is deplored in an epithalamium attributed to Sappho: frag. 114 Voigt (see above ch. VI, §2.3, n. 31). N. Loraux, *Façons tragiques de tuer une femme* (Paris 1985), 68ff. (English translation: A. Forster, *Tragic Ways of Killing a Woman* [Cambridge, Mass. 1987]), lists the girls in tragedy who are sacrificed before acceding to marriage. An anecdote from Miletus, recorded by Plutarch, *Fem. Virtut.* 249bc, attributes to the girls of this Ionian city a longing for death that impelled them to commit suicide by hanging; only an appeal to their modesty could cure these *parthenoi* of this "distraction of the mind."

[28] See *Danais* frag. 1 Bernabé; also Hes. frag. 127 Merkelbach-West and Apoll. 2.1.4ff., with the commentary by M. Detienne, "Les Danaïdes entre elles," *Arethusa* 21 (1988): 159–75 (reprinted in 1989, 41–57).

The power of the goddess of desire is likened to that of Zeus and Hera. With farsighted wisdom, the servants sense that the Danaids, like so many women before them, will eventually come to experience marriage. Whatever the outcome of the completed trilogy (predicted in the above fragment to be legitimate marriage), and whatever the social context of this tragic union, the endogamous nature of which provokes the kind of fears that might be felt by any Athenian woman subjected to the rules governing an *epikleros* daughter, this chorus sung by the Danaids' servants reminds us that, like it or not, once a woman becomes an adult, she cannot escape the power of Aphrodite and Eros; and at the end of the trilogy that power is envisaged from the point of view of its potential procreative effects.[29]

The Danaids will have to submit to marriage in the end, even if it leads them into crime. So what the tragedy challenges is not so much the violence of the institution itself but that of the subjection that the inflexible Aphrodite imposes. It should be remembered that this domestication, conveyed here by the image of the yoke, is of a twofold nature: it involves not only submission to the desire that is aroused by Eros but also, for an Athenian woman, subjection to the authority of her husband through her sexual union with him and her moving to live with him in his house. In social practice, the function of the ritual of marriage was, precisely, to convert sexual constraint, as symbolized by pursuit and rape, into a form of domestication that was culturally sanctioned and socially approved: it led to the acceptance of the power of the male, an acceptance that was part and parcel of the social role or gender of an adult woman and that found expression in the metaphor of her ritual passage into civilization.

Significantly enough, in tragedy the actual celebration of the marriage rite could only be parodied by a woman totally possessed by Dionysus. In Euripides' *Trojan Women*, it is only when seized by Bacchic madness that young Cassandra can imagine celebrating her own marriage with her future master Agamemnon and can express her vision in a parodic marriage hymn, which she sings on her own:

---

[29] Aesch. *Suppl.* 1034ff., in H. W. Smyth (trans.), *Aeschylus* I (Loeb 1922), and 144ff. and 817ff.; see also 830ff., 904, 943, and 1035ff.; see frag. 44 Radt. The institutional and legal context of the problem of marriage posed in *The Suppliant Maidens* is studied by Seaford 1987, 110ff., who returns to the hypothesis of the eventual marriage, or even remarriage, of the Danaids, in the last tragedy in the trilogy: see above ch. VI, §2.3, with n. 38. On the lesson of moderation offered in conclusion by the chorus members, see E. Lévy, "Inceste, mariage et sexualité dans les *Suppliantes* d'Eschyle," in Vérilhac 1985, 29–45; Zeitlin 1992, 226ff. = 1996, 153ff., has skillfully shown that even the relationship between the daughters of Danaus and Zeus bears the stamp of Eros.

Up with the torch! — give it to me — let me render
  Worship to Phoebus! — lo, lo how I fling
wide through his temple the flash of its splendor! —
  Hymen! O Marriage-god, Hymen my king!
Happy the bridegroom who waiteth to meet me;
Happy am I for the couch that shall greet me;
  Royal espousals to Argos I bring: —
  Bridal-king, Hymen, thy glory I sing.

Mother, thou lingerst long at thy weeping
  Aye makest moan for my sire who hath died,
Mourn'st our dear country with sorrow unsleeping:
  Therefore myself for mine own marriage-tide
Kindle the firebrands, a glory outstreaming,
Toss up the torches, a radiance far-gleaming! —
Hymen, to thee is their brightness upleaping:
  Hekate, flash thou thy star-glitter wide,
  After thy wont when a maid is a bride.[30]

When Cassandra recovers her senses, she vows that in her the king of Argos will find a wife more baleful than even Helen was; their marriage will lead to crime and ruination; it will ultimately be celebrated in Hades. When the madness of the maenad gives way to the clairvoyance of the prophetess, that solipsistic vision of marriage is replaced by crime and bloodshed. Once again, a conjugal union with the betrothed in the halls of Hades is a metaphor.

## 2.2. The Fateful Tyranny of Eros and Aphrodite

What tragedy attacks in marriage is not so much its institutional aspect as the implacable nature of a sexuality that is personified by certain deities. This brings us back to the main theme of the present study. What the tragic authors who seized the opportunity offered by the ritual of the Dionysia chose to bring into question was the excessive power of Eros and his mistress Aphrodite.

Thus in Sophocles' *Antigone*, when Haimon, confronted with his father Creon's inflexibility, hints that he has decided to follow his loved one to the grave, the chorus of Theban old men launch into a veritable hymn to Eros. Using terms that we have already encountered in archaic

---

[30] Eur. *Tr.* 308ff. and 341, 349, 366ff., 357ff., 404ff., and 445ff., in A. S. Way (trans.), *Euripides* I (Loeb 1912). The crossovers between Cassandra's marriage hymn and a bacchant's singing are raised by S. A. Barlow, *Euripides. Trojan Women* (Warminster 1981), 173ff.; R. Schlesier, "Der Stachel der Götter," *Poetica* 17 (1985): 1–45, notes the way in which Euripides interlinks the madness of love and Dionysiac possession.

poetry, they praise the invincible power of Desire, which holds sway in the animal kingdom and also brings a flush to the fresh cheeks of maidens:

Love invincible in battle,
Love who falls upon men's property,
you who spend the night
upon the soft cheeks of a girl,
and travel over the sea
and through the huts of dwellers in the wild!
None among the immortals can escape you,
nor any among mortal men,
and he who has you is mad.
    You wrench just men's minds aside from justice,
doing them violence;
it is you who have stirred up this quarrel
between men of the same blood.
Victory goes to the visible desire
that comes from the eyes of the beautiful bride,
desire that has its throne beside those of the mighty laws;
for irresistible in her sporting
is the goddess Aphrodite.[31]

Eros, in the form of *himeros*, beams from the eyes of betrothed girls destined for the marriage bed, but his victory brings with it no hope that justice will be restored. In the perspective of the tragic plot of conflict between a son, his father, and his betrothed, Eros takes a just man, led astray by an unjust heart, to a degrading death. The members of the chorus declare that, whatever its outcome, victory for Eros constitutes one of the primordial laws (*thesmoi*) of the universe. In consequence, and in a ring composition that follows the pattern of archaic argumen-

---

[31] Soph. *Ant.* 781ff., in H. Lloyd-Jones (trans.), *Sophocles* I (Loeb 1994): see H. Erbse, "Haimons Liebe zu Antigone," *Rhein. Mus.* 134 (1991): 252–61; for bibliography on the question of Haimon's motivation, see Des Bouvrie 1990, 181. On the cosmic power of Eros celebrated in these lines, see below ch. X, n. 1; Aphrodite's affinities are not only with madness but also with Hades himself: Soph. frag. 941.1ff. Radt, with the commentary by D. Pralon, "L'éloge d'Aphrodite (Soph. fr. 941 Radt)," in A. Machin and D. Pernée (eds.), *Sophocle. Le texte, les personnages* (Aix-en-Provence 1993), 125–31. As for echoes of this hymn to Eros in other tragedies, see R. Garner, *From Homer to Tragedy* (London and New York 1990), 78ff. In a little-known satyr play, Sophocles is more faithful to tradition when he describes the contrasting effects of Eros upon lovers: frag. 149 Radt. In *Sophocles' Tragic World* (Cambridge, Mass., and London 1995), 69–94, C. P. Segal shows that the tragedy of the *Women of Trachis* likewise questions not so much the institution of marriage but rather the divine powers that are involved; see also B. Effe, "Die Emanzipation des Eros in der griechischen Dichtung," in G. Binder and B. Effe (eds.), *Liebe und Leidenschaft* (Trier 1993), 25–44.

tation, the invincibility of this power is traced back to the goddess Aphrodite herself. After that trenchant statement, all that is left for the chorus to do is remind themselves to remain on their guard: at the sight of Antigone approaching the nuptial couch of death, they must not allow themselves to be carried away or risk thereby contravening those very laws (*thesmoi* again)! The freedom to speak out and criticize that is afforded by the masked dramatic performances that are a feature of the cult of Dionysus is subject to limitations imposed by the power of the gods, however objectionable that power may be; and that is particularly true when Aphrodite and Eros are involved.

This sheds new light upon the fateful aspects of Euripides' hymn to Eros quoted at the end of this study. While an entity through whose eyes desire is distilled can fill the soul with the pleasures of love, it should be remembered that such a being also brings reversals of fortune and ruination. Along with Hippolytus who, in his exclusive devotion to the virgin Artemis, imitates the behavior of a girl, the female victims of Aphrodite are all women in the grip of possession: Iole, who is compared to a Bacchant, Semele the mother of Bacchus, and Phaedra herself who, though a married woman, dreams of dashing through the wild woods in pursuit of a dappled doe. It is as if the Dionysiac aspect of the dramatic ritual bewitched love-smitten women, subjecting them to all that is most destructive and death-dealing in the power of Eros and Aphrodite. Certainly, when the body of the dying Hippolytus is carried on stage, the chorus sings of the power of Aphrodite and her companion Eros. Nobody can resist Cypris or her winged servant, who reigns over both land and sea, assailing maddened hearts and bewitching them; all the beasts and mortals under the sun fall victim to them. Even the chorus members, who are respectable matrons of Troezen, must strive, in their turn, not to be carried away: their earnest prayer is that where they are concerned Eros should not intervene with damaging effect. So it is that the plot of the *Hippolytus*, a play that constitutes a denunciation of the excessive power of Aphrodite, closes with the institution of a prematrimonial rite in which locks of hair are offered up in a ceremony designed to consecrate the passage of girls from the jurisdiction of Artemis into that of Cypris, the very passage that Hippolytus rejected when, in his madness, he identified himself as one of their number.[32]

---

[32] Eur. *Hipp.* 525ff. (see above my introduction to this book), 215ff., 1268ff., and 1422ff.; on the prenuptial offering of locks of hair, see the references given below, n. 24. On the meaning of this gesture in relation to the death of Hippolytus, see P. Pucci, "Euripides: The Monument and the Sacrifice," *Arethusa* 10 (1977): 165–95, and B. E. Goff, *The Noose of Words. Reading of Desire, Violence and Language in Euripides' Hippolytos* (Cambridge 1990), 117ff.; also F. I. Zeitlin, "The Power of Aphrodite," in P. Burian (ed.),

In the *Medea*, also by Euripides, the chorus of women expresses exactly the same fervent hope that Love's intervention will not prove destructive. Here too, its prayer to Aphrodite comes at a turning point in the plot, when Jason definitively abandons his first wife, who then turns to Aegeus for help in implementing her vengeful plans. Here, in a remarkable reversal, the members of the chorus appeal to Cypris herself to show the moderation and control that the gods normally expect from men. For when the Erotes and Aphrodite intervene with violence, they deny humans any pleasure, force women into alien beds, fill the sleep of wives with anguish, depriving them of homeland and hearth, and precipitate them into distress and death.[33] In the light of this commentary, the tragic destiny of Medea results from the excesses in which both Eros and Aphrodite sometimes indulge. The fatal madness of their victim is simply a consequence of the excesses of the deities of love. Euripides makes the most of the means that tragedy consecrated to Dionysus offered to produce an indirect critique of those gods, denouncing those very excesses. The chorus, reverting to a Homeric metaphor, begs the gods of love to allow there to be beds without conflict, the beds that go with marriage as it should be.

The ritual of the Dionysia and the means that masked ritual drama provided made it possible to represent not only the extremes of madness into which the onslaught of erotic desires drives us, along with all its dire consequences, but also the affinities that the Greeks of the archaic and classical periods perceived between the states of love and death.[34] At the same time, the chorus is generally there to remind us of the constructive and civic effects that the interventions of Eros and Aphro-

---

*Directions in Euripidean Criticism* (Durham, N.C., 1985), 52–110 and 198–200 = 1996, 219–84; parallels to the power of the two deities are shown in Barrett 1964, 393ff. Des Bouvrie 1990, 242ff., has clearly argued, like so many others before her, that Hippolytus' rejection of the power of Aphrodite is equivalent to a rejection of matrimonial sexuality and its reproductive function; see also M. R. Halleran, "Gamos and Destruction in Euripides' *Hippolytus*," *Trans. Am. Philol. Assoc.* 121 (1991): 109–21, Adrados 1995, 267ff., and D. L. Cairns, "The Meadow of Artemis and the Character of the Euripidean *Hippolytus*," *Quad. Urb. Cult. Class.* 86 (1997): 51–75. On the religious connection between Aphrodite and Hippolytus in Athens, see Pirenne-Delforge 1994, 40ff.

[33] Eur. *Med.* 627ff.; see also 835ff; see P. Pucci, *The Violence of Pity in Euripides' Medea* (Ithaca and London 1980), 121ff. This "moral" concept of Eros expressed by the chorus stands in opposition to the concept conveyed by the plot, which identifies love with madness and divinity: see A. Rivier, *Essai sur le tragique d'Euripide* (Paris, ²1975), 41ff. and 183ff.

[34] The comic poets were clearly also happy to criticize the power of Eros, in particular in the fourth century B.C.: see, for example, Alexis frag. 247 Kassel-Austin (on the duplicity of Eros) and Aristophon frag. 11 Kassel-Austin (Eros should be excluded from the pantheon); according to the hypothesis of Lasserre 1946, 110ff., those authors were probably influenced by the Sophists.

dite may produce. The words sung by the chorus take over the practical function of melic poetry and assume a pragmatic value. Even as it comments upon the plot, deploring all the violence wreaked by love, the voice of the chorus addresses the public composed of citizens, exhorting them to practice moderation.

The advice proferred by the wise chorus members of Greek tragedy to some extent anticipates the concept of love elaborated several centuries later by the moralist Plutarch, who transferred all the ethical and educative values of the homophile relationship to the relationship between a husband and his legitimate wife. As he saw it, in conjugal union the seductive ploys of the deities of love could be combined with both pleasures that were measured and controlled and also the inculcation of ethical values:

> [Women] are, in fact, fond of their children and their husbands (*philoteknoi, philandroi*). . . . Just as poetry adds to the prose meaning the delight of song and metre and rhythm, making its educational power more forceful and its capacity for doing harm more irresistible, just so nature has endowed women with a charming face, a persuasive voice and a seductive physical beauty and has thus given the dissolute woman great advantages for the beguilment of pleasure, but to the chaste great resources also to gain the goodwill and friendship (*philia*) of her husband.[35]

[35] Plut. *Amator.* 769cd, in W. C. Helmbold (trans.), *Plutarch's Moralia* IX (Loeb 1961): see M. Foucault, *Histoire de la sexualité* 3. *Le souci de soi* (Paris 1984), 234ff. (English translation: *The History of Sexuality* 3. *The Care of the Self* [New York 1988]).

## PART FOUR

### THE SPACES OF EROS

## Chapter VIII

## THE MEADOWS AND GARDENS OF LEGEND

WHEN THE INTERVENTIONS of Eros and Aphrodite were dramatized in Attic theater, within a space consecrated to the cult of Dionysus, those deities were sometimes bitterly criticized by human beings, as just noted above. Let us now pursue our inquiry into the poetic representations of their modes of intervention by considering the spaces in which the powers of deified love are deployed. As we have seen, Eros' activity in Greek educative institutions of an initiatory type takes place not so much in the domain of wild nature — as the anthropological pattern of tribal initiation might lead us to expect — but rather in spaces that were integrated into the city territory, that is to say in banquet halls or in the vicinity of gymnasia. Now, to return to the realization of love that involves women, let us examine one kind of erotic space that is often overlooked. This tends to be eclipsed, as a result of all the attention that is focused upon the domain of wild nature, because of both the structural opposition established between nature and culture and the prevailing interest in the three phases of the initiatory pattern. The erotic space to which I refer is the flower-studded meadow (*leimôn*), sometimes all too easily confused with the garden (*kêpos*).[1]

As we make our way first into these erotic meadows, then into the gardens of Aphrodite, we shall again be presented with the various essential moments that mark the transition from adolescence to fully assumed sexual maturity. We shall, however, be moving away from the level of rituals and institutions and reentering the domain of poetry, with its images of plant-filled spaces in which the deities of love manifest their powers (frequently in a metaphorical manner).

The paradigm, both mythical and theological, of a meadow used for erotic purposes is represented for us by the famous love scene in the *Iliad* in which Hera manages to lure Zeus away from the battlefield of Troy, using the seductive ploys described above, in the second chapter of this study. With his heart bursting with the sweetest desire he has

---

[1] The fundamental study on this subject is by Motte 1973; as it frequently proceeds by association, the work tends to efface a number of essential spatial and metaphorical distinctions, which are partially restored by the brief essay of W. Burkert, "Die Betretene Wiese," in H. P. Duerr (ed.), *Die Wilde Seele* (Frankfurt am Main 1989), 32–46; Bremer 1975, 272ff., has shown that the study Motte is not entirely complete.

ever known, Zeus refuses to adjourn to the private marriage chamber as his wife suggests, and insists upon being forthwith united with her on the very summit of Mount Ida, where she has met with him, determined to arouse his passion. The earth responds by putting forth a sward of fresh grass that, enveloped in a golden mist and freshened with the gleaming dew, serves as a bed for the divine couple. Clover, crocuses, and hyacinths adorn this newly grown lawn. The choice of flowers reflects more than a straightforward preoccupation with ornamentation, for in the *Cypria*, too, the clothing of Aphrodite is colored by the hues of those very spring flowers — crocuses and hyacinths, as well as violets and roses.[2]

## 1. EROTICIZED MEADOWS

Meadows of love. Before returning to consider the particular significances of the flowers that flourish best in them, it is worth noting that in Hesiod just such a meadow, covered with fresh grass and spring flowers, is the place where Poseidon is united with Medusa. And in the myth that even Socrates is prepared to recognize, the love of Boreas for the Nymph Oreithyia is consummated not far from a meadow through which the clear waters of the Ilissus flow. It is there, to the shade cast by a plane tree and a fragrantly blooming agnus castus (chaste tree) that he leads Phaedrus. This is a particularly suitable spot to engage in dialogue on the subject of Eros, since it is the place that, at the end of the dialogue, turns out to be the sanctuary of the Muses, where Socrates first began to philosophize with his disciples, his *erômenoi*. Actually, to be altogether precise, the soft meadow of the Ilissus was the place where the Nymph was seized by the North Wind, who then carried her off and was united with her somewhere else. A parallel version of the myth adds that Oreithyia is busy gathering flowers when Boreas seizes hold of her.[3]

Similarly, in the version of the legend dramatized by Aeschylus, Zeus provides the bull that carries off the young Europe with a meadow in which to graze. But it is not there that the god is united with the daughter of Cadmus: she is forced farther afield, where she loses the modesty

---

[2] Hom. *Il.* 14.312ff. and 346ff.: see above ch. I, §1, n. 8, and the commentary by Janko 1992, 206ff., who notes that the Greeks linked fecundity with the dew (see also below ch. IX, §3, n. 13). See also *Cypr.* frag. 4 Bernabé.

[3] Hes. *Theog.* 276ff.; Plat. *Phaedr.* 229a ff. and 278b ff.; Choeril. Sam. frag. 7 Bernabé: the other versions of the abduction of Oreithyia are collected and intelligently analyzed by Brulé 1987, 291; on the iconography, see Kaempf-Dimitriadou 1979, 36ff. Herodotus, 7.189, testifies to the Athenian orientation of the legend.

that befits a maiden (*parthenos*) and becomes a woman (*gunê*). In a metaphor borrowed from agriculture and frequently used to allude to the process of human generation, Europe herself then becomes a plowed field that, after receiving the god's seed, gives birth to Minos. In a more sentimental vein, much to the taste of his Alexandrian contemporaries, the author of a Hellenistic poem devoted to this heroine does not hesitate to turn the pasture of Zeus' bull into a meadow where the girl is surrounded by companions of her own age as she gathers spring flowers, placing them in a golden basket wrought by Hephaestus on the occasion of the marriage of Libye and Poseidon: fragrant narcissi, hyacinths, violets, wild thyme, and roses that evoke Aphrodite, to whom the young flower gatherer is herself compared. The sight of her is enough to arouse the overpowering desire of Zeus who, metamorphosed into a bull with breath even sweeter and more spellbinding than the fragrance of the meadow, carries her off to Crete. It is there, on a bed prepared by the Hours, that the maiden (*kourê*) becomes a young bride (*numphê*) and subsequently the mother of children engendered by the son of Cronos.[4]

The Hellenistic author of this poem may have drawn the spatial model for his idyll from the famous scene of abduction of Core that is described in the *Homeric Hymn to Demeter*. Once again, the place where the girl is seized is a meadow of fresh grass, where Demeter's daughter is enjoying herself in the company of the full-breasted daughters of Ocean, gathering roses, crocuses, irises, and hyacinths. But it is the narcissus, with its heady scent, that proves her undoing, luring her to the gaping hole through which Hades drags her down to the underworld. Without going into the secondary function of the meadow, from which it is possible to pass into the underworld, it is worth noting that, in the retrospective account at the end of the *Hymn*, in which Core gives her own version of the abduction, the scene is highly eroticized: the meadow that inspires desire (*himertos*) and the flowers that arouse *erôs* (*eroenta*) are reflected by the amorous desire (*himeroessa, erateinê*) that is evoked by the youthful charm of the daughters of Ocean.[5]

---

[4] Aesch. frag. 99 Radt, the text of which is, admittedly, uncertain; Mosch. *Eur.* 27ff., which is no doubt inspired by the Hesiodic version (frags. 140 and 141 Merkelbach-West) in which Europe, gathering flowers in a meadow, with the Nymphs, is seduced by the saffron-fragrant breath emanating from Zeus; in the shape of a bull, the god carries the girl off to Crete, where he is united with her. In the description of the painting that introduces the novel of Achilles Tatius, 1.1.5, Europe is carried off from a meadow blooming with narcissi, roses, and myrtle, which changes into a *locus amoenus*. Other mentions of parallel abductions of girls gathering flowers, and lists of flowers, are in W. Bühler, *Die Europa des Moschos* (Wiesbaden 1960), 75 and 110ff.

[5] *Hhom. Cer.* 5ff. and 417ff., where lilies take the place of violets in this paradise of flowers. It should be noted that Persephone is accompanied not only by the Oceanids, but

Only occasionally does a flower-filled field provide the god with the actual bed on which he is united with the girl whom he has seduced. More often, the meadow represents a space filled with Eros, which serves as an immediate prelude to the gratification of sexual desire. That is certainly the case in the story of Creusa, who is seized and carried off by Apollo of the golden locks while she is gathering crocuses into the folds of her clothing. The god, her husband-to-be, takes her to a cave where, on an improvised bed, he forces her to do homage to the powers of Aphrodite. The child born from this union is Ion, the eponymous hero of the Ionians. On the other hand, Io, driven by nocturnal visions and oracles, leaves her dwelling as a girl (*parthenos*) to roam through the lush grass of the meadow of Lerna, and it is in this meadow itself, among her father's cowsheds and sheep pens that she is metamorphosed into a cow by either Hera or Zeus himself; and there she is united with the god, who accommodatingly turns himself into a bull for the occasion. For this maiden, the marriage bed (*lekhos*) where Zeus satisfies his desire does turn out to be the soft pasture. It is worth remembering, in this connection, that in poetry Eros himself is frequently to be found, in the guise of a child, playing amid fragrant flowers; and in the most ancient representations that associate Eros with some form of plant, he is often presented as an adolescent in flight, holding a rose.[6]

Whether as a prelude meadow or, more rarely, as a marriage-bed meadow, a flowery pasture is always a framework for games that lead to the fulfillment of amorous desire. Take, for instance, the musical games to which Pan, with his pipes, summons the sweetly singing mountain Nymphs: the frolics of these young women around a spring of deep waters, in a fresh meadow where the grass is interwoven with crocuses and fragrant hyacinths, are merely the prelude to an account of the conjugal lovemaking of Hermes the shepherd and the daughter of Dryops, a productive union from which Pan is born. The poet skillfully constructs his narrative in such a way that the framework for the enunciation of the account of the love affair between Hermes and the

---

also by the two *parthenoi* goddesses, Artemis and Athena: on this tradition, see Richardson 1974, 290ff. The scene of the abduction of Core is compared to the rape of Europe by M. Campbell, *Moschus, Europa* (Hildesheim and New York 1991), 71ff. On the local affinities between Persephone and Aphrodite, see C. Sourvinou-Inwood, "Persephone and Aphrodite at Locri," *Journ. Hell. Stud.* 98 (1978): 101–21 (reprinted in 1991, 147–88). On meadows and their links with the Underworld, see Motte 1973, 119 and 233ff.

[6] Eur. *Ion* 881ff.; Aesch. *Prom.* 645ff.; see also *Suppl.* 538ff. On Eros, see in particular Plat. *Symp.* 196ab and Alcm. frag. 58 Page together with the references that I provided in 1983, 555ff.; on iconography, see Hermary 1986, 864ff. The abduction of Persephone from a flowering meadow has naturally been given an initiatory interpretation: see B. Lincoln, "The Rape of Persephone," *Harv. Theol. Rev.* 72 (1979): 223–35.

Nymph creates the very spatial circumstances that probably led to its consummation. According to myth, it was likewise in a green meadow by the clear waters of the springs of the Nymphs that the rival goddesses gathered to compete in beauty before Paris the cowherd. There forgathered Pallas, Cypris, and Hera to pick roses and hyacinths, Athena with her lance, Aphrodite strong in the power of the amorous desire that she inspired, and Hera with all the confidence of the wife who shared the bed of the king of the gods.[7]

In the epithalamium already cited, which presents the story of the marriage of Helen and Menelaus as an idyll, Theocritus, in the manner characteristic of Hellenistic poetry, turns that idyll into a myth that founded a ritual, thereby transposing the functions of the flowering meadow of legend to the level of religion. Helen's transition from the state of a "charming girl" (*khariessa kora*) to that of a "housewife" (*oiketis*) is celebrated by her still adolescent companions close to the river Eurotas, in blossoming meadows where they weave her a sweetly scented crown of flowers, which they consecrate in the shade of the plane tree close to which tradition situated a sanctuary devoted to Helen.[8] In this neat intertwining of myth and religion, the fragrant pastureland is the scene of the rite that prepares for a paradigmatic conjugal union. The meadow prelude to love prefigures the meadow marriage bed.

## 2. THE ORCHARDS AND GARDENS OF APHRODITE

The above-mentioned spaces are meadows, not gardens. But in the world of the gods, Aphrodite has a proper garden, a fragrant and enclosed garden that the *Homeric Hymn* to the goddess locates at Paphos, on the island of Cyprus, where it is bounded by the same limits as a sanctuary that is centered on an altar consecrated to her. Certainly, as soon as she was born, the beautiful goddess was welcomed in Cyprus by a carpet of grass that sprang up beneath her feet. Later, when she is united in love with Anchises, soon to produce Aeneas, Aphrodite is de-

---

[7] *Hhom.* 19.19ff.; Eur. *IA* 1291ff. Note also that in Ap. Rhod. 3.896ff., it is after gathering flowers amid soft grass, accompanied by her friends, that Medea meets Jason. Elsewhere, even if the landscape that surrounds the cave of Calypso in Hom. *Od.* 5.55ff. falls outside the framework of a *locus amoenus* (despite the efforts made to restrict this landscape to that model), Motte 1973, 210, may well be correct in suggesting that the soft violet-filled meadows that surround the Nymph's abode may represent a spatial prelude to her lovemaking with Odysseus. In the Euripidean version (*Hel.* 241ff.) of the abduction of Helen, the heroine is carried off by Hermes while she is gathering into a fold of her *peplos* roses intended for Athena.

[8] Theocr. 18.38ff.; see Calame 1977, I, 335ff., and above ch. VI, §2.

scribed as simply disappearing into the forests that cover Mount Ida. There, the mortal Anchises leads the goddess, without more ado, to a soft bed covered with bear- and lionskins.[9] Gardens, meadows, and beds: these are three distinct spaces that, however, sometimes come to overlap, but only in particular circumstances.

Similarly, in Pindar's version of the myth of Cyrene, the eponymous heroine of the fertile colony of Libya, the girl's father is born in the deep forests of Mount Pindus, from the union of Creusa, one of the daughters of Earth, and a son of Ocean, the river Penaeus. However, it is from the windy valleys of Pelion that his daughter, Cyrene, who is a virgin huntress, is carried off by Apollo, who then takes her to the fertile land of Libya. There, she is welcomed by Aphrodite, who propels the divine couple into the soft bed of conjugal union. Apollo's mention of their gathering grass, as sweet as honey, prior to making love, is a metaphor for the union itself. Then, as he goes on in similar vein, his words transform the whole of Libya, with all its vast fields, into a garden for Zeus: for not only Aphrodite, but the king of the gods too, has a mythical *kêpos* to enjoy. In Plato's *Symposium*, Diotima declares that it was in this garden of Zeus that Poverty (Penia) and Expedience (Poros) were brought together in a union that resulted in the birth of Eros, destined to be Aphrodite's servant and companion. It is also in this garden that, in the *Argonautica*, the goddess of love comes across her son, Eros, playing knucklebones with Ganymedes, the *erômenos* of Zeus.[10] A *kêpos*, which is carefully fenced, is not to be confused with a *leimôn*, filled with the blooms of love, which, in its turn, is distinct from the conjugal *lekhos*, the matrimonial couch. Where it is gods who are involved, it sometimes happens that the meadow prelude is immediately metamorphosed into a marriage bed, whereas the marriage beds of the heroes of legend are always distinct from that flowering meadow and

---

[9] *Hhom. Ven.* 58ff.; Hes. *Theog.* 188ff.; Hom. *Il.* 2.819ff., Hes. *Theog.* 1008ff., *Hhom. Ven.* 155ff.; only Theocritus, 1.105ff., adds oaks trees and cyperus to this wooded scene on Mount Ida. It is likewise on a bed artistically adorned that Aphrodite meets with her lover Adonis: Theocr. 15.125ff.

[10] Pind. *Pyth.* 9.5f., 36ff., and 51ff. This garden of Zeus should not be confused with the garden of Aphrodite, which was probably a real place, where the fifth *Pythian* was presented: see 1.24 and M. R. Lefkowitz, "Pindar's *Pythian* V," in A. Hurst (ed.), *Pindare. Entretiens sur l'Antiquité classique* XXXI (Vandoeuvres and Geneva 1985), 33–63. Plat. *Symp.* 203bc, Ap. Rhod. 3.114ff. (see above ch. I, §1, n. 4); see also Soph. frag. 320 Radt (see below n. 14). Furthermore, contrary to the connection suggested by F. Bornmann, *Callimachi Hymnus in Dianam* (Florence 1968), 79, the garden of Zeus should not be identified with the meadow of Hera mentioned by Call. *Dian.* 164 (see also Eur. *Phoen.* 24); this meadow is more reminiscent of the union of the divine couple in the *Iliad* (Hom. *Il.* 14.347; see above ch. II, §2). On the religious linke between Hera and grass, see Paus. 2.17.2.

are usually located in a space of their own, a space that, in some cases, is set inside a divine garden.

And even in the category of well-fenced gardens, there are further distinctions to be made. In parallel to the eroticized gardens of the gods, in the *Odyssey* there are orchard gardens constantly in bloom in an eternal springtime, while elsewhere we find even more idealized ones that harbor the frolics of the Charites or springs gushing with honey, gardens that, with the help of Eros, encourage the blooming of poetry and philosophy.[11]

Within the confines of the present study it is not possible to roam at leisure through all these gardens that differ one from another both in aspect and in function. However, a kind of synthesis of the three types may be found in the Garden of the Hesperides, all too often assimilated to the meadow on Mount Ida that provides the setting for the passionate union of Zeus and Hera in the *Iliad*. This orchard garden is situated on the westernmost edge of the world, beyond the river Ocean, and its sole products are the golden apples that Earth offered to the divine couple Zeus and Hera on the occasion of their marriage. The apples were either protected or coveted — depending on the version of the myth — by the "western" Nymphs, *parthenoi* and the daughters of Night, whom Hesiod names the Hesperides and represents as singers with spellbinding voices. Nonnus, in his much later epic, has no compunction about taking over the products of the Garden of the Hesperides for his reformulation of the legend of the marriage of Cadmus and Harmonia. In the form of golden flowers, rather than apples, these products from the garden at the world's end enhance the splendor of this wedding, which is celebrated in Libya. Cypris and Eros gather the miraculous flowers of the Hesperides and present some to the bride, using others to crown the heads of the young couple and to deck the *thalamos* and marriage bed.[12] The chorus of Euripides' *Hippolytus* adds another touch to the inaccessible orchard of the far west, suggesting that it lies close to the sources of ambrosia and the birthplace of Zeus. On the strength of this suggestion, the tragedy's Alexandrian commentator hastened to identify the garden in the west as the place

---

[11] Hom. *Od.* 7.112ff. (the garden of the Phaeacians; see also 6.293, and Vidal-Naquet [2]1983, 60ff.) and 24.336ff. (the garden of Laertes): the common features of these two gardens are noted by C. Vatin, "Jardins et vergers grecs," in *Mélanges helléniques offerts à Georges Daux* (Paris 1974), 345–57; Pind. *Ol.* 9.26ff. (metaphorical garden of the Charites) and *Pyth.* 6.1ff. (plowed field of the Charites and Aphrodite); Plat. *Ion* 534ab (garden with springs of honey); on the gardens of the philosophers, see Motte 1973, 372ff.

[12] Pherec. *FGrHist.* 3 F 16a–c; Hes. *Theog.* 213ff., 274ff., 333ff., and 518, and also frag. 360 Merkelbach-West; Nonn. *Dion.* 13.333ff.: see Rocchi 1989, 16ff. and 74ff.

where the marriage between Zeus and Hera took place.[13] As a miraculous orchard and as a probable source of poetic inspiration, the Garden of the Hesperides certainly contributed with its fruitful blooms to the paradigmatic union of the gods; however, it was not where that union took place, nor should it be confused with either the prelude meadow or the garden of Zeus.[14]

## 3. FLOWERS, FRUITS, AND CEREALS

The carefully bounded garden thus stands in opposition to the open meadow that, for its part, is freely accessible to grazing flocks; and this contrast is reflected in the respective products of these opposed spaces.

Gardens, which are tended carefully, as orchards need to be, produce fruits, chiefly apples, quinces, and pomegranates. Now, as used in ritual and also in its literary representations, the apple, along with its predecessor the quince, happens to be associated with sexual union, particularly within marriage, as is frequently attested: one of the laws attributed to Solon decreed that as a bride entered the marriage chamber and lay down next to her husband she should be biting into a quince. Then there was a Greek proverb that maintained that to accept the gift of an apple was tantamount to being drawn into an amorous relationship; furthermore, quinces, myrtle leaves, and crowns woven from roses and violets were said to have been tossed in the path of the wedding procession of Helen and Menelaus.[15] Apples and quinces could symbolize

---

[13] Eur. *Hipp.* 741ff., with the scholion cited and commented on by Barrett 1964, 303ff. The song of the Hesperides is also mentioned by Eur. *HF* 394, Ap. Rhod. 4.1396ff., etc.; for other references, see iconography and bibliography in I. McPhee, "Hesperides," in *LIMC* V.1 (Zurich and Munich 1990), 394–406. The garden of the Hesperides is thus not the nuptial space that Motte, after many others, believes it to be (Motte 1973, 113, and 223ff.); see also C. Jourdain-Annequin, *Heraclès aux portes du soir* (Besançon and Paris 1989), 564ff. For references on the erotic significances attributed to the apple, see below n. 15.

[14] Perhaps it is with this imaginary garden that we should identify the gardens of Zeus in which perfect felicity can be enjoyed (Soph. frag. 320 Radt), or with the gardens of Ocean in which Aristophanes' Clouds (*Nub.* 271) form a chorus in the company of the Nymphs. All these are, at any rate, gardens on the edge of the world, similar to the one that tradition attributed to Apollo in the far North: Soph. frag. *956* Radt; it is true that this garden, to which Boreas brings Oreithyia after abducting her (see above, §1) may have been where the wind god and the Nymph were united.

[15] Sol. frag. 127 Ruschenbusch, cited in particular by Plut. *Praec. conj.* 138d; Aristoph. *Nub.* 997 together with the sch. *ad loc.* (III.2. 141 Koster); attestations to the sexual powers attributed to apples and quinces are in J. Trumpf, "Kydonische Aepfel," *Hermes* 88 (1960): 14–22, and A. R. Littlewood, "The Symbolism of the Apple in Greek and Roman Literature," *Harv. Stud. Class. Philol.* 72 (1968): 147–81; complementary refer-

either the beginning of an amorous relationship or sexual consumma tion. The golden apples of the Garden of the Hesperides provided the mythical model here. Not only were the fruits of gardens and orchards the products of agricultural activity very different from the cultivation of cereals, but they also stood in sharp contrast to the seedlings of the short-lived "gardens" of Adonis. In a kind of ritual parody of real agriculture, which entailed a lengthy process of ripening for the cereals and fruits involved, the women of Athens would plant and set out in the summer sunshine seeds that would inevitably wither away. These sterile little gardens of Adonis, which women would grow on their own in saucepans, pots, or baskets, were the very antonyms not only of plowed fields but also of proper gardens that were cultivated continuously over long periods and were, as a result, productive.[16]

In contrast to the products of cultivated trees, which evoked consummated love, the flowers that grew wild in the prelude meadows symbolized the preparation for that crowning consummation. Although we have no contemporary botanical study to consult, myth — once again — provides easy access to an understanding of the meanings of the flowers that filled the meadows where girls loved to roam. Hyacinths, crocuses, and violets, the flowers most commonly found there, were all the subjects of anthropomorphic metamorphoses in mythical tales of unhappy love affairs. Hyacinthus, the son of either the Muse Clio and Pierus, or of Amyclas of Laconia and Diomede, was none other than the young lover of Apollo, whom the god, in competition with his rival Zephyr, killed by mistake when he threw a discus that felled the young hero at the very moment when his desirable beauty was at its youthful peak. An admittedly late-attested myth attributed a similar fate to Crocus, a young man loved by the wind Smilax, who was likewise killed by a discus thrown, in his case, by Hermes. It was said that the crocus flower sprang from his blood. As for the violet, it was the flower used to weave the crown that the Ionian Nymphs made for their beloved Ion, when the young hero bearing the name of the flower went hunting on the site of the future Olympia.[17]

---

ences are in I. Chirassi, *Elementi di culture precereali* (Rome 1968), 73ff. (on the pomegranate), Detienne 1977, 102ff. (English translation: M. Muellner and L. Muellner (trans.), *Dionysos Slain* [Baltimore 1979]), and Burnett 1983, 267 n. 102.

[16] Aristoph. *Lys.* 389ff., Plat. *Phaedr.* 276b, etc.; M. Detienne, *Les Jardins d'Adonis* (Paris ²1989), 191ff. (English translation: J. Lloyd [trans.], *The Gardens of Adonis* [Princeton 1994]), which presents all the details as well as an analysis of the opposition he reconstructs between the ephemeral gardening in honor of Adonis and the agriculture of Demeter; see also the critical remarks of Winkler 1990, 189ff., and of J. D. Reed, "The Sexuality of Adonis," *Class. Ant.* 14 (1995): 317–47; see also references in W. Attalah, *Adonis dans la littérature et l'art grecs* (Paris 1966), 211ff.

[17] Hyacinthus: Eur. *Hel.* 1465ff., Apoll. 1.3.3 and 3.10.3, Paus. 3.19.5, etc.; see S. Ami-

These three meadow flowers all produce an overpowering scent, as do the narcissus and the rose, which are also frequently mentioned. The story of Narcissus' love and death in his own reflection is well known. It was Aphrodite's way of punishing the recalcitrant young man for repeatedly rejecting the love that a series of Nymphs offered him. One of these was Echo, whose name was to determine the manner of the young hero's death. However, there is a less well known version that tells of the youth's passionate love for his twin sister. Looking into the waters of a spring, Narcissus mistook his own reflection for the face of his beloved and proceeded to fade away in sorrow. At the point of death he was metamorphosed into a narcissus. As for the rose, born from the blood of Adonis whom Aphrodite had loved, I need only refer the reader to the scholarly studies that have already been devoted to its many connections with the goddess of love and her entourage of other divine figures, such as the Hours, the Charites, and Eros.[18]

In myth, the flowers that adorn the meadow of love thus first appear at the precise moment when their respective eponymous heroes are themselves in the flower of youth, arousing amorous desire but as yet innocent of physical love. This moment of transition between two states of sexuality is matched by a death that constitutes not so much an initiation or a ritual as simply a narrative representation. The metamorphoses that in some cases result from such deaths are also of a narrative and figurative nature, as is the fact that flowers, which may be either of the masculine or the feminine gender in Greek, are nevertheless regularly represented in these myths by young heroes. Of course, in the delicate flower of their adolescent beauty, such heroes arouse "homosexual" passions as much as heterosexual ones. But as a result of the use of metaphor that characterizes the symbolic process, these flowers attached to legends involving boys, which symbolize a preliminary phase

---

gues, "*Hyakinthos* fleur mythique et plantes réelles," *Rev. Et. Gr.* 105 (1992): 19–36; crocus: Ov. *Met.* 4.283ff., and Plin. *Hist. Nat.* 16.63.154; violet: Nicander frag. 74.2ff. Gow-Schofield; see also P.M.C. Forbes Irving, *Metamorphosis in Greek Myths* (Oxford 1990), 133ff., and D. Auger, "A l'ombre des jeunes garçons en fleurs," in D. Auger (ed.), *Enfants et enfances dans les mythologies* (Paris 1995), 77–101.

[18] Narcissus: Ov. *Met.* 3.509ff., Paus. 9.31.8, *Anth. Pal.* 5.147, etc.; see Chirassi, above, n. 15, 143ff., and E. Pellizer, *La peripezia dell'eletto* (Palermo 1991), 46ff. Rose: Bion *Ad.* 1.65ff., *Anacreont.* 32.13ff. and 44 West, Paus. 6.24.7; other references in J. Murr, *Die Pflanzenwelt in der griechischen Mythologie* (Innsbruck 1890), 78ff., and also, for archaic poetry, Ibyc. frag. 288 Page, Stes. frag. 187 Page, and Bacch. 17.115ff. On the botanical identification of these various flowers, see Richardson 1974, 142ff., who points out, on the basis of Soph. *Oed. Col.* 684 and frag. 451 Radt, that the narcissus and saffron are more specifically associated with Demeter and Core; see also E. Irwin, "The Crocus and the Rose," in D. E. Gerber (ed.), *Greek Poetry and Philosophy* (Chicago 1984), 147–68.

of love, are transposed into meadows that tend to be connected with myths about love affairs that involve girls. The effect of the metaphor is to elide the distinction between the social roles of the two sexes, that is to say between the genders. For it is always girls who encounter the first stirrings of erotic love in these flower-strewn meadows, always *parthenoi* who, once enveloped in an amorous embrace on a marriage bed become, not *gunaikes*, adult women, but — as is clearly indicated by the law of Solon cited above — *numphai*, that is to say young brides.

Legendary meadows associated with the blooming of spring flowers and pastures where grazing flocks can roam freely are clearly distinguished not only from well-fenced gardens that need to be tended like orchards if they are to bear fruit, but also from the conjugal beds in which those fruits are consumed (and love is consummated). Those beds of shared love are, furthermore, frequently described metaphorically in agricultural terms, as has been indicated above. The movement from flowers growing wild in the meadows, through fruits cultivated in orchards, to the cereal products of agriculture symbolizes a progress toward civilization, as does the spatial progression from the borderland territory of the nomadic activities of herdsmen, possibly followed by a passage through an enclosed garden, leading ever closer to the central *oikos*. The transition that these tales of Nymphs construct at the levels of plant life and space clearly refers to the stages through which girls not yet brought under the yoke must pass on their way to the civilizing domestication achieved by marriage. As they gather flowers that symbolize amorous desire, in the company of their friends, *parthenoi* like themselves, or as they sing and dance in a ring in meadows where the flocks come to pasture, these Nymphs invariably fall victim to the violent advances of some god whose love they have provoked. Only after having bitten into the fruits grown in a garden do they at last come to experience love on a bed secluded within the well-defined space of the *oikos*. There, Eros manifests himself, usually as a promoter of reproduction. Sometimes legend even seems to reflect the instability of the status of a young bride, for some of the Nymphs that it represents as *numphai*

| Social Status | Legendary Space | Activity | Geographical Space |
|---|---|---|---|
| *parthenos* | meadow | herding | outdoors, quasi wild |
| *numphê* | garden | tree cultivation | transition |
| *gunê* | bed | agriculture | indoors, *oikos* |

subsequently expose their unwanted infants produced from the unions forced upon them. The status of a fully established wife is, as a matter of fact, quite distinct from that of a young bride.

Of course, it is important to be aware of the inevitable distortions that tend to mar schematic representations such as the one above; but it is tempting—and may be helpful—to use a table to convey the various ways in which the Greeks of the classical period represented the three successive statuses that were assigned to women.

# Chapter IX

## THE MEADOWS AND GARDENS OF THE POETS

MELIC POETRY, the speech of which is assumed by the locutor, who thus becomes its main protagonist, refers the reader not to a mythical situation, but to circumstances that directly affect that locutor. These circumstances, which are situated in the immediate past, may, through the interplay of deictics and verb tenses, be made to coincide with the actual enunciative situation of the poem. Let us see whether, through these enunciative means, the meadows and gardens of myth play a role in the real institutional circumstances of the initiation of girls into the seductive manners of reproductive sexuality.

### 1. THE METAPHORICAL SPACES OF LOVE

One singer of love poetry, Anacreon, places the beautiful young girl to whom his poem is addressed in a meadow of hyacinths, where Cypris is tethering young fillies that have been released from the reins held by their mothers. The imposition of this new yoke seems to represent the transition that is required in order for a girl to be allowed to appear amid citizens, no doubt to fill their hearts with desire. The poet's original use of the metaphor of the domestication that marriage customarily imposes includes a mention of flower-filled meadows. Whatever the girl is doing there — the text does not make this clear — is itself an image intended to convey that the maiden is now invested with the power of Aphrodite.[1] The metaphor of the hyacinth meadow thus represents the girl's passage from her mother's house into the civic community, where she appears in the full flower of youth, filling men's hearts with amorous desire.

Theognis uses a similar metaphor to describe the return of the youth whom he loves. In his poem, the adolescent boy becomes the satiated

---

[1] Anacr. frag. 346.1 Page (cf. above ch. I, §3); see also Sappho frag. 105b Voigt; commenting on these lines in his work of 1958, 181ff., Gentili rightly points out that the term *aroura* is here used with the wider sense of "field" (not necessarily plowed) and that its designation integrates it into the erotic metaphorical gist of the whole verse: see, for example, Sappho frag. 96.11 Voigt, in an equally erotic context; a complex interpretation is in S. R. Slings, "Anacreon's Meadows," *Zeitschr. Pap. Epigr.* 30 (1978): 38. On love and marriage conceived as reins or a yoke imposed on a filly or a heifer, see above ch. VI, §2.3, n. 25. It is worth noting that if line 13 belonged to another poem, these lines could equally well be addressed to a boy!

horse that was earlier described returning to his stable. Now, in a lovely meadow watered by a cool spring and bordered by shady copses, he longs for a good rider. It may be found surprising that here it should be a young boy who frolics in the very fields that provide Anacreon with a pasture for his Thracian filly with sidelong glances (probably some *hetaira*). In Anacreon's poem, it is she who frolics there freely until such time as she is dominated by the reins held by a skilful and experienced rider:

> Thracian filly, why do you look at me from the corner of your eye
> and flee stubbornly from me, supposing that I have no skill?
> Let me tell you, I could neatly put the bridle on you
> and, with the reins in my hand, wheel you round the turnpost of the race-
>    course;
> instead, you graze in the meadows and frisk and frolic lightly,
> since you have no skilled horseman to ride you.[2]

However, we should remember that in a homophile relationship between a Greek adult and an adolescent boy, the latter, with his youthful, beardless beauty, was, precisely, assimilated to a girl. With its inversion of the signs of sexuality, this was a relationship that facilitated the transition from the sexual ambivalence of adolescence into the full sexuality of adulthood. The fact that a boy is sometimes represented in the fresh pastureland that is usually the scene of a prelude to love involving a girl is an indication of the purely metaphorical nature assumed by the flowering meadow in these poems, which may be directly addressed to either adolescent girls or adolescent boys. The metaphor is a poetic way of referring to the initiation of Eros that the melic narrator dreams of forcing upon his young addressee (whether a boy or a girl), verbally at least, if not in deed.

Notwithstanding the use of a far more direct language, this is probably likewise how we should read the lines already cited in which the young Archilochus recounts his first amorous encounter with the maiden pointed out to him by the daughter of Amphimedo. It would thus be upon a bed of flowers that is purely metaphorical that the poet lays the girl before veiling her nudity with a soft cloak and lavishing upon her beautiful body caresses that lead to a union that may have been prudently arrested before completion. The space in which this

---

[2] Anacr. frag. 417 Page, in D. A. Campbell (trans.), *Greek Lyric* II (Loeb 1988); see above ch. I, §3.1, n. 30. Thgn. 1249ff.: the metaphor developed in these lines by Theognis (see also 1267ff.) is explained by Vetta 1980, 55ff., who, however, is wrong to assimilate this erotic landscape to a simple *locus amoenus*. Alcaeus, frag. 296b Voigt (see also frag. 115a), places the youth whose praises he is singing in a similar setting: see A. Bonnafé, *Poésie, nature et sacré* II (Lyon 1987), 108ff.

youthful lovemaking takes place is probably purely metaphorical, not that that prevents it from operating as a rite of passage since, in the course of it, in Archilochus' eyes at least, the young girl becomes a woman. As for the grassy gardens toward which the poet declares he wishes to move, through yet another frequently used metaphor, they simply constitute an erotic allusion to female anatomy. Empedocles refers in similar fashion to the female reproductive organs as "the cleft meadow of Aprodite."[3] It is thanks to this metaphorical transposition that, when a poet replaces the actions of mythical figures by his own lived (or imagined) experiences, the space of the flowery meadow continues to provide a framework within which girls can be prepared for love and initiated into it. In Archilochus' *Cologne Epode*, a touch of irony is added to the metaphor by the narrator's allusion to his withheld amorous gratification.

## 2. THE IDEAL DOMAINS OF THE GODS

And what about gardens? Over the years many attempts have been made to identify one of them as the garden close to the sanctuary in which Sappho prayed to Aphrodite, inviting her to take part, as a cup-bearing deity, in the mysterious celebrations that were held there. This was a sacred precinct that comprised an orchard (*alsos*) of apple trees watered by a cool stream, altars that emitted the fragrant fumes of incense, and shady rose bushes beneath which one could slip into a deathly slumber. It was lapped by the gentlest of breezes and also included a meadow (*leimôn*), where horses grazed and flowers bloomed in the springtime. Is this a fictional representation of the world of the gods, a poetic metaphor, or a real site of religious activities? There can be no doubt at all that everything about this breeze-cooled, watered landscape — from the apple trees to the rose bushes, and including the fragrant wafts of incense and the slumber and death that the Greeks equated with the state of erotic love — evokes the presence of the goddess of love. It is a real landscape, which corresponds to the spot (*deuru*, "here") where the narrator (*me*) stands at the beginning of her appeal to the goddess, but which, by very reason of that goddess's inter-

---

[3] Archil. frag. 196a West; see the comments of S. R. Slings, "Archilochus: First Cologne Epode," in J. M. Bremer (ed.), *Some Recently Found Greek Poems* (Leiden and Cologne 1987), 24ff., who provides all the necessary data for a reading of this fragmentary poem; see also the complementary references provided above ch. I, §4, n. 34 and n. 48; some interpreters have seen this eroticized meadow as a garden of Hera: see Nagy 1990, 399ff.; Emped. frag. 31 B 66 Diels-Kranz.

vention as the dispenser of nectar, is at the same time removed to the "there" (*entha*) of the divine place that belongs to the goddess (*su*).[4]

This poetic use of the metaphor of a field in which horses graze to describe a flower-studded meadow integrated into the garden sanctuary of Cypris clearly refers us to the meadow that, in the legend, provides the setting for a prelude to love. And sure enough, in one of her famous "memory poems," Sappho describes a meadow filled with flowers and bathed in dew in which a beautiful Lydian woman longingly recalls her love for the young Atthis. On the other hand, a parallel poem declares that it is on a soft bed that erotic love finds fulfilment.[5] The meadow thus consecrated to Aphrodite lies within a sacred precinct that, we are led to believe, is real enough, even if the poems do suggest that it belongs to Aphrodite. So, over and above the textual construction of the metaphor, it could in truth also represent one of the places in which Sappho dispensed the teaching that prepared for the beauty and love of mature women. It was no doubt there that, under the protection of Aphrodite, the girls of Lesbos or Lydia learned, by dint of performing ritual dances and songs, to become fully fledged women. It was a meadow of initiation where the poems composed by Sappho themselves acquired an initiatory function, a meadow where girls were initiated into a love that some of them might come to satisfy among themselves, elsewhere, on a bed beyond the space consecrated to Cypris, until such time as their transitory relations of homophilia were superseded by lasting conjugal ones.[6]

In light of the above, it becomes easier to understand the function of a no less famous, pristine garden for girls, evoked in one of Ibycus' poems cited earlier. Here, in the springtime, Cydonian apple trees grow, watered by passing streams, and on the vines buds flourish in the shade of the spreading leaves. Set in strong opposition (*men . . . de*) to this springtime space, an implacable love, which has been mentioned earlier on in the poem, a love at once icy and burning, which may strike what-

---

[4] Sappho frag. 2 Voigt; the long analysis by Burnett 1983, 259ff., who, while showing the erotic connotations of the various elements that go to make up this landscape, suggests that it may be a garden of the Nymphs, should be complemented by R. Merkelbach, "Sappho und ihr Kreis," *Philologus* 10 (1957): 1–29, and by Lanata 1966, 68ff.; the spatial movement conveyed in this poem is studied by M. Steinrück, *Rede und Kontext* (Bonn 1992), 380ff. On the erotic qualities of the apple and the apple tree, see above ch. VIII, §3, n. 15.

[5] Sappho frags. 96.9ff. and 94.21ff. Voigt; see also the commentary by Burnett 1983, 300ff. and 290ff., and the reflections of Gentili 1984, 116ff.

[6] This is no doubt the meaning of the *numphaioi kêpoi* that Dionysius of Halicarnassus, *Compos.* 132, attributes to the nuptial and erotic poetry of Sappho (= frag. 215 Voigt). As for the "initiatory" nature of the education dispensed within the poet Sappho's group, see the references given above in ch. V, §1.2, n. 17.

ever the season, seems to prompt the narrator to take to poetic flight, seeking refuge in this ideal garden. This seems to constitute a regression into not untouched nature in the wild, but rather one of the gardens situated on the very edge of the inhabited world, gardens that belong to a legendary geography the model of which is the Garden of the Hesperides (who are themselves *parthenoi*!): these are spaces to which a specific location is attributed, but which lie beyond the reach of mortals, spaces where, as the chorus members of Euripides' *Hippolytus* tell us, the Blessed live in happiness, feeding upon ambrosia. The narrator of Ibycus' poem contrasts the gusting passion that assails his heart to his paradoxical dream of a love that is still intact, in the distant beyond of a landscape at the world's end, where the quince trees are watered by streams and the vines are in bud, but where there is no inviting meadow to provide a prelude that leads on to the consummation of desire. In this poem, the apple trees mentioned right at the beginning are set in this garden reserved solely for girls (not for Nymphs), simply in order to maintain the symmetry of the current of amorous desire that runs through Ibycus' poem. It is important to remember that it is only the garden's product, namely the apples themselves, that act as a spell to establish an amorous relationship, and that the apples only produce that effect when eaten outside the confines of the magical garden.[7]

In metaphor, in dreams, and in religious ritual, the meadows described by the melic poets constitute a space where the amorous desire felt and expressed in the here and now of the singing of their poems can never be realized other than ideally. They are meadows rather than gardens because it is generally an adolescent boy or girl that arouses the poet's love, and that love plunges the protagonists subjected to Eros into a relationship that is asymmetrical. The erotic poetry of archaic "lyric" is designed, practically, to seduce the beloved and, with its educative role of initiating him or her into the civic sexuality of maturity, constitutes no more than a prelude to erotic fulfillment. It thus assumes both the function of a prelude meadow and the probably religious role of Aphrodite's garden. However, having conveyed this transitional

---

[7] Ibyc. frag. 286 Page (text cited above in ch. I, §1); Eur. *Hipp.* 742ff. (see above ch. VIII, §2, n. 13). The study by Trumpf (see above ch. VIII, §3, n. 15) on the symbolism of apples tends to confuse the space where they grow with the space where they are eaten; the structural analysis suggested by Bremer 1975, 271, is also mistaken in that, when comparing the garden of Ibycus to that of Sappho, it assimilates the precinct and the meadow without retaining the distinctive feature of the latter in its landscape of wild flowers; on the other hand, Trumpf rightly points out the contrast between the tufty meadow in which Phaedra longs to assuage her passion (Eur. *Hipp.* 208ff.) and the untouched meadow evoked by Hippolytus, which is merely the fruit of a distracted imagination perverted by the power of Artemis, which turns the hero into a *parthenos*; on this subject, see also S. Saïd, "L'espace d'Euripide," *Dioniso* 59 (1989): 107–36.

phase on three different levels (pragmatic, metaphorico-mythical, and religious), it may go on to evoke the ultimate phase of the intitiation to love, that is to say the fulfillment of erotic desire on a soft bed (possibly in the course of a banquet). Each poetic mention of a meadow, a garden, or a bed needs to be interpreted in context, bearing in mind that it is in all probability metaphorical.

## 3. Religious Gardens

In Athens there existed a space that enables us at last to move on from myth and poetic metaphor to institutional practice: this was the now famous sanctuary on the northern face of the Acropolis, which was consecrated to Aphrodite "in the Gardens."[8] The precinct was associated with the sanctuary that was similarly dedicated to the goddess in the plain, not far from the river Ilissus, where one rite, at least, was performed, a rite to which the antiquarian Pausanias refers for the benefit of any interested reader. First he describes the sanctuary of Pandrosos, which was situated on the Acropolis alongside the Erechtheion, and within which a sacred olive tree grew; he then goes on to note that two of the *arrhêphoroi* lived close by. The duties of these little girls in the service of the priestess of Athena culminated in a nocturnal festival. It has not been hard to identify this with the famous rite of the *Arrhêphoria*, which is known to us from other sources. Pausanias' text is the subject of much controversy, and I can do no more than provide the following translation:

> Having loaded on to their heads whatever the priestess of Athena gives them to carry (and neither she who gives it nor those who are to carry it know what they will be giving and carrying), the maidens (*parthenoi*) go down to the place in the town where there is a precinct of Aphrodite said to be situated in the Gardens, which lies not very far away and across which runs a natural underground passage. Once they arrive down there, they deposit the objects that they have brought and pick up something else, which they bring back, well concealed. They are then dismissed and are replaced on the Acropolis by other *parthenoi*.[9]

[8] On situation and traces of the sanctuary: Travlos 1971, 228ff.; this sanctuary has often mistakenly been confused with the sanctuary consecrated to Aphrodite Ourania. Cypris possessed other religious gardens, in particular in Cyprus: references in Motte 1973, 122ff.

[9] Paus. 1.27.2f. Contrary to the belief of E. Kadletz, "Pausanias 1, 27, 3, and the Route of the Arrhephoroi," *Am. Journ. Arch.* 86 (1982): 445–46, who is followed by Brulé 1987, 89ff., the expression *ou porrhô* cannot refer to the genitive that precedes it since the latter designates not the place but Aphrodite's ownership of the place (*peribolos*), itself

It is uncertain whether the name *arrhêphoroi*, by which these two young girls are known, is derived from the secrecy surrounding the objects that they carry or from the life-giving dew (two explanations that are volunteered by the Ancients), or whether the etymology of this term is linked with the basket that they carry (a modern suggestion). But there can be no doubt that they were two of the four little girls aged between seven and eleven who were entrusted with the task of weaving a *peplos* for Athena. It is also most likely that the rite that they performed in the sanctuary of Aphrodite in the Gardens was ideologically founded upon the legend of the three daughters of Cecrops. Two of these were destined to commit suicide as a result of disobeying the injunction not to open the round basket entrusted to them by Athena. At the sight of the infant Erichthonios and the snake lying there in the sacred basket, the two panic-stricken girls hurled themselves off the Acropolis. Only their sister Pandrosos, who had remained obedient, survived. A one-time event is not a custom: the way that the plot of this myth unfolds could really reflect the sequence followed in the ritual.[10]

Uncertainties are bound to dog any archaeological interpretation of the ancient texts, and it would be risky to use such an interpretation as the basis of a topographical identification of the secret route taken by the *arrhêphoroi* as they performed this rite. However, there seems little doubt that the path that the girls took linked the sanctuary of Pandrosos on the Acropolis (or the precinct believed to have been reserved for the *arrhêphoroi* a little farther to the south) with the sanctuary consecrated to Aphrodite in the Gardens. The latter, backing on to the rock, was situated on the path that encircled the Acropolis, down at the level of the city. It is not clear whether the little *arrhêphoroi* required the skills of a speleologist to reach this sanctuary by climbing down the vertical course of the waters from the Mycenaean Fountain, or whether they simply followed the narrow track that passed through the rocks situated to the north of the Erechtheion. But it is at least certain that the "natural underground passage" described by Pausanias cannot have led

---

mentioned in the nominative case; the phrase is thus used as an adverb here. According to E. Langlotz, *Aphrodite in den Gärten* (Heidelberg 1954), 8ff., representations of Aphrodite amid growing plants constitute reproductions of the sanctuary gardens consecrated to the goddess.

[10] The whole of the literary, iconographical, epigraphical, and archaeological dossier is studied in relation to myth and cults by Brulé 1987, 68ff. and 79ff.; see the classic article by W. Burkert, "Kekropidensage und Arrhephoria," *Hermes* 94 (1966): 1–25, reprinted in *Wilder Ursprung* (Berlin 1990), 40–59, and see also E. Specht, *Schön zu sein und gut zu sein* (Vienna 1989), 37ff.

as far as the second sanctuary consecrated to Aphrodite of the Gardens, which lay on the banks of the Ilissus river.[11]

This ritual coming and going of the two *arrhêphoroi* girls who made the trip from the Acropolis down to the sacred garden of Aphrodite set at the foot of the rock, and back up again, was no doubt linked to the legendary story. But what was its purpose? For many years this strange rite has been interpreted as a kind of initiation by scholars who, on the basis of the little girls' nocturnal descent to make contact with Aphrodite, and above all by projecting the myth on to the sequences of the ritual, have explained it as a symbolic death. But neither the extreme youth of the *arrhêphoroi* nor the social setting of their journey are suggestive of the distinctive characteristics of tribal initiation. If it is true that the time passed on the Acropolis by these little girls aged between seven and eleven represented a period of segregation, their incursion into the sanctuary of Aphrodite would represent an initiation into an initiation. If the girls' contact with the goddess of love indeed constituted a preparation for the end of their service as *arrhêphoroi* (as has been argued), their descent to the garden could have been a kind of rite of integration; but, given that at the age of eleven the *arrhêphoroi* would still have been prepubescent, the question is: Integration into what and accession to what status?

Finally, if one accepts that the sacred space constituted by the Acropolis of classical Athens may have represented an area for segregation situated right at the center of the political space rather than outside it, the sanctuary of Aphrodite of the Gardens, with its remarkable position on the lower slopes of the Acropolis, must, for its part, have been situated on one of the "internal" boundaries of that space! Perhaps we could make more progress instead by interpreting these proceedings as a rite of "fecundity." If it is not too presumptuous to seem to be claiming more clairvoyance than the *arrhêphoroi* themselves or even the priestess of Athena, it may be worth noting that a number of indications suggest a phallic interpretation of the "unmentionable" objects that were carried to the precinct reserved for Aphrodite and were then substituted by another "carefully concealed" object, possibly a newborn infant, to be conveyed back up to the Acropolis.

The very fact that one classical inscription attests the celebration of a festival in honor of Eros in this sanctuary of Aphrodite in the Gardens suggests that the secret objects transported by the two little *arrhêphoroi*

---

[11] That at least is the thesis upheld by N. Robertson, "The Riddle of the Arrhephoria at Athens," *Harv. Stud. Class. Philol.* 87 (1983): 241–88, partly repeated by Brulé 1987, 84ff., on the basis of Paus. 1.27.3; this second sanctuary of Aphrodite in the Gardens, close to the Ilissus, was probably outside the precinct marked out by Themistocles: see Travlos 1971, 291. Pirenne-Delforge 1994, 50ff., does not touch upon this question.

were connected with an initiation into sexuality.[12] Meanwhile, the etiological legend, which tells of young girls discovering the newborn Erichthonius, may well refer to the reproductive aspect of sexuality. The following interpretation might thus be worth considering: this was no rite of tribal initiation, no "fertility" rite, but instead a ritual procedure that, through a coming and going between a religious space and a civic one, introduced two of the very best of the youngest Athenian girls to their future function as mothers of citizens-to-be. It was a procedure that involved provisionally stepping down from the service of Athena in order to do homage to Aphrodite and possibly Eros, in a space where the tending of plants and trees might appositely symbolize the rearing of children and the education of boys and girls.

Seen in this perspective, the inclusion of the sacred olive tree in the sanctuary of Pandrosos from which the little girls probably set out seems, along with the plants that certainly grew in Aphrodite's Garden at the foot of the Acropolis, to refer to an *isotopia* of tree cultivation that was totally distinct from the cereal cultivation over which Demeter presided.[13] The little girls' stay on the Acropolis, where they learned the special skills of women, and their visit to the cultivated precinct consecrated to Cypris and Eros, made these *arrhêphoroi* the potential mothers of the children of Athena; likewise, the daughters of Cecrops, as nurses of Erichthonius, were the tenders (*kourotrophoi*) of one of the earliest kings of Athens, who was born from Earth when it was fertilized by the sperm ejaculated by Hephaestus in his passion for Athena.

From the twofold structural point of view of the space that it consti-

---

[12] Inscription published by O. Broneer, "Eros and Aphrodite on the North Slope of the Acropolis in Athens," *Hesperia* 1 (1932): 31–55; see Fasce 1977, 32ff. The age of the *arrhêphoroi* is given by the *EMag.* 149, 18ff. Gaisford, which partially coincides with the famous text of Aristoph. *Lys.* 641ff.; see C. Sourvinou-Inwood, *Studies in Girls' Transitions* (Athens 1988), 136ff. In his recent study, "Der Heros in der Kiste," *Ant. und Abendl.* 28 (1992): 1–47, G. J. Baudy again suggests an agrarian interpretation of the rite, suggesting that the *arrhêphoroi*'s basket contains seeds to be offered, both materially and metaphorically, to the fertilizing dew.

[13] The numerous metaphorical links in classical Greece between the growth of young shoots and the development of children and adolescents are noted by Detienne 1989, 71ff., with the references given in n. 55. The young bride and young husband are themselves compared to flowering plants: references in Seaford 1987, 111ff. E. Simon, *Festivals of Attica* (London 1983), 39ff., stresses the relations between Pandrosos and the dew with its fertilizing powers: see on this subject D. Boedeker, *Descent from Heaven* (Chicago 1984), 10ff. and 100ff., who, after analyzing the metaphorical meanings of the fertilizing powers attributed in Greece to water that falls from the sky (see also above ch. VIII, n. 2), shows that the very names of the *arrhêphoroi* and the daughters of Cecrops reflect their affinity with the dew, which should be related to the autochthonous birth of Erichthonios. See also now R. L. Fowler, "Greek Magic, Greek Religion," *Ill. Class. Stud.* 20 (1995): 1–22, who criticizes the initiatory interpretation of the Arrhephoria.

tuted and the moment of feminine sexuality for which it provided a setting, the garden would thus appear to be situated somewhere in between the flowering meadow, accessible to the grazing herds, and the marriage bed within the shelter of the *oikos*. But legend, poetry, and social institutions all had their own ways of representing the various spaces inhabited by Eros and Aphrodite, and might ascribe to them particular, different uses. In myth, the prelude meadow could be transformed, without mediation, into a marriage bed; in religious practice, a flowering meadow could be incorporated into a garden; in poetry, the ideal garden was transported to the edge of the inhabited world, while religion in contrast incorporated it within civic space. While myth located the beds of its gods in wild, mountainous spots, social practice confined the marriage couch to the intimacy of the *thalamos*. But over and above all these essential nuances, and over and above the various spaces that were assigned to it in different contexts, the power of love that was personified by Eros was given two functions, the one propaeudeutic, the other reproductive. And these two complementary roles are precisely those that we find used and reelaborated first in theogonic speculation, then in philosophical thought. Let us therefore conclude the present study by considering those two types of reflection, each in turn.

# PART FIVE

## THE METAPHYSICS OF EROS

# Chapter X

## EROS AS DEMIURGE AND PHILOSOPHER

WHATEVER THE particular spaces in which it operates, the power of Eros extends to the whole universe, from the sea to the sky and encompassing the earth, and from the animal kingdom to the realm of the gods and including the human race. That is how it is represented throughout the whole of Greek literature, from the *Homeric Hymns* to Longus' novel, and including tragedy, Hellenistic poetry, and the formulae of magical spells.[1] There is thus a cosmic dimension to the power of Eros and, consequently, also to that of Aphrodite; and it is constructive rather than destructive. Although the tragic authors chiefly exploited the destructive powers of deified amorous desire, Eros and Aphrodite are essentially productive in that, through education and marriage, they create social links, that they strengthen even as they reproduce them. Clearly, the cosmic impact of their fecund reproductive power did not escape the notice of poets and philosophers in quest of cosmogonic and theogonic explanations for the origin of the world. Contrary to the frequently advanced hypothesis of the existence of two parallel traditions, the cosmic role of an Eros elevated to the role of a demiurge and the philosophical developments by which this figure was affected fit neatly into the poet's representation of desire personified by a god who was also a forger of social relations.[2]

It was no doubt on the basis of the institutional role played by Eros in practices relating to education of an initiatory nature and in the rite

---

[1] Among many other examples, *Hhom. Ven.* 2ff. (the power of Aphrodite over the gods, mortals, and animals of both the earth and the sea), Hes. *Theog.* 121ff. (the power of Eros over men and gods), and Soph. *Ant.* 787ff. (the power of Eros over the gods and ephemeral men): see above ch. VII, §2.2, n. 31) and frag. 941.12 Radt (the power of Cypris over beasts, mortals, and gods), Eur. *Hipp.* 1268ff. (the power of Aphrodite over men and gods; the power of Eros over the earth and the sea, animals and human beings) and 447ff. (the power of Cypris over the sky, the water, and the earth), Ap. Rhod. 3.158ff. (the ubiquity of Eros), *Anth. Pal.* 5.177 (the paternity of Eros denied by Aether, Earth, and Sea), Long. 2.7.2 (the power of Eros, greater than that of Zeus, over the elements, the stars, and the gods), Ach. Tat. 1.2.1 (the power of the babe over Sky, Earth, and Sea), etc.; for the magic hymns, see for example *P.G.M.* 4.2915ff. (Aphrodite the generator of the gods and men, reigning in the ether and on the earth, "nature the mother of all things"!).

[2] See the demonstration given by J. Rudhardt, *Le rôle d'Eros et d'Aphrodite dans les cosmogonies grecques* (Paris 1986); more hesitation is shown by Lasserre 1946, 24ff., and Fasce 1977, 73ff.

of passage leading to feminine maturity that a deified Eros acquired a place and a function in first theogonic, then philosophical representations of the cosmos. The power of love, which maintained the social fabric of the civic community, likewise organized the ordering of things.

## 1. Eros as a Cosmogonic Principle

In the first Greek theogonic construction known to us, Eros appears right at the beginning of the cosmogonic process, as a principle born without generation: first there was Chaos, an undifferentiated and formless yawning gap, then came Gaia, the seat of all things, then possibly the misty Tartarus, and finally Eros, "the most beautiful of the immortal gods." If Eros initially remains singularly inactive in the cosmogonic process, that is because the first physical entities — Erebus and Night were born from the Abyss by parthenogenesis. However, reading on in the unabridged text as it has come down to us, we find that Night is then united in love (*philotêti migeisa*) with Erebus and produces Aether and Day. Earth likewise starts off by producing physical entities by parthenogenesis: the starry Heaven, the great Mountains, and the fruitless deep of Pontus. But as soon as this initial cosmos is in place, primordial gods come to inhabit it — gods born from the embraces of Earth and Heaven. The transition from a cosmogony to a proper theogony is also brought about by *philotês*, through the commitment inspired by desire that unites Gaia and Ouranos on the same bed. Eros thus brings about the same effects as he does in the legends of archaic poetry and is from the start presented in the same terms: he "loosens limbs," and constrains not only hearts but even the wise will of gods and men alike.[3] Desire thus exists, with all its traditional attributes, to bring about the birth of further beings from the loving and mutual union of two separate, sexed entities. Division, differentiation, and distinctions are paradoxically born from the union of two entities, under the aegis of Eros, the unique, unificatory principle that engenders plurality. To rephrase in abstract terms what Hesiod says, using the means of genealogical narrative, it is as if, in the representation of Greek cosmotheogony, Eros served as the fecund mediator between duality and plurality.

In this same theogonic process, Aphrodite is born solely from the

---

[3] Hes. *Theog.* 116ff. A Bonnafé, *Eros et Eris* (Lyon 1985), 9ff. and 25ff., while stressing the contribution made by *philotês* to the action of Eros, shows the intermediary role played by that entity in the struggle between Eros and Eris: the harmful effects of amorous desire are also mentioned in the theogonic genealogy. For the qualities of Eros in Hesiod, see the commentary by M. L. West, *Hesiod. Theogony* (Oxford 1966), 195ff.

sperm of Ouranos. After castrating his father, Cronos hurled into the sea the testicles of the god who, by hiding the many offspring produced by his wife, had thwarted the process of differentiation, which was a consequence of the dual union brought about by Eros. In the company of beautiful Himeros — who appears at this point (his birth unaccounted for) — Eros hastens to fall in behind the goddess, who is allotted the seductive means of easy pleasure (*terpsis*) and sweet *philotês*. Philotes, for her part, only appears as a deified entity at a later stage, as the daughter of Night, when she, like Eros, is found to be instrumental in setting up the first amorous unions that result in offspring.[4] Aphrodite, followed by Philotes, in a sense takes over the work initiated by Eros. Although they, like him, were engendered without any sexual union, they nevertheless work to promote fertile and productive unions, usually intent on stimulating the amorous liaisons of Zeus, the king, and those of his descendants.

But the intervention of a being created in the absence of any sexual generation, who then undertook its promotion, was not the only narrative solution to be adopted by the cosmogonic tradition in order to account for plurality and differentiation springing from a dual union. In parallel to the long genealogical line traced by Hesiod to explain the cosmos and all its components, a line of theological speculation was elaborated one century later by Pherecydes of Syros. Here too, Eros played a role of prime importance. The function of demiurge was assumed by Zeus-Zas, who had appeared at the same moment as Chronos, Time, and Chthonia, the Earthly One. For this creative act, he not only entered into union with Chthonia, who changed into Earth, but then seems himself to have undergone a metamorphosis that changed him into Eros. By this assimilation, Eros, through sexual union and in a paradigmatic marriage, became the direct creator of the cosmos. The nuptial cloak created by Zeus on the occasion of his marriage with Chthonia appears to have been adorned by an image of this cosmogonical act: embroidered upon it was a representation of the primordial couple formed by Ge, Earth, and Ogenos, Ocean. In yet another genealogical account that began with a cosmogony, Acousilaus of

---

[4] Hes. *Theog.* 188ff., 125, 224ff. For Vernant 1989, 153ff. (English translation in Halperin, Winkler, & Zeitlin (eds.) 1990, 465–78), Eros — an immediately productive force — does not engender the diversity born of sexual union and duality until the castration of Ouranos and the birth of Aphrodite: but he forgets the intervention of *philotês* already in lines 125 (the authenticity of which is questioned) and 177 (Ouranos seized with the desire of *philotês* just before being castrated); he also overlooks the fact that Night continues to engender by parthenogenesis after the appearance of Aphrodite (1.211ff.): on the progressive interventions of *philotês*, see Bonnafé, above n. 3, 30ff., 48ff., and 102ff., and above ch. II, §1, n. 4. The scene of the birth of Aphrodite is interpreted by G. Devereux, *Femme et mythe* (Paris 1982), 97ff.

Argos represented Eros as being born from the union between the very first two sexed entities: Erebus (or Aether), the masculine "principle," and Night, the feminine "principle," both of which had come into existence immediately after the sole first "principle" that, as in Hesiod, was Chaos. Such, at least, are the reconstructions produced by the much later and fragmentary summaries written for the most part by neo-Platonic philosophers. One of these, commenting upon the demiurgic action of Eros in Pherecydes' cosmogony, favors a modern line of interpretation: he explains the intervention of Love by the twofold need to introduce concord (*homologia*) and reciprocal relationships (*philia*) in a cosmos composed of contraries, and to implant unity and identity in all things.[5]

The generating and demiurgic power of Eros thus seems to possess two complementary aspects: it is an agent both of unification and differentiation. But of the division created by union is born an order in which, to use a neo-Platonic idea, differences become harmonized.

The generating and differentiating aspect of Eros is even recognized by Parmenides, who makes Love the first of all the gods in the process of theogonic reproduction, a god probably "imagined" by Generation (*Genesis*) itself. As for his unificatory aspect, this is exploited by Empedocles, who effects a transition from a line of descent, a feature peculiar to cosmogonies, to the systematic type of concept that is typical of cosmologies. For him, Love, embodied by Philia or Philotes, if not Aphrodite in person, constitutes the eternal principle that intermingles the four primordial elements. These are subsequently separated by Neikos, Discord.[6] The process of creation thus led from a narrative explanation of an order conceived as static to a more philosophical conception of a cosmos that resulted from the contrasted actions of two fundamental entities. But it was still Eros who animated the positive principle of becoming and the cosmic variety developed from four simple elements of a physical nature. Neikos, in negative fashion, merely represented its reverse, a principle that was indispensable in a cyclical and systematic conception of change.

[5] Pherec. Syr. frags. 7 B 1a.2 and 3a Diels-Kranz (see also 7 A 11), the last being cited by Proclus *In Plat. Tim.* 32c: the nature of the "metamorphosis" of Zeus into Eros is discussed by H. S. Schibli, *Pherekydes of Syros* (Oxford 1990), 57ff., and the nuptial cloak that shelters the union of Zeus and Gaia is studied by Scheid and Svenbro 1994, 45ff.; see also Fasce 1977, 88ff., on Proclus' interpretation of Pherecydes' theogony; Acus. frags. 9 B 1 and 3 Diels-Kranz, and the allusion in Plat. *Symp.* 178b, as compared to Hesiod. See the commentary by H. Schwabl, "Weltschöpfung," *Realenc. Alt.-Wiss. Supplb.* IX (Stuttgart 1962), coll. 1433–582 (coll. 1459f.).

[6] Parm. frag. 28 B 13 Diels-Kranz, cited in particular by Plat. *Symp.* 178b: see G. Casertano, "L'infanzia di Eros (da Omero a Parmenide)," *Aufidus* 4 (1988), 3–22. Emped. frags. 31 B 16, 17, 18, 22, and 71 Diels-Kranz: see J. Bollack, *Empédocle* I (Paris 1965), 97ff. and 171ff.

Eros was thus at once a primordial entity and a metaphysical principle, a generating power that constructed and animated the relations between things, between men, and between gods. This double aspect of Eros was definitely recognized in the double genealogy attributed to him by melic poetry, despite the fact that it is generally reputed to be solely concerned with the kind of love that strikes the hearts of mortal men and the immortal gods: Sappho declared that his parents were Earth and Sky, thereby identifying Love itself as a primordial entity; Simonides, for his part, imagined him to be descended from Ares and Aphrodite, thereby placing him among the Olympian gods but genealogically subordinating him to the goddess of love.[7]

## 2. EROTIC FORMS OF THE INITIATION TO BEAUTY

In the domain of cosmogonic and cosmological thought, the notions of love put forward by the various participants reclining on beds around the table set up in Plato's *Symposium* are for the most part underpinned by the idea of an erotic fusion of a limited plurality with an ephemeral unity, which produced multiplicity. What better place than a banquet to talk about love? The probably fictional dialogue situates this occasion at the end of the fifth century B.C. and makes it the subject of an account told at second hand. This symposium is somewhat paradoxical since, after the meal itself, the libations to the gods, the singing of a paean, and a decision to drink no more than moderately, the female flute-player is dismissed, at the very point when it is decided to place Eros at the center of the discussion. What better opportunity than this literary fiction of a sympotic dialogue could there be to pass in review the entire narrative, poetic, and philosophical traditions about Eros?

The introductory address, by Phaedrus, emphasizes the unity and divinity of Eros, the one who is the first, the most ancient, and the most powerful of all the gods. In support of this concept of Love as a primordial god, Phaedrus cites Hesiod, of course, but also Acousilaus of Argos and Parmenides. But then Eros also turns out to be an ethical power, since it is he who contrives the relationship between a lover and his beloved and impels the latter to rival the older man in valor. Love is divine, if not cosmic, and it is also a moral force: such is the double

---

[7] Sappho frag. 198a Voigt (frag. 198b substitutes Aphrodite for Earth as the mother of Eros) and Simon. frag. 575 Page, both cited by sch. Ap. Rhod. 3.26 (216 Wendel); see also Paus. 9.27.3 and sch. Theocr. 13.1/2a (p. 258 Wendel); genealogies commented upon by Lasserre 1946, 130ff., who also mentions the Hellenistic poems of Antagoras, frag. 1 Powell (Eros the end of Night and Erebus), and Simias, frag. 24 Powell (Eros the son of Chaos).

concept of Eros that thereafter inspires the entire discussion between the symposiasts set on stage by Plato.

It is precisely upon that moral quality of Eros that Pausanias dwells, in order to introduce a distinction between the body and the soul never imagined in the archaic poetry of erotic love. Just as in Hesiod's *Theogony* Eros was represented both as being one of the primordial gods and also as the companion of Aphrodite, who was born later than him, in Pausanias' account Aphrodite is given a double genealogy: she is both the daughter of Ouranos and, according to a different tradition, a descendant of Zeus. In accordance with this double genealogical tradition, he suggests that Eros Ouranios ought to be distinguished from Eros Pandemos. This moralizing theory appropriated for itself and for Eros both the cults that the Athenians, in complementary fashion, devoted to the goddess of love. It produced a new semantic interpretation of the two titles under which Cypris was revered in those two cults. "Celestial" love was attributed to the soul; "popular" love to the body. Aphrodite Ourania presided over homophile relationships that committed the young *erômenos* to virtue, while Aphrodite Pandemos presided over sexual relations oriented toward physical gratification![8]

It subsequently fell to Eryximachus to engineer a return to unity, starting from the multiplicity of the relations imagined by Pausanias. As a doctor and a master of his own particular art, it was not hard for him to explain that doctors knew how to restore equilibrium to the body and concord between the cold and the hot, the bitter and the sweet, and the dry and the wet. In similar fashion, Eros, that universal power, was able to reconcile contraries: he could maintain men's harmony with other men and also their harmony with the gods. The implication was that the technical know-how of the doctor could reconcile Sappho and Empedocles: the bittersweet Eros was the guarantor of cosmic harmony.

But, to explain the multiplicity of beings, it was necessary for differentiation to be born from this refound unity. In his parodic fable of androgonous beings, Aristophanes, the comic poet, devised an explanation for this strange process. It was founded upon the postulate that at the very beginning, there were bisexual beings formed of two halves, one of each sex, and also — ironically enough — beings formed of two feminine halves or two masculine halves. All beings were thus double, and they could be divided into three genders: the masculine, descended

---

[8] Plat. *Symp.* 176e ff., 178a ff. and 180c ff.; see A. Lesky, *Vom Eros der Hellenen* (Göttingen 1976), 87ff. Aphrodite Pandemos, the civic goddess, is not related to prostitution in Athens as the (false) parallel presented by her cult in Corinth suggests: see V. Pirenne-Delforge, "Epithètes cultuelles et interprétation philosophique," *Ant. Class.* 57 (1988): 142–57, and 1994, 26ff. and 446ff., and also Calame 1989, 103ff. and n. 6; *pace* Halperin 1990, 104ff.

from Sun, the feminine, descended from Earth, and the androgynous, descended from Moon. To neutralize the excessive power of these over-autonomous and doubly human beings, Zeus was obliged to perform a surgical operation on them: he cut them in half, ordering Apollo to switch first the faces, then the sexual organs of each half to the side of the cut. It was at this point that a strange sense of incompleteness became manifest, impelling each half, now in the shape of a new human being, to seek its complement through different forms of love. The explicit reference — much to the taste of comedy — to the organs of sexuality explained not only the existence of masculine homophilia and feminine homoeroticism alongside heterosexual lovemaking, but also man's capacity, under the influence of Eros, to engender new halves from the union of the two of them. Furthermore, what might at first sight appear to be a physiological justification for homosexuality leads to a moral defense of homophilia, the love of adults for boys; and these boys were by nature (*phusei*) the most "manly" (*andreiotatoi*) of all; loving men as they did, as adults they became the best of politicians. It was homophilia that provided the example for the feelings of *philia*, *oikeiotês*, and *erôs* that impelled amorous couples to fuse. Despite the separation decided upon by Zeus, love thus restored the singleness of human beings in nostalgic quest of their primordial complementarity and at the same time made it possible for them not only to survive and multiply physically, but also to reproduce themselves morally.

On the basis of this allegorical plea for a return, through Eros, to an original unity, the tragic poet (and host of the banquet), Agathon, manages to show that, far from being the most ancient of the gods, Love is, in truth, the youngest of them. Ultimately, it all depends upon the moment selected to define Eros; whether this comes at the beginning or, on the contrary, at the end of the process for which he is the inspiration! The reign of necessity, of division, and of the quarrels described by the poets — among them Hesiod — is set in opposition to the reign of an Eros who is the principle of order, the chorus leader of both gods and men, who sing his praises in perfect harmony. For, at the climax of the Platonic satire of tragedy, which Agathon represents at this banquet, Eros is presented as the god of the four cardinal virtues of the philosopher: wisdom (*sophia*) and courage (*andreia*), and at the same time moderation (*sophrosunê*) and justice (*dikaiosunê*). Just as truly as Eros is "the finest and best of guides," he is also a creator (*poietês*), the master of the art of the Muses:

> He it is who casts alienation out, draws intimacy in; he brings us together in all such friendly gatherings as the present; at feasts and dances and oblations he makes himself our leader; politeness contriving, moroseness outdriving;

gracious, benign; a marvel to the wise, a delight to the gods; coveted of such as share him not, treasured of such as good share have got; father of luxury, tenderness, elegance, graces and longing and yearning; careful of the good, careless of the bad; in toil and fear, in drink and in discourse, our trustiest helmsman, boatswain, champion, deliverer; ornament of all gods and men; leader fairest and best, whom everyone should follow, joining tunefully in the burthen of his song, wherewith he enchants the thought of every god and man.[9]

Agathon's speech, which is studded with literary references and itself abides by the conventions of poems of praise, concludes by maintaining the equivalence (with which we are by now familiar) between the effects of poetry and the effects of Eros. It is an equivalence that was not only implicit in archaic poetry but was also illustrated, at the very time when this dialogue was supposed to have taken place, in the beguiling prose elaborated by the rhetor Gorgias in his *Encomium of Helen*, mentioned above. However, the organ that was now said to be affected by the charms of Eros (*thelgôn*) was no longer the affective center (*thumos*), but the center of intellection (*noêma*). Eros as the generator of multiplicity, the sole conciliator of contraries, the creative guide for poetry: the whole of the rhetoric that Plato develops in this dialogue to convey concepts that are complementary to love is designed for one purpose; namely, to introduce the intervention of Diotima, the priestess from Mantinea, whose words of wisdom are reported by Socrates in another discursive shift that introduces an external perspective. Poetry is now replaced by incantation, divination, and initiation, in all of which domains the reversal of sexual roles frequently plays a part.

In a maneuver that is somewhat reminiscent of procedures favored by Socrates himself, the question of the beauty, goodness, and divinity of Eros shifts into that of the Beautiful. For what Diotima — and probably, through her, Plato himself — proposes in place of a static eulogy of Eros is a way of acceding to what does not yet quite constitute a Form, but does represent the very basis of love. This way is initially pedagogical since it involves an apprenticeship (*mathêma*) to the understanding of the Beautiful. It also constitutes a dynamic expression of the philosophical problem of the one and the many that is embodied by the figure of

---

[9] Plat. *Symp.* 197de, in W.R.M. Lamb (trans.), *Plato* V (Loeb 1925); see 185e ff., 189d ff., and 194e ff. The literary allusions contained in the encomium of Eros pronounced by Agathon are explained by K. J. Dover, *Plato. Symposium* (Cambridge 1980), 123ff.; see also J. Reale, *Eros dèmone mediatore* (Milan 1997), 117ff. and 149ff. On the role of Eros in Gorgias' *Encomium of Helen*, see above ch. VI, §2.3.

Eros. Here is the famous summary of the problem provided by Diotima herself:

> So when a man by the right method of boy-loving ascends from these particulars and begins to descry that beauty, he is almost able to lay hold of the final secret. Such is the right approach or induction to love-matters. Beginning from obvious beauties, he must for the sake of that highest beauty be ever climbing aloft, as on the rungs of a ladder, from one to two, and from two to all beautiful bodies; from personal beauty he proceeds to beautiful observances, from observance to beautiful learning, and from learning at last to that particular study which is concerned with the beautiful itself and that alone, so that in the end he comes to know the very essence of beauty.[10]

The "woman revered by Zeus," the only woman admitted, through the intermediary of Socrates, into the symposium, thus urges a return from duality and plurality to the unity embodied in an extremely abstract beauty. To lead him all the way along this philosophical path, man has at his disposal a guide, in the shape of Eros: Eros the double one, the mediator, the son of Poverty (*Penia*) and Expedience (*Poros*), himself born after a banquet, in the garden of Zeus mentioned earlier. Eros is also a remarkable enchanter, a veritable bewitcher, a true sophist. He has shed his wings and his adolescent baby fat, lost his looks of an *erômenos*, and become an *erastês*. As such he bears an uncanny resemblance to Socrates. However that may be, his nature as a mediator makes him, as an *erastês*, an altogether exceptional guide to initiation. This new function of his attests to love's moral role, for his cosmic quality is now directed toward the ideal to which he provides access. But the main effect of the indirect intervention of a woman in this banquet of men is to topple the essentially pedagogical relationship of institutional homophilia: the graceful charms of the young *erômenos* now serve only to propel the *erastês* into commitment to the philosophical path that leads to an understanding of the Beautiful. Eros has become the guide of the adult *erastês*, and for now leaves the adolescent to his own superficial and immature form of beauty.

---

[10] Plat. *Symp.* 211bc, in W.R.M. Lamb (trans.), *Plato* V (Loeb 1925), see already at 201d ff. The "pedagogical" access to transcendence offered by love is explained by H. Büchner, *Eros und Sein* (Bonn 1965), 133ff., while S. Graefe, *Der gespaltene Eros — Platons Trieb zur "Weisheit"* (Frankfurt am Main and Paris 1989), 110ff., examines the attempts to identify Diotima's pronouncements with the theory of Ideas. See also P. Hadot, *Qu'est-ce que la philosophie antique?* (Paris 1995), 71ff., and also Vernant 1989, 164ff.; Halperin 1986, 71ff., who lists all the passages in which Plato presents the philosopher as an *erastês*; and C. Osborne, *Eros Unveiled. Plato and the God of Love* (Oxford 1994), 93ff.

## 3. LOVE AS A METAPHYSICIAN

In Plato's *Phaedrus*, the argumentative procedures adopted to arrive at analogous conclusions on the subject of love are quite different. What is at stake here is not the divinity of the figure of Eros, but the function of the state of being in love. This dialogue does not set before a gathering of symposiasts the contrast between a number of different concepts of Eros, each one influenced by the particular profession or discipline of its respective defender. Instead, it is a matter of a competition of wits, using all the ploys of rhetoric in a debate inspired by the landscape — green banks of the Ilissus river — in an atmosphere redolent of the love stories of legend. The subject of the debate is the amorous relationship between an *erastês* and his *erômenos*. The words of the foremost logographer of the day, Lysias, who is absent, start off the debate in a speech that is read out by Phaedrus, in which Lysias presents the ethical aspect to such a relationship. His thesis, which is a paradoxical one, runs as follows: far from granting his favors to the man who loves him, the young beloved should bend to the will of a man who feels no desire for him.[11]

As is well-known, Socrates responds to Lysias' written speech with a double riposte. His critique of Eros is intertwined with a critique of writing. Given that Socrates simply repeats the paradoxical thesis propounded by Lysias, and given that by the time he has finished with it the love (*philein*) of an *erastês* for a boy can be ironically likened to the love of a wolf for a lamb, this first part of Socrates' first speech calls for a rectification, a palinode in the manner of the archaic poet, Stesichorus. The lying speech must be opposed by a truthful one that recants the former. In this particular case, it is the god Eros himself, the son of Aphrodite, who demands it, for first Lysias, and then Socrates, in this first phase of his argument, have shown a lack of respect for him.

We thus move on from the subject of the moral aspect of amorous desire and its social and institutional aspects to that of its divine nature. The introduction of the figure of Eros itself is reminiscent of the theme put before the symposiasts in the *Symposium*. However, the way that it is treated, in a palinode, is quite different. Three essential points are made, all relating to the classical and literary notion of the effects of love; and it should be remembered that in this new *logos* of Socrates, which he addresses to Phaedrus, the role that the philosopher adopts

---

[11] Plat. *Phaedr.* 229a ff. and 229e ff.; the reverse of the paradoxical thesis defended by Lysias is already formulated in the *Dissoi Logoi*, frag. 90 B 2.2 Diels-Kranz. The relation to the spatial setting in which the dialogue on love takes place is indicated above in ch. VIII, §1.

toward his interlocutor, here granted the rank of a "beautiful boy," is that of an *erastês* seeking to seduce his *erômenos*. We thus find our-selves, once again, in a dialogue that calls into question the art of rheto-ric itself and, along with it, the words of love and all their beguiling effects.

Initially then, the subject of the debate is the state of being in love, a state that we have often found to be experienced as a rapture, a mad-ness (*mania*). But now this madness turns out — through etymology — also to be what seizes hold of diviners: *mantikê*, the art of divination, is also *manikê*, the art of delirium. Thanks to the etymological play on the morphology of the words, we now gain a better understanding of the role of Diotima, the *Mantinikê*, the wise woman of Mantinea. Through her origin, she is a woman who is both possessed (from *manikê*) and at the same time a diviner (from *mantikê*). Not only is she the sole female guest (*xenê*, meaning both guest and stranger), introduced through the mediation of Socrates' words, into the *Symposium*; she is also the only person qualified to speak of the madness of love, since she alone knows what she is talking about. Essentially, only women are capable of cop-ing with divine possession: the priestess of Delphi, the priestess of the oracle at Dodona, and that wise female diviner, the Sybil. *Mania*, which is inspired by the gods and which provides access to the domain of the gods, is thus superior — as the tradition shows — to the kind of wisdom that is learned (*sôphrosunê*), which depends on men. The same goes for the Dionysiac spells and initiatory rites that have the power to deliver men from diseases and misfortunes; and also for the delirium of the Muses, which transports the soul of the poet, enabling him to sing of the exploits of the ancients, and which thereby furthers the education of future generations. All these comparisons not only show that the nature of erotic *mania* is divine, since it too is inspired by the gods, but also indicate how beneficial it is to a lover and his beloved.[12] The divine dimension of love is a moral one.

The next point to note from the long allegory of the harnessed team of horses and its driver, by which the soul is carried along in the wake of the gods, is the great advantage from which such a soul benefits: thanks to its extracelestial flight, it is able, through the sense of sight, to gain direct perception of the realities (*ta onta*), of truth (*ta alêthê*). At last we glimpse the meaning that informs the philosopher's thought: through reflection, he will rise above the plurality of sensations, and move toward unity; the soul will then remember the altogether real real-

---

[12] Plat. *Phaedr.* 243e and 244a ff.; see also 265b. On the relation of Diotima of Man-tinea to prophecy, see *Symp.* 201d, 202e, and 211d, with the pertinent commentary by Halperin 1990, 120ff.; on the "madness" of the Pythia, see Sissa, above ch. VI, §2.2, n. 31, 40ff.

ity (*to on ontôs*) that it has perceived as it followed in the wake of a deity. Now, amorous madness provides us with the means to accomplish that philosophical journey that takes the form of reminiscence. As he seizes upon the beauty of the world through his sense of sight, a philosopher is assailed by the memory of truth: seized by erotic madness at the sight of these beautiful goddesses, he takes off and soars toward reality. At that point he proves himself to be the very best of *erastai*. But how is it that love provides access to philosophy? It is partly because, by putting us in contact with the gods, the madness of love reveals itself to be the most opportune of all forms of divine possession, but also because beauty is what is proferred to the most acute of all our senses, namely sight, in the clearest fashion, like the coming of a Homeric deity (*enargestata*). In the erotic rapture that it provokes, a vision of human beauty shares many affinities with the soul's contemplation of transcendant reality:

> All my discourse so far has been about the fourth kind of madness, which causes him to be regarded as mad who, when he sees the beauty on earth, remembering the true beauty, feels his wings growing and longs to stretch them for an upward flight, but cannot do so and, like a bird, gazes upward and neglects the things below. My discourse has shown that this is, of all inspirations, the best and of the highest origin to him who has it or who shares in it, and that he who loves the beautiful, partaking in this madness, is called a lover.[13]

The role played by vision in erotic *mania* finally brings us back to the physiology of desire, at the same time evoking the moral consequences of the state of being in love. It is the distinction between an initiate of long standing and a new initiate that makes it possible to establish the difference between the one who, having forgotten the sight of beauty, indulges like an animal in the pleasure of reproduction or even in unnatural pleasures and the one who, at the sight of a countenance that is an image of beauty, allows his soul to be inflamed and take to flight, in pursuit of the god whose progress it has been following. As for the physiological explanation, it is a twofold one: first, there is a stream of particles, which gushes from the beauty of the boy who is beloved and which affects the lover through the intermediary of the boy's gaze. This concept of *himeros* prompts a reference to the etymology of *erôs* sug-

---

[13] Plat. *Phaedr.* 249de, in H. N. Fowler (trans.), *Plato* I (Loeb 1953). The account of the team of horses begins at 246a and leads into the passage translated, on the path forward offered by the vision of beauty. The verbs of seeing, upon which the term *eidos* used at 249b is based, punctuate the telling of this allegory and also the account of the procedure of reminiscence (248a, 248c, 249b, 249e, etc.): see G.R.F. Ferrari, *Listening to the Cicadas* (Cambridge 1987), 171ff.

gested in the *Cratylus*: the terms from which *himeros* is said to be composed denote the rush (*rheonta*) of particles (*merê*) as the erotic desire (*erôs*) that is supposed to flow into the man (*es-rei*) from outside, through the eyes. Second, though, these visual streams then provoke a sensation of heat and boiling in which the soul believes it has recovered the wings that once allowed it to follow in the wake of the gods as they progressed on their extracelestial way: this represents the onset of the state of rapture and joy that, according to one epic distich, men call Eros, but the gods call the Feathered One. Similarly, at the end of the *Symposium*, Socrates explains to Alcibiades, who is ready to grant his favors to the philosopher, that the vision of thought only gains in sharpness when one desists from physical gazing. For Socrates, beauty is simply an illusion; one needs to look farther afield.[14]

The philosopher takes over the processes of the traditional physiology of love-in-the-Greek-fashion and incorporates them into his metaphysics. As a result, the social and pedagogical relationship between an *erômenos*, a beloved, and an *erastês*, a lover, is transfigured. By dint of an effort of memory, the loved one becomes for the lover a kind of visual representation (*agalma*) of the god to whom the soul has gained access. Through his devotion to the boy, the *erastês* ends up by focusing upon him his admiration for the deity. Reverting to the image of the horse-drawn chariot, Plato describes the *erastês* following the *erômenos*, just as his soul had once been drawn in the train of the god. The reversal hinted at at the end of the *Symposium* is confirmed: the adolescent is there to enable the adult to rise above appearances. But, in contrast to Diotima, Socrates does not abandon the *erômenos* to his adolescence. For, as the relationship between lover and loved one deepens, in the gymnasium or in the course of other meetings, the stream of desire (*himeros*) felt by the *erastês* overflows and spurts, in a visual echo, over the boy who, through his beauty, is its source. At last the soul of the *erômenos* is, in its turn, filled with desire (*erôs*) and is thus borne toward the truth.

Does this mean that Plato introduces into the relationship of homophilia the reciprocity that so many interpreters have ascribed to it? Only an over-hasty reading of the text could lead to such a conclusion. In

---

[14] Plat. *Phaedr.* 250e ff. and *Symp.* 218e ff.; on the function of the concluding episode of Alcibiades and its relation to the words of Diotima, see R. Luca, *Platone. Simposio* (Florence 1982), 21ff. A similar materialistic explanation of perception is to be found in some Presocratics: see above ch. I, §2, n. 18. Plato's *Cratylus*, 419e ff., provides a different etymology for *himeros*, conceiving it to be an "impetuous flow" (*hiemenos rhei*). On the two epic lines, attributed to the Homeridae, with their wordplay on *Erôta* and *Pterôta*, see G. J. De Vries, *A Commentary on the Phaedrus of Plato* (Amsterdam 1969), 159ff., and Carson 1986, 156ff., in connection with written discourse.

truth, the loving desire of the *erômenos* is simply an *anterôs*, not a love reciprocated or a "counter-love," as has all too often been suggested, but instead a mirrored love that is born in the loved one and that reflects for him an image not of the lover but of himself. The rules of asymmetry and mismatch are still respected: the young man in his turn comes to know the state of being in love and will, as a result, in his turn become an adult philosopher — for the *erômenos* as well as for the *erastês*, there is a path that leads to truth. And, sure enough, this love that invades the *erômenos*, as an echo of the love felt by the *erastês*, is called *philia* by the boy, not *erôs*! It is only when this situation is reached that the undisciplined horse in the chariot team succeeds in convincing the driver and that the *erômenos* then grants the *erastês* his favors: the loved one and the lover are thus at last to be found lying together on the same bed, even if the charioteer and the horse have still to behave with modesty and reason.[15] Any reciprocity that there is between the adult and the adolescent exists, as ever, solely at the level of trust, the mutual trust that, in the iconography of the late archaic period, often seems to be indicated by an exchanged look of complicity.

In Xenophon's *Symposium*, Socrates defends exactly the same thesis, albeit in a more schematic fashion than in the *Phaedrus*. The *erômenos* will only respond to the advances of an *erastês* who possesses a soul characterized by the beauty, modesty, and nobility of a free man. His response will be provoked not by amorous desire, but by a mutual trust. This response of "love" is designated by the verb *antiphilein*. It is an intellectual love, the goal of which is moral and social worth. Whatever happens, the boy is not capable of erotic love. Even if he gives himself to his lover, it will be without love (*erônti ouk erôn*), for only adult men and women can share the enjoyment of the pleasures of Aphrodite. Through a shift in Athenian theology similar to that introduced by Plato, for Xenophon physical love affairs are the province of the "popu-

---

[15] In connection with the interpretation of this passage (255a ff.) suggested by Vernant 1989, 159ff., who follows other interpreters and bases his remarks in particular on the concept of the gaze set out in Alc. 132e ff. (which is not concerned with the amorous gaze), it is worth pointing out that Plato, for his own purposes, distorts the traditional figure of the conflictual *anterôs* (see above in ch. V, §1.1, and n. 22) and applies it solely to the *erômenos*. In homophilia, the erotic desire is not itself reciprocated (Foucault makes the same mistake [1984, 262ff.], although he elsewhere rightly refers to the "asceticism of the subject"), and strictly speaking there is no "specular" erotic relationship: see also *Phaedr.* 232d ff., and above ch. I, §3, and ch. III, §1. Although more prudent, the interpretation of Halperin 1990, 131ff., also mistakenly takes *anterôs* to mean a counterlove (see also Halperin 1986, 66ff.).

In the simplifying paraphrase provided by Plutarch, *Amator.* 758d ff., of this passage in the *Phaedrus*, the erotic fervor by which the *erômenos* is seized is reduced to a passion for *philia* and virtue (759d).

lar" Aphrodite, while the love affairs that concern the soul and fine actions, those that aim for *philia*, belong to the "heavenly" Aphrodite.[16]

The paradoxical argument developed by Lysias the logographer in the *Phaedrus* now makes more sense: for whoever wishes to achieve true *philia*, it is definitely better to do without erotic desire and all its temptations. So, for an adolescent, a mutual friendship can only develop with a man who feels no desire for him. Lysias' thesis is summarized in Socrates' first speech, which draws a sharp distinction between an *erôs*, which is an innate desire for pleasure (*epithumia hêdonôn*), and a *doxa*, which is an aspiration toward the good. In the philosopher's second speech, that thesis is overturned by his showing that in a pedagogical relationship there is an overlap between physical desire and spiritual aspiration.[17]

Thus *philia*, even when it does lead to sexual satisfaction, can only be generated by the loving desire of the *erastês*. That is why, in the concluding passage of this dialogue, Phaedrus, who has been playing the role of an *erômenos*, becomes the incarnation of Eros himself (*ô phile Eros*). By reason of its acknowledged poetic form, the palinode pronounced by Socrates falls outside the framework of a rhetorical dialogue. In a sense, it becomes a seductive gift that, in the course of an erotic courtship, the philosopher-*erastês* presents to his young *erômenos*, in order to obtain his *kharis*, his favor.

---

[16] Xen. *Symp.* 9ff. and 16ff., with the mythological examples of homophile relationships given at 28ff.: see Dover 1978, 53ff., and Foucault 1984, 256ff.; see also *Mem.* 2.6.28 and *Hier.* 1.35ff., in which the looks and words exchanged by the *erastês* and the *erômenos* who "loves" in return (*antiphilôn*) are contrasted to the constraint imposed by the fondling done by whoever is seized by Eros.

[17] Plat. *Phaedr.* 232e ff. and 237d ff.

# Chapter XI

## MYSTIC EROS

IN BOTH THE *Symposium* and the *Phaedrus* of Plato, the ways proposed for progressing toward beauty or toward truth, through the mediation of Eros, are of an initiatory nature. The way indicated by Diotima is conceived as a path that rises in steps (*epanabasmoi*) toward beauty and also as a giving birth, the metaphorical meaning of which can only be explained by a woman and, what is more, only by one who is a "diviner." Also, more directly, the proposed itinerary is described in the very same terms that were used to designate initiation into the mystery cults: *muêsis*, *teletai*, and above all *epoptika*. In the context of classical Athens, the most precise allusion is clearly a reference to the Mysteries of Eleusis, an allusion that Plato does not fail to exploit to his own advantage: he transforms *epopteia*, a vision of mystic action and objects, which constituted the ultimate step in the Eleusian initiation ritual, into the contemplation of metaphysical beauty and reality.[1]

The Eros of the philosophers certainly takes on a double role: cosmic and metaphysical to the extent that he serves to mediate between the multiplicity of appearances and the unity of the ideal beauty or the transcendant reality; and moral when he intervenes in the institutional relationship of homophilia, to get the soul of the youth who is beloved to follow the example of his lover and to rise toward the supracelestial realities. But the initiatory aspect to the interventions of Eros also produces a reversal: in the cosmotheogonies of the archaic period, the power of love made it possible to pass from duality, through unity, to multiplicity, by going through a process of generation and differentiation; in contrast, in the initiatory process indicated by Diotima and by Socrates, an erotic relationship made it possible, through a plurality of bodies here on earth, to rediscover the unity to be contemplated in the Beyond. For we need to take into consideration not only the initiatory

---

[1] The initiatory aspects of the eroticophilosophical progress described by Plato are noted by I. Chirassi Colombo, "L'Inganno di Afrodite," in *Labirinti dell'Eros* (Florence 1985), 109–21. *Symp.* 211c and 206b ff., along with the fine interpretation suggested by Halperin 1990, 116ff. and 137ff. (a first version of this study was published in Halperin, Winkler, and Zeitlin 1990, 257–308). On the use of the technical lexicon of initiation, see *Symp.* 209e ff. (see also 202e) and *Phaedr.* 250b ff.; this vocabulary is explained by W. Burkert, *Ancient Mystery Cults* (Cambridge, Mass., and London 1987), 7ff.; on the content of the Eleusian *epopteia*, see Richardson 1974, 26ff. and 310ff.

path followed by the mystics of Eleusis, but also the speculative thought of Orphism. By manipulating traditional cosmotheogony in a number of ways, the metaphysics of the Orphics even managed to reconcile the generative movement from the one to the many with a mystic passage from the many to the one.

## 1. Eros in the Orphic Theogonies

Discounting a number of reconstructions that are over-hasty and risky, our most reliable evidence for the configuration of the earliest Orphic cosmogony and theogony is provided by the *parabasis* in Aristophanes' *Birds*.[2] It is, to be sure, a parodic text, but it nevertheless sets out the essential features of the architecture of the cosmos elaborated by the disciples of Orpheus, in which Eros occupies an even more strategic role than he does in Hesiod's theogony.

In the beginning, seemingly without any hierarchical organization, there were Chaos, Night, the black Erebus, and the vast Tartarus. In the midst of these elements characterized by an absence of light and limitations, there then appeared an egg "borne by the wind." It was produced by Night, which laid it in the limitless lap of Erebus. From this primordial egg, Eros emerged, "full of desire." In contrast to the indistinct nature of the primordial entities, he was equipped with sparkling golden wings and is compared to the tornadoes created by the wind. The "windy" aspect of the primordial egg should be referred to the fact that it was produced without fertilization, just as Eros was; and Aristophanes clearly makes the most of the "windy" qualities of these primordial beings, incorporating them into the cosmic Utopia that is the basis of the ideal city imagined by the birds in his comedy. In vast Tartarus, Eros was united in the night with Chaos, now likewise equipped with wings. From this dual — and probably homosexual — union was born, not the race of the blessed gods, as might have been expected, but the species of flying creatures. Subsequently, it was through the effect of Eros that dual and sexed unions took place, engendering the various elements that were to constitute the cosmos: the sky, the ocean, and the earth, and also the indestructible race of the gods.[3]

---

[2] The most recent of these hypothetical reconstructions of the archaic Orphic cosmogony is that presented by M. L. West, *The Orphic Poems* (Oxford 1983), 68ff. and 264. For a critical attitude and for all the technical details of the outline presented here, I refer the reader to my study, "Eros initiatique et la cosmogonie orphique," in P. Borgeaud (ed.), *Orphisme et Orphée* (Geneva 1991), 227–47.

[3] Aristoph. *Av.* 676ff. = *Orph.* frag. 1 Kern; see G. S. Kirk, J. E. Raven, and M. Schofield, *The Presocratic Philosophers* (Cambridge [2]1983), 26ff.; see also Fasce 1977,

Not until the nineteenth century did scholars perceive the Orphic nature of Aristophanes' ornithological parody. It was through an erudite comparison with the *Sacred Speeches*, reelaborated much later by the "rhapsodes," who were disciples of Orpheus, that the mystic provenance of the comic construction was brought to light. The neo-Platonic tradition, which in its turn strongly influenced the development of this cosmogonic and theogonic system reconstructed in the Orphic rhapsodies, produced several summaries of it, from which its organization can be deduced. In the beginning, there were a few primordial entities such as Chronos, then Aether, Chaos, and probably Night. The scenario imagined by Aristophanes' birds turns out to be remarkably similar as soon as we come across the egg of dazzling whiteness that Chronos creates within Aether. In another version, the primordial egg is produced from the union between Aether and Chaos. But, whatever the egg's origin, from it Phanes, the Brilliant One, was hatched. In a process of superposition characteristic of Orphic thought, the rhapsodic theogony soon goes on to identify this new being with a number of different figures: Protogonos, the First-Born, Metis (Intelligence), and, above all, the graceful Eros.[4]

Exactly as in the cosmogony reinvented by Aristophanes, the Phanes-Eros of the Orphic rhapsodes is conveyed around the universe by his golden wings. But according to a genealogy attributed to the mysterious Orphic "theologians," Hieronymus and Hellanicus, and subsequently reinterpreted in a neo-Platonic fashion by Damascius, he was also equipped with a number of animal heads, including one of a lion and one of a bull. He was at once masculine and feminine, and had two pairs of eyes. However he appears to have lost the use of these once he had engendered—either through parthenogenesis or with the participation of Night—the various constitutive elements of the universe. A comparison with the "theology" attributed to Hieronymus and Hellanicus fully confirms the bisexual nature of Eros: in their reinterpretations of the Orphic cosmogony, the primordial egg contains a dyad formed from the masculine principle and the feminine principle and also a winged god with two bull-headed bodies, who introduces order into the cosmos. This being, who complements the bisexual dyad, is Protogonos

---

91ff., and the contributions of G. Ricciardelli Apicella, "Teogonie orfiche nell'ambito delle teogonie greche," and A. Pardini, "L'*ornitogonia* (Ar. *Av.* 693 sgg) tra serio e faceto: Premessa letteraria al suo studio storico-religioso," in A. Masaracchia (ed.), *Orfeo e l'orfismo* (Rome 1993), 27–51 and 53–65.

[4] Reconstruction based on the *Orph.* frags. 60, 65, and 73–82 Kern; see in this connection L. Brisson, "Proclus et l'Orphisme," in J. Pépin and H.-D. Saffrey (eds.), *Proclus, lecteur et interprète des anciens* (Paris 1987), 43–104.

(or Phanes, or Zeus, or Pan), who, thanks to the light that emanates from him, is the creator of all things.[5]

In the light of all this, it seems clear that the hemispherical beings in quest of their original unity, invented by Aristophanes in his parody of Plato's *Symposium*, refer back to the Orphic allusion in his dramas, in particular to the cosmotheogony of the *Birds*. In these texts, bisexuality appears to be one of the essential features of Eros, the creator and organizer of the cosmos.[6] That bisexuality is reminiscent of the paradoxical nature of the contrary aspects credited to Eros by archaic poetry.

## 2. THE MYSTIC ASPECTS OF EROS

Is the distinctly bisexual nature of Eros enough to account for his inclusion in a cosmogony and a theogonic genealogy that is said to represent a mystic system?

There is one further step we must take: we must try to make out the genealogical thread that runs through the famous *Derveni papyrus*—a task of papyrological detection that is made the more delicate by the fact that this text has not yet been officially published; and that in any case it provides us with no more than a commentary on an Orphic poem, which may, however, go back to the classical period.[7]

The line of ancestors described by the commentary and, presumably, also by the text, makes it possible to reconstruct a cosmic and theogonic genealogy. It begins with the sudden leap into the ether of a "first-born king" (*prôtogonos basileus*). This first being, identified with Sun, has a son, Cronos, who seems to appear after Ouranos, the son of Night, who probably symbolizes a primordial state of indifferentiation. At any rate, it is Cronos who assumes the task of setting the cosmos in move-

[5] The version of Hieronymus and Hellanicus is known to us through Damascius, *Princ.* 123 bis = *Orph.* frag. 54 Kern; see L. Brisson's commentary, "Damascius et l'Orphisme," in Borgeaud (see above n. 2), 157–209. The sexual role attributed to the figure of Eros in these various cosmogonies is explained by L. J. Alderink, *Creation and Salvation in Ancient Orphism* (Chicago 1981), 40ff.

[6] This affiliation is pointed out by L. Brisson, "Eros," in Y. Bonnefoy (ed.), *Dictionnaire des mythologies* I (Paris 1981), 351–59. Confirmation is to be found for the oviparous birth of Phanes-Eros, for his winged and double nature, and for his role as a generator in *HOrph.* 6 and in *Arg. Orph.* 12ff. and 421ff. The hermaphrodite aspects of the figure of Eros are noted by Fasce 1977, 97ff.; it sometimes happened that, in her cult in classical Greece, Aphrodite took on a bisexual character: see the references given by M. Delcourt, *Hermaphrodite* (Paris 1958), 43ff.

[7] The *P. Derv.* has appeared in a pirated form in *Zeitschr. Pap. Epigr.* 47, 1982, 1–10, but see now the complete translation by A. Laks and G. W. Most (eds.), *Studies in the Derveni Papyrus* (Oxford 1997), 9–22; see, among other studies, that of M. Henry, "The Derveni Commentator as a Literary Critic," *Trans. Am. Philol. Assoc.* 116 (1986): 149–64.

ment and making everything in it distinguishable, with the aid of Sun in particular. Then, in a development that puts one in mind of Hesiod's myth of the succession of the gods, Zeus intervenes. The god swallows the penis of Sun before the latter has time to spurt forth the whole of creation: the gods and the goddesses, the flowers and the springs, and all things that now exist in the world are thus forced to go through the process of birth.[8] This act of "castration" and swallowing—which comes at a different juncture from in the Hesiodic tradition, and is concentrated and given a different meaning—is essential: it marks a return to unity through Zeus, in between two processes of distinction and differentiation. Given that the relation between Sun and his penis seems reminiscent of the relation between Aristophanes' egg and the generating power of Eros, the most ancient versions of the Orphic cosmogony do appear to be comparable. They seem to be organized as a sequence comprising first an indifferentiated state (Night, Tartarus, Erebus, Chaos), followed by an initial differentiation under the effect of light (the egg, Sun), then the intervention of sexuality (Eros, penis), and then, with the appearance of Zeus, a first return to unity.

Now we can perceive the mystic orientation that the Orphic thinkers succeeded in imposing upon the traditional cosmotheogony. In the system suggested by the text of the Derveni papyrus and also by the theogonic construction of the *Rhapsodies*, Zeus is no longer the sovereign who, chiefly under the influence of Eros, guarantees the differentiated and sometimes conflictual order produced by the process of generation. By swallowing Phanes-Eros and the whole of the creation that depended upon him, Zeus, the king of the gods instead restores to all created beings their original unity and then goes on to confer a new order upon the universe. This Zeus, who is single, like the cosmos that he will eventually recreate, is praised in the *Orphic Hymn* cited by Eusebius: he is the master of the gods and is all-powerful; upon him rest the earth and the sky, and he engenders all things, he is both masculine and feminine, husband and wife, and is finally assimilated to Eros of a thousand charms.[9]

The unity of Eros born from an egg in his single and perfect form,

---

[8] *P. Derv.* coll. IX.4 and XII.3ff. with the commentary by J. S. Rusten, "Interim Notes on the Papyrus of Derveni," *Harv. Stud. Class. Philol.* 89 (1985): 121–40, who, however, regards the term *aidoion* as an adjective and therefore rejects its sexual meaning: see in this connection the study cited above in n. 2, 232ff. and n. 12. On the Sun god of the Orphics, see Detienne 1989, 127f.

[9] *Orph.* frags. 129 and 167, and also 168 Kern, cited by Eus. *Praep. Ev.* 3.9.1f. The central figure of Orphic Zeus, who is a principle of both unity and multiplicity, is well described by H. Schwabl, "Zeus (Teil II)," in *Realenc. Alt.-Wiss., Supplb.* XV (Stuttgart 1978), coll. 993–1411 (col. 1327ff.).

and his bisexuality, which allowed him to engender life by parthenogenesis, opened up the possibility of a return to the primordial unity.
Mediating between indifferentiation and differentiation, Eros was no
longer quite the midterm between duality and multiplicity. In his singleness, he could be absorbed by Zeus, who thereby recreated in himself
the unity of the earliest times. This cosmogonic return to unity was
repeated in the sixth generation of the deities, when Dionysus was absorbed by the Titans. The line followed is homologous to that of the
mystic progress suggested by Orphic morality.[10] Those initiated into Orphism were encouraged to adopt a series of ascetic practices in order to
recover their initial state, ruled by Eros: the golden age that existed
before all the differentiations that had resulted from the hatching of the
primordial egg. Eros was no longer simply a guide to initiation; to the
mystics in quest of the lost unity, he represented both the beginning and
the end. He had no more to do with social sexual roles or gender.

[10] The path of the *bios orphikos* is traced by Detienne 1977, 163ff., and by West, above
n. 2, 140ff.; see now my study, "Figures of Sexuality and Initiatory Transition in the
Derveni Theogony and Its Commentary," in Laks and Most, above n. 7, 65–80.

*Elegiac Coda*

## EROS THE EDUCATOR

EROS THE ORGANIZER of the cosmos, Eros the mapper of metaphysical spaces, Eros the constructor of social relations, hence Eros the educator, Eros the incarnation of the power of love — to reverse the order of the guises in which we have so far discovered him. What strikes one above all about the cosmic or civilizing relations woven by Eros, under the control of Aphrodite, is the dynamic, if not the dialectical and polemical aspects of this web. It is the fact that, through amorous desire, Eros is first and foremost a force of reproduction, above all of social reproduction.

There is a remarkable similarity between, on the one hand, the young pupil of Theognis who, by the end of the apprenticeship in which he absorbs the aristocratic values of the symposion, in his turn masters the kind of speech that enables him to celebrate the qualities of the poet, and, on the other, the *erômenos* who, thanks to his intimacy with his lover, accedes to the maturity of an adult citizen capable, in his turn, of becoming a good *erastês*. As for a girl, she tolerates the violence perpetrated by men in the grip of Eros, and allows herself to be seduced by the perfumes of the flowering meadows. She ends up by submitting to the yoke of marriage, to be united in love on a soft bed, in a relationship of reproductive reciprocity.

In a relationship of *philotês* and *philia* in which erotic desire is established in all its implacable power, women — through marriage — and men — through the process of initiatory education — produce good citizens. In both cases, the erotic "mismatch" is productive: the girl is subjected to Eros and Aphrodite, and in their company and in the fullness of amorous unity accedes to the maturity that will lead to the production of fine children; the adolescent boy, for his part, is subjected to the seductive words of the poets before himself becoming an adult citizen and an educator who uses the very same means of erotic seduction. The different statuses of the two genders are, on both sides, produced by the action of the deities of love, but the relations between them are bound to be conflictual. Like the organization of the cosmos, they require the constant readjustments that are effected by Eros and the symbolic speeches that he inspires.

In this dynamic interplay, the categories elaborated by the twentieth-century anthropology of sexuality lose their pertinence. In archaic and classical Greece, the "active/passive" opposition does not coincide with the "masculine/feminine" polarity, for this is regularly confused during the period of adolescence. Nor does it coincide with the "young/adult" contrast, the terms of which sometimes cross. The "heterosexuality /homosexuality" dichotomy does not coincide with a clear division between normality and deviance. The "public/private" opposition cannot be applied either to the educative erotic practices of the symposium, or to the supposed segregation of adult married women, neither in the cities of the archaic period nor in fifth-century Athens. And it is very hard to assess to what extent Greek women were regarded as "sexual objects," given that virtually all the documents that refer to them were the work of men! As for "sexual asymmetry," this has less to do with amorous relationships between adult men and women than, in a very partial manner, with relationships of homophilia that, despite their essential mismatch, could recuperate reciprocity through *philia*.

It may be that only the notion of "gender," understood as a social representation constructed on the basis of the relations between the sexes, is of help to us as we try to understand the various social statuses that became defined in relationships inspired by Eros and Aphrodite. So there would appear to be good reason to question the pertinence of our own operational concepts, which so far as the humanities are concerned seem bound to establish ill-defined categories; good reason to look with a reflective eye at our own academic and eurocentric erudition.

Greek civilization is so rich that, although it constantly gives rise to new cultural interpretations, it equally constantly eludes the categories that we, with our own perspective, impose upon it. It is as if it were itself possessed by the dynamism of the deities of love. For, as Euripides has the other Phaedra represented by Stheneboea declare, Eros is an educator; he teaches the poet, turning him into a man inspired:

ποιητὴν δ'ἄρα
Ἔρως διδάσκει, κἂν ἄμουσος ἦ τὸ πρίν

Eros surely teaches the poet, even the one who was
previously uninspired.

(frag. 663 Nauck²)

# BIBLIOGRAPHY

Adrados, F. R. *Sociedad, amor y poesia en la Grecia antigua*. Madrid: Alianza Universidad, 1995.

Arrigoni, G. "Amore sotto il manto e iniziazione nuziale." *Quaderni Urbinati di Cultura Classica* 44 (1983): 7–56.

Barrett, W. S. *Euripides. Hippolytos*. Oxford: Clarendon Press, 1964.

Benveniste, E. *Le vocabulaire des institutions indo-européennes*. Paris: Minuit, 1969 (Engl. transl.: *Indo-European Language and Society*. Trans. E. Palmer. London: 1973).

Bethe, E. "Die dorische Knabenliebe." *Rheinisches Museum* 67 (1907): 438–75.

Brelich, A. *Paides e Parthenoi*. Rome: Ateneo, 1969.

Bremer, J. M. "The Meadow of Love and Two Passages in Euripides' *Hippolytos*." *Mnemosyne* IV.28 (1975): 268–80.

Bremmer, J. M. "Adolescents, *Symposion*, and Pederasty." In Murray (1990), 135–48.

Brendel, O. J. "The Scope and Temperament of Erotic Art in the Graeco-Roman World." In T. Bowie and C. V. Christenson, eds. *Studies in Erotic Art*. New York: Basic Books, 1970, 3–107. Rpt. in Calame (1983b), 211–45.

Brulé, P. *La fille d'Athènes. La religion des filles à Athènes à l'époque classique. Mythes, cultes et société*. Besançon and Paris: Université de Paris and Belles Lettres, 1987.

Buffière, F. *Eros adolescent. La pédérastie dans la Grèce antique*. Paris: Belles Lettres, 1980.

Burnett, A. P. *Three Archaic Poets. Archilochus, Alcaeus, Sappho*. London: Duckworth, 1983.

Calame, C. *Les choeurs de jeunes filles en Grèce archaïque*. I, *Morphologie, fonction religieuse et sociale*. Rome: Ateneo, 1977 (Engl. transl.: *Choruses of Young Women in Ancient Greece. Their Morphology, Religious and Social Functions*. Trans. J. Orion and D. Collins. Lanham and London: Rowman & Littlefield, 1997).

————. II, *Alcman. Introduction, texte critique, témoignages et commentaire*. Rome: Ateneo, 1983a.

————. ed. *L'amore in Grecia*. Rome and Bari: Laterza, 1983b.

————. "Entre rapports de parenté et relations civiques: Aphrodite l'hétaïre au banquet politique des *hetaîroi*." In F. Thélamon, ed. *Aux sources de la puissance: Sociabilité et parenté*. Rouen: Université de Rouen, 1989, 101–11.

————. *Thésée et l'imaginaire athénien. Légende et culte en Grèce antique*. 2d ed. Lausanne: Payot, 1996.

Cantarella, E. *Secondo natura. La bisessualità nel mondo antico*. Rome: Editori Riuniti, 1988 (Engl. transl.: *Bisexuality in the Ancient World*. Trans. C. Ó. Cuilleanáin. New Haven: Yale University Press, 1992).

Carson, A. *Eros the Bittersweet. An Essay*. Princeton: Princeton University Press, 1986.

Cohen, D. *Law, Sexuality and Society. The Enforcement of Morals in Classical Athens*. Cambridge: Cambridge University Press, 1991.

Contiades-Tsitsoni, E. *Hymenaios und Epithalamion. Das Hochzeitslied in der Frühgriechischen Lyrik*. Stuttgart: Teubner, 1990.

Delivorrias, A. "Aphrodite." In *Lexicon Iconographicum Mythologiae Classicae*, II.1. Zurich and Munich: Artemis, 1984, 2–51.

Des Bouvrie, S. *Women in Greek Tragedy. An Anthropological Approach*. Oslo and Oxford: Norwegian and Oxford University Presses, 1990.

Detienne, M. *Les maîtres de vérité dans la Grèce archaïque*. Paris: Maspero, 1967 (Engl. transl.: *The Masters of Truth in Archaic Greece*. Trans. J. Lloyd. New York: Zone Books, 1996).

———. *Dionysos mis à mort*. Paris: Gallimard, 1977 (Engl. transl.: *Dionysos Slain*. Trans. L. and M. Muellner. Baltimore and London: Johns Hopkins University Press, 1979).

———. *L'écriture d'Orphée*. Paris: Gallimard, 1989.

Dover, K. J. *Greek Homosexuality*. London: Duckworth, 1978.

Dowden, K. *Death and the Maiden. Girls' Initiation Rites in Greek Mythology*. London and New York: Routledge, 1989.

duBois, P. *Sappho Is Burning*. Chicago and London: University of Chicago Press, 1995.

Fasce, S. *Eros. La figura e il culto*. Genova: Università, 1977.

Fischer, E. *Amor und Eros. Eine Untersuchung des Wortfeldes "Liebe" im Lateinischen und Griechischen*. Hildesheim: Gerstenberg, 1973.

Figueira, T. J., and G. Nagy, eds. *Theognis of Megara. Poetry and the Polis*. Baltimore and London: Johns Hopkins University Press, 1985.

Foley, H. P., ed. *Reflections of Women in Antiquity*. New York and London: Gordon and Breach, 1981.

Foucault, M. *Histoire de la sexualité 2. L'usage des plaisirs*. Paris: Gallimard, 1984 (Engl. transl.: *The History of Sexuality. 2, The Use of Pleasure*. Trans. R. Hurley. New York: Pantheon Books, 1985).

Gentili, B. *Anacreon*. Rome: Ateneo, 1958.

———. *Poesia e pubblico nella Grecia antica. Da Omero al V Secolo*. Rome and Bari: Laterza, 1984 (Engl. transl.: *Poetry and Its Public in Ancient Greece from Homer to the Fifth Century*. Trans. Th. Cole. Baltimore and London: Johns Hopkins University Press, 1988).

Goldhill, S. "The Dance of the Veils: Reading Five Fragments of Anacreon." *Eranos* 85 (1987): 9–18.

———. *Foucault's Virginity. Ancient Erotic Fiction and the History of Sexuality*. Cambridge: Cambridge University Press, 1995.

Gould, J. "Law, Custom and Myth: Aspects of the Social Position of Women in Classical Athens." *Journal of Hellenic Studies* 100 (1980): 38–59.

Greifenhagen, A. *Griechische Eroten*. Berlin: de Gruyter, 1957.

Halperin, D. M. "Plato and Erotic Reciprocity." *Classical Antiquity* 5 (1986): 60–80.

———. *One Hundred Years of Homosexuality and Other Essays on Greek Love*. New York and London: Routledge, 1990.

Halperin, D. M., J. J. Winkler, and F. I. Zeitlin, eds. *Before Sexuality. The Construction of Erotic Experience in the Ancient Greek World*. Princeton: Princeton University Press, 1990.

Hatherly Wilson, H. *Sappho's Sweetbitter Songs. Configurations of Female and Male in Ancient Greek Lyric*. London and New York: Routledge, 1996.

Henderson, J. *The Maculate Muse. Obscene Language in Attic Comedy*. 2d ed. Oxford and London: Oxford University Press, 1991.

Hermary, A. "Eros." In *Lexicon Iconographicum Mythologiae Classicae*, III.1. Zurich and Munich: Artemis, 1986, 850–942.

Janko, R. *The Iliad: A Commentary. Vol. IV, Bks. 13–16*. Cambridge: Cambridge University Press, 1992.

Kaempf-Dimitriadou, S. *Die Liebe der Götter in der attischen Kunst des 5. Jahrhunderts v. Chr.* Bern: Francke, 1979.

Kennedy, D. F. *The Arts of Love. Five Studies in the Discourse of Roman Elegy*. Cambridge: Cambridge University Press, 1993.

Keuls, E. *The Reign of the Phallus. Sexual Politics in Ancient Athens*. New York: Harper & Row, 1985.

Koch-Harnack, G. *Knabenliebe und Tiergeschenke. Ihre Bedeutung im päderastischen Erziehungssystem Athens*. Berlin: Mann, 1983.

———. *Erotische Symbole. Lotosblüte und gemeinsamer Mantel auf antiken Vasen*. Berlin: Mann, 1989.

Konstan, D. *Sexual Symmetry. Love in the Ancient Novel and Related Genres*. Princeton: Princeton University Press, 1994.

———. *Friendship in the Classical World*. Cambridge: Cambridge University Press, 1997.

Kurke, L. "Inventing the *Hetaira*: Sex, Politics, and Discursive Conflict in Archaic Greece," *Class. Ant.* 16 (1997): 106–50.

Lanata, G. "Sul linguaggio amoroso di Saffo." *Quaderni Urbinati di Cultura Classica* 2 (1966): 63–79.

Laqueur, Th. *Making Sex: Body and Gender from the Greeks to Freud*. Cambridge, Mass.: Harvard University Press, 1990.

Lardinois, A. "Lesbian Sappho and Sappho of Lesbos." In J. Bremmer, ed. *From Sappho to de Sade. Moments in the History of Sexuality*. London and New York: Routledge, 1989, 15–35.

Lasserre, F. *La figure d'Eros dans la poésie grecque*. Lausanne: Imprimeries Réunies, 1946.

———. *Sappho. Une autre lecture*. Padua: Antenore, 1989.

Latacz, J. *Zum Wortfeld "Freude" in der Sprache Homers*. Heidelberg: Winter, 1966.

Lewis, J. M. "Eros and the *Polis* in Theognis Book II." In Figueira and Nagy (1985), 197–222.

Lissarrague, F. "De la sexualité des satyres." *Mètis* 2 (1987): 63–79 (Engl. transl.: Halperin, Winkler, and Zeitlin, eds. [1990], 53–81).

Loraux, N. *Les expériences de Tirésias. Le féminin et l'homme grec*. Paris: Gallimard, 1989 (Engl. transl.: *The Experiences of Tiresias*. Trans. C. Levine. Princeton: Princeton University Press, 1994).

Luca, R. "Il lessico d'amore nei poemi omerici." *Studi Italiani di Filologia Classica* 53 (1981): 170–98.

Lyons, D. *Gender and Immortality. Heroines in Ancient Greek Myth and Cult.* Princeton: Princeton University Press, 1997.

Motte, A. *Prairies et jardins de la Grèce antique. De la religion à la philosophie.* Brussels: Royal Academy, 1973.

Müller, H. M. *Erotische Motive in der griechischen Dichtung bis auf Euripides.* Hamburg: Buske, 1980.

Murray, O., ed. *Sympotica. A Symposium on the* Symposion. Oxford: Oxford University Press, 1990.

Nagy, G. *The Best of the Achaeans. Concepts of the Hero in Archaic Greek Poetry.* Baltimore and London: Johns Hopkins University Press, 1979.

———. *Pindar's Homer. The Lyric Possession of an Epic Past.* Baltimore and London: Johns Hopkins University Press, 1990.

Parker, R. *Miasma. Pollution and Purification in Early Greek Religion.* Oxford: Clarendon Press, 1983.

Peschel, I. *Die Hetäre bei Symposion und Komos in der attischrotfiguren Vasenmalerei des 6–4 Jahrh. v. Chr.* Frankfurt am Main and Bern: Lang, 1987.

Pirenne-Delforge, V. *L'Aphrodite grecque. Contribution à l'étude de ses cultes et de sa personnalité dans le panthéon archaïque et classique.* Athens and Liège: CERGA, 1994.

Powell, A., ed. *Euripides, Women and Sexuality.* London and New York: Routledge, 1990.

Redfield, J. "Notes on the Greek Wedding." *Arethusa* 15 (1982): 181–201.

Reinsberg, C. *Ehe, Hetärentum und Knabenliebe im antiken Griechenland.* Munich: Beck, 1989.

Richardson, N. J. *The Homeric Hymn to Demeter.* Oxford: Clarendon Press, 1974.

Robinson, D. M., and E. J. Fluck. *A Study of the Greek Love-Names, Including a Discussion of Paederasty and Prosopographia.* Baltimore: Johns Hopkins University Press, 1937.

Rocchi, M. *Kadmos e Harmonia. Un matrimonio problematico.* Rome: "L'erma" di Brettschneider, 1989.

Rosenmeyer, P. A. *The Poetics of Imitation. Anacreon and the Anacreontic Tradition.* Cambridge: Cambridge University Press, 1992.

Rosenmeyer, T. G. "Eros-erotes." *Phoenix* 5 (1951): 11–22.

Scheid, J., and J. Svenbro. *Le métier de Zeus. Le mythe du tissage et du tissu dans le monde gréco-romain.* Paris: La Découverte, 1994 (Engl. transl.: *The Craft of Zeus: Myths of Weaving and Fabric.* Trans. C. Volk. Cambridge, Mass., and London: Harvard University Press, 1996).

Schmitt-Pantel, D., ed. *Histoire des femmes en Occident. I, L'Antiquité.* Paris: Plon, 1991 (Engl. transl.: *A History of Women. I, From Ancient Goddesses to Christian Saints.* Cambridge, Mass., and London: Harvard University Press, 1992).

Schnapp, A. "Eros en chasse." In *La cité des images. Religion et société en Grèce antique.* Paris and Lausanne: Nathan and L.E.P., 1984, 67–84 (Engl.

trans.: *A City of Images: Iconography and Society in Ancient Greece.* Trans. D. Lyons. Princeton: Princeton University Press, 1989).

Seaford, R. "The Tragic Wedding." *Journal of Hellenic Studies* 107 (1987): 106–30.

Segal, C. "Eros and Incantation: Sappho and Oral Poetry." *Arethusa* 7 (1974): 139–60.

Sergent, B. *L'homosexualité dans la mythologie grecque.* Paris: Payot, 1984 (Engl. transl.: *Homosexuality in Greek Myths.* Trans. A. Goldhammer. Boston: Beacon Press, 1986).

Sourvinou-Inwood, C. *"Reading" Greek Culture. Texts and Images, Rituals and Myths.* Oxford: Clarendon Press, 1991.

Stehle, E. *Performance and Immortality. Heroines in Ancient Greek Nondramatic Poetry in Its Setting.* Princeton: Princeton University Press, 1997.

Travlos, J. *Bildlexikon zur Topographie des antiken Athen.* Tübingen: Wasmuth, 1971 (Engl. transl.: *Pictorial Dictionary of Ancient Athens.* New York: Praeger, 1974).

Vérilhac, A.-M., ed. *La femme dans le monde méditerranéen.* I, *Antiquité.* Lyon: Maison de l'Orient, 1985.

Vernant, J.-P. *Mythe et société en Grèce ancienne.* Paris: Maspero, 1974 (Engl. transl.: *Myth and Society in Ancient Greece.* Tr. J. Lloyd. New York: Zone Books, 1988).

———. *L'individu, la mort, l'amour. Soi-même et l'autre en Grèce ancienne.* Paris: Gallimard, 1989.

———. *Figures, idoles, masques.* Paris: Julliard, 1990.

Vetta, M. *Teognide. Libro secondo. Introduzione, testo critico, traduzione e commento.* Rome: Ateneo, 1980.

———. "Poesia simposiale nella Grecia arcaica e classica." In M. Vetta, ed. *Poesia e simposio nella Grecia antica.* Rome and Bari: Laterza, 1983, xiii–lx.

Vidal-Naquet, P. *Le Chasseur noir. Formes de pensée et formes de société dans le monde grec.* 2d ed. Paris: La Découverte, 1983 (Engl. transl.: *The Black Hunter: Forms of Thought and Forms of Society in the Greek World.* Trans. A. Szegedy-Maszak. Baltimore and London: Johns Hopkins University Press, 1986).

Wickert-Micknat, G. *Die Frau (Archaeologica Homerica* III R). Göttingen: Vandenhoeck and Ruprecht, 1982.

Winkler, J. J. *The Constraints of Desire. The Anthropology of Sex and Gender in Ancient Greece.* New York and London: Routledge, 1990.

Zeitlin, F. I. "The Politics of Eros in the Danaid Trilogy of Aeschylus." In R. Hexter and D. Selden, eds. *Innovations in Antiquity.* New York and London: Routledge, 1992, 203–52. Rpt. in Zeitlin (1996), 123–71.

———. *Playing the Other: Gender and Society in Classical Greek Literature.* Chicago: University of Chicago Press, 1996.

N.B. I have not been able to take into account the new book of Thornton, B. S. *Eros. The Myth of Ancient Greek Sexuality.* Boulder, Colo., and Oxford: Westview Press, 1997.

# NAME INDEX

Academy, 101, 106
Achilles, 115, 139, 143
Acousilaos of Argos, 179, 181
Acropolis, 170–173
Adonis, 161–162
Aegisthus, 35, 128
Aeschines, 103, 111, 139–140
Aeschylus, 3, 127–129, 142, 144, 154
—*Agamemnon*, 142
—*Supplices*, 144
—*Xantriai*, 127
Aether. *See* Erebus
Agamemnon, 42, 143, 145
Alcaeus (of Messene), 58–59
Alcaeus (of Mytilene), 19, 33, 86, 93, 99
Alcibiades, 121, 140, 189
Alcman, 15, 19–20, 22, 26, 30, 32, 36–
  37, 54, 133
Amphitrite, 67
Amymone, 66, 122
Anacreon, 15, 18–19, 21–24, 26–28, 32,
  37, 54, 86, 93, 95, 97, 132, 165–166
Anchises, 45–47, 62, 157
Anteros, 101–102
Antigone, 142–143, 146–148
Aphrodite (Cypris), 3–9, 18, 21, 24–26,
  29, 31–34, 37, 39–40, 42, 44–47, 53–
  55, 57–62, 66, 71–72, 88, 95, 98–99,
  110, 113, 115, 118–122, 125, 127,
  129–132, 144–150, 153–158, 162,
  165, 167–174, 177–182, 186, 191,
  198–199
—Aphrodite Hetaira, 115
—Aphrodite of the Gardens/"in the
  gardens," 168–173
—Aphrodite Ourania, 182
—Aphrodite Pandemos, 182
Apollo, 34–35, 37, 46, 62, 66, 103, 105–
  106, 126, 128, 156, 158, 161, 183
—Apollo Carneios, 106
—Apollo Delphinios, 105, 106
—Apollo the shepherd, 128
Apollonius of Rhodes, 15, 126
Archilochus, 19, 27, 30, 35–36, 53, 86,
  119, 140, 166–167

Ares, 42, 120, 181
Ariadne, 121–122
Aristaeus, 67, 126
Aristogeiton. *See* Harmodios
Aristophanes, 3, 104, 115, 117, 119, 121,
  133–136, 182, 193–195
—*Acharnians*, 134
—*Birds*, 117, 119, 193
—*Frogs*, 3, 135
—*Women at the Assembly*, 115, 133
Aristotle, 51, 84, 103, 133–134, 138
Arrhephoria, 110
Artemis, 3, 5, 7, 102, 131, 144, 148
—Artemis Philomeirax, 102
Asclepiades (of Samos), 56, 58
Atalanta, 24–26, 126
Athena, 45, 101, 170–173
Athens, 93–94, 101–102, 106, 110–115,
  118, 122, 125, 128, 130–132, 136,
  161, 170, 173, 192, 198

Bacchylides, 24, 30, 133
Bellerophon, 42
Boreas, 17, 154
Briseis, 42

Cadmos, 120, 154, 159
Callimachus, 59
Calliope. *See* Muse(s)
Cassandra, 145
Centaur, 34, 94
Chaos, 178, 180, 193–194, 196
Charites (Graces), 120, 133, 136, 159,
  162, 184
Cheremon (tragedian), 84
Circe, 41
Clio. *See* Muse(s)
Clytemnestra, 35, 128, 143
Core. *See* Persephone
Corinth, 34, 112–113
Creusa, 66, 156, 158
Cronos, 124, 155, 179, 195
Cypris. *See* Aphrodite
Cyrene (nymph). *See*
  Nymph(s)

Danaids, 129, 144–145
Delphi, 5, 187
Demeter, 101, 125, 127, 129
Demosthenes, 111–112, 139–140
*Derveni* (papyrus), 195–196
Dionysus, 3, 5, 8, 18, 21, 32, 67, 121–
122, 130–135, 145, 148–149, 153, 197
Diotima, 184–185, 187, 189, 192
Dryope. *See* Nymph(s)

Echo, 162
Eleusis, 112, 125, 192–193
Empedocles, 167, 180, 182
Eos, 66
Epic cycle (*Cypria*), 42, 154
Erato. *See* Muse(s)
Erebus (Aether), 178, 180, 193, 196
Euripides, 3–6, 16, 119, 128, 135, 136,
143, 145, 148–149, 159, 169, 199
— *Hippolytus*, 5–6, 8, 148, 159, 169
— *Iphigenia at Aulis*, 143
— *Medea*, 149
— *Phaethon*, 119
— *Trojan Women*, 145
Europe, 34, 52, 155

Galatea. *See* Nymph(s)
Ganymedes, 15, 21, 28, 59, 62, 66, 71,
122, 136, 158
Gnathon, 62–63
Gorgias, 123, 140, 184
Graces. *See* Charites

Hades, 46, 142–143, 146, 155
Harmodios (Aristogeiton), 139
Harmonia, 120, 159
Helen, 19, 35, 39, 41–42, 52, 54, 119,
123–124, 126, 141–142, 146, 157, 160
Hera, 21, 35, 41, 44, 47, 52, 117, 124,
127, 144–145, 153, 157, 159–160
Heracles, 5, 35, 41, 101–103, 135
— Heracles Parastates, 102
Hermes, 35, 37, 156, 161
Hesiod, 8, 40–41, 45, 130, 154, 178–
179, 182–183, 193, 196
— *Catalogue of Women*, 41
— *Shield*, 40
— *Theogony*, 45, 130–131, 182
— *Works*, 45
Hesperides, 159–160
Hippolytus, 3, 5, 7, 34, 52, 148

Hipponax, 137
Homer, 54, 120
— *Homeric Hymns*, 177
— *Homeric Hymn to Aphrodite*, 44–46,
157
— *Homeric Hymn to Demeter*, 155
— *Homeric Hymn to Hermes*, 37
— *Iliad*, 22, 24, 43, 46–47, 52, 124, 130,
153, 159
— *Odyssey*, 40, 130, 159
Hours, 162
Hyacinthus, 103, 161

Ibycus, 17, 19–21, 32, 54, 97, 103, 133,
168–169
Io, 141, 144, 156
Iole, 5, 148
Ion, 156, 161
Iphigenia, 143
Ixion, 21, 34

Laius, 103
Libya, 155, 158–159
Longus, 62–63, 177
Lysias, 112, 186, 191

Medea, 141, 149
Medusa, 154
Meleager, 56–60
Menelaus, 39, 47, 119, 124, 126, 142,
157, 160
Mimnermus, 29, 53–54
Minos, 24, 30, 34, 131, 155
Muse(s), 14, 35, 37, 45, 47, 59, 99, 120,
133, 154, 161, 183, 187
— Calliope, 37
— Clio, 161
— Erato, 47
Myiscus, 58, 107

Narcissus, 162
Nymph(s), 18, 32, 127–128, 132, 156
— Cyrene, 34, 66, 126, 135, 158
— Dryope, 156
— Echo, 162
— Galatea, 59
— Oreithyia, 154
— Syrinx, 156

Oceanids, 155
Odysseus, 40–42
Olympia, 5, 101, 161

Oreithyia. *See* Nymph(s)
Orpheus, 8, 193–197
Ouranos, 33, 41, 45, 178–179, 182

Pan, 128, 156, 195
Pandora, 41, 45
Pandrosos, 171
Paris, 24, 39, 41, 43, 52, 54, 103, 130
Parmenides, 180–181
Peitho, 144
Penelope, 40, 47
Persephone (Core), 36, 127, 142, 155
Phaedra, 3–4, 6, 148
Phaedrus, 101, 154, 181, 186, 190–191
Pherecydes of Syros, 179
Pindar, 14, 17, 19–21, 52, 86, 95, 106, 128, 158
Plato, 8, 21, 30, 44, 51, 101–102, 121, 140, 181–182, 184, 186, 189–190, 192, 195
Plutarch, 37, 62, 83, 150
Poseidon, 21, 34, 67, 122, 154–155

Sappho, 16–19, 21–22, 25–26, 31–33, 35–36, 45, 54, 58, 98–99, 111, 115, 126, 133, 142, 167, 181–182
Semele, 5, 34, 67, 127, 148
Semonides, 33, 120, 124
Silenus, 136

Simonides, 83, 181
Socrates, 30, 101, 121, 140, 154, 186, 189–192
Solon, 29, 37–38, 53, 93, 102–103
Sophocles, 128, 143
Stesichorus, 186
Strato, 56, 61
Syrinx. *See* Nymph(s)

Tartarus, 178, 193–194, 196
Theocritus, 59, 119, 124, 126, 157
Theognis, 15–16, 18, 21–22, 24, 27–28, 36, 44, 46, 54, 56, 86, 93–95, 97, 120, 165, 198
Theseus, 4, 17, 24, 67, 125, 130
Thetis, 21, 34, 66
Timarchus, 139
Titans, 41, 94, 197

Xenophon (of Athens), 121, 190
Xenophon (of Ephesus), 119–120
Xenophon (of Corinth), 113

Zephyr, 33, 161
Zeus, 4–5, 15, 21, 28, 32, 34, 40–46, 52, 58–59, 62, 66, 71, 97, 117, 122, 124, 127, 136, 141–142, 144–145, 153–156, 158–160, 179, 182–183, 185, 195–197

# SUBJECT INDEX

abduction (rape, violence), 28, 66–68, 71–72, 121–122, 144–145, 154–156
acclamation(s), pederastic (graffiti), 85–86, 105–109, 137
agriculture, 131, 154, 165
*akoitis. See* wife
Alexandrine (poetry), 56–64, 86. *See also* epigram
*alokhos. See* wife
anal (relationship), 62, 70, 137, 140
animal, 68, 70, 84, 95, 104
—bear, 158
—bull, 155–156, 194
—cock, 63, 71
—donkey, 33, 70
—filly, 27, 166
—hare, 104
—horse, 166
—lamb, 187
—lion, 158, 194
—mare. *See* filly
—mouse, 108
—panther, 104
—ram, 63
—snake, 171
—wolf, 187
apple. *See* fruits
arboriculture, 161–164, 173
asymmetry (sexual), 23–29, 52–53, 60, 67–68, 71, 85, 97, 101–103, 137–138, 191
*aulos. See* flute

banquet. *See* symposium
banqueter. *See* symposiast
beauty, 22, 44, 62, 84, 99, 120, 155, 162, 166, 181–186
bed (*eunê, lekhos, lektron*), 29–43, 52, 54, 65–67, 111–113, 121–129, 133–134, 144–150, 153–174, 198
bisexuality, 194–197
blame (*mômos, psogos*), 84, 91–95, 107–109, 132. *See also* praise

cereal culture, 117, 161, 173

chamber (nuptial). See *thalamos*
chest. See *stêthea/sterna*
chorus, 4, 26, 30, 37, 44, 54, 116–120, 135, 144, 146–148, 168
city (*polis*)/citizen, 3, 91–109, 131–132, 171–174, 198–199
cithara. *See* lyre
civilization, 116–117, 163, 199
cloak (*himation, khlaina, khlanis*), 30, 69, 113, 121–123, 166
comedy, 8, 34, 51, 60, 83, 133–141
concubine. See *hetaira*
cosmogony, 8, 178–181, 193–195
courtesan. See *hetaira*

death, 3–6, 20, 36, 72, 132, 141–143, 147–148, 162, 167
descendance. *See* procreation
desire. See *pothos*
*diamerismos*, 138
diaphragm. See *phrenes*
*dikaiosunê. See* justice
domestication (yoke), 3–6, 27, 104, 119, 123, 144–145, 165–166, 198
*dôron. See* gift
drunkenness, intoxication, 19, 23, 36, 86, 132, 134

education, 7, 62–63, 91–98, 101–109, 137, 147, 169, 177, 185, 198
elegiac (poetry), 56, 61, 86, 94–96, 112
*egkômion. See* praise
enunciation, 39, 51–56, 65, 85, 94, 156, 165
*epainos. See* praise
epigram, 56–59, 142
epic (poetry), 39–43, 51–52, 65–66, 132
*epithalamium. See* marriage
*erastês*, 19–23, 62, 71, 98–109, 114–115, 186–191
*erômenos. See erastês*
*eunê. See* bed

fiancée, 116–120, 128. See also *numphê*
flower(s), 15, 30, 58, 160–164, 165, 196

—hyacinth, 62, 154–156, 161, 165
—iris, 155
—melittis, clover, 154
—myrtle, 160
—narcissus, 155, 162
—rose, 154–156, 160, 162
—saffron, crocus, 154–155, 161
—wild thyme, 155
—vine, 17, 169
—violet, 154–155, 160–161
flute (*aulos*), 37, 47, 93, 111–112, 139
fragrance (odor), 155, 163
fruit(s), 160–164
—apple, 160–161, 169
—pomegranate, 160
—quince, 160, 169

garden (*kêpos*, orchard), 14, 101, 153–
174, 186
gaze. *See* sight
gift (present, *dôron*), 24–25, 33–34, 40,
53, 59, 68–72, 104, 116, 142
graffiti. *See* acclamations
(pederastic)
gymnasium (palaestra), 83, 93, 101–109,
137
*gunê*. *See* wife

heart. See *kardia*
Hellenistic (poetry). *See* Alexandrine
(poetry)
*hetaira* (concubine, courtesan), 33, 98–99,
110–115
*hetairêsis*. *See* prostitution
*hetairos*, 28, 33, 95–97, 115
heterosexuality, 55, 64, 68–69, 121, 162
*himation*. *See* cloak
*himeros* (Himeros), 30–32, 36–38, 44–
47, 135, 141, 179, 188–189
homoeroticism. *See* homophilia
homophilia (homoeroticism,
homosexuality), 38, 55, 57–62, 68–69,
94–109, 121, 134–141, 150, 165–166,
183, 199
homosexuality. *See* homophilia
*hymen*. *See* marriage
Hymenaeus, 119, 121
hymn, 4, 94, 144–146

iambic (poetry), 84, 137, 141

iconography, 34, 51, 65–88, 104, 114,
122, 130, 190
initiation, 63, 96–98, 102–109, 125,
165–174, 181–185, 192

justice (*dikaiosunê*), 24–27, 91, 147, 183

*kardia* (heart), 13–19, 31–32, 37, 57
*kêpos*. *See* garden
*kharis*, 5, 32, 99, 191
*khlaina*. *See* cloak
*khlanis*. *See* cloak
*kômos* (procession), 83, 111–117, 130,
160

*leimôn*. *See* meadow
*lekhos*. *See* bed
*lektron*. *See* bed
lyre (cithara), 37, 47, 86, 93
lyric (poetry). *See* melic
(poetry)

madness, 14–19, 23, 132, 148–149, 187–
188
*mania*. *See* madness
marriage (wedding), 4–6, 25, 34–35, 40,
54, 62–64, 67, 91–92, 100, 110, 116–
133, 141–148, 154–165, 179, 198
meadow (*leimôn*), 27, 53, 153–170, 198
melic (lyric, poetry), 13–15, 22, 27, 29–
31, 34, 37, 39, 44, 51–57, 67, 92–93,
123, 133, 141, 146–148, 165, 169,
179–183
*mômos*. *See* blame

nature. See *phusis*
*nous*, 19, 28, 37, 44, 46
novel, 62–64, 119, 177
*numphê*, 119, 125–129, 143, 163
nuptial chamber. See
*thalamos*

obscenity, 86, 134, 137
odor. *See* fragrance
*oikos*, 100, 110–129, 131, 157, 163–164
orchard. *See* garden

*paidophilein/paiderastein*, 28–29, 54, 85,
103
palestra. *See* gymnasium

*parthenos*, 53, 126, 129, 163
passivity (sexual), 101–102, 137–141
perfume (odor). *See* fragrance
*philia* (*philê/phílos*), 29, 35, 55, 62, 69, 95–104, 114, 121, 139, 178–179, 183, 190–191, 198–199
*philotês* (Philotes), 25–29, 34, 36, 39–47, 54–55, 69, 98, 100, 198
*phrenes* (diaphragm), 17, 19, 21, 28, 31, 39, 43, 46
*phusis* (nature), 63–64, 117, 137–141, 150, 187, 188
poetry. *See* Alexandrine (poetry); elegiac (poetry); epic (poetry); iambic (poetry); melic (poetry)
*polis*. *See* city
pomegranate. *See* fruit(s)
*pothos* (Pothos), 5, 30–32, 36, 40, 57, 133, 135, 144
praise (*egkômion, epainos*), 72, 83–88, 94–98, 108, 132. *See also* blame
present. *See* gift
procession. See *kômos*
procreation (descendance, reproduction), 35, 117, 120–125, 145, 163, 174, 183, 192, 198
prostitution (*hetairêsis*), 111, 139
*psogos*. *See* blame

quince. *See* fruit(s)

rape. *See* abduction
reciprocity, 24–25, 27–29, 34, 43, 45, 52–53, 61, 102, 122, 133, 190–191, 198–199
reproduction. *See* procreation

rite (ritual), 91, 96, 116–122, 142, 157, 170–174

satyr(s), 63, 70–88, 130
satyr play, 135
seduction, 43–46, 56, 68–71, 121, 147, 165, 169, 179
sexuality, 13, 35, 57, 65, 72–88, 96, 146, 162, 165–166, 173, 183, 196, 198
sight (gaze), 4–5, 20–23, 32–33, 36, 46, 58, 60, 69, 127, 141, 147, 166, 186–188
sleep, 5, 14, 20, 36, 44, 47, 72, 167
sodomy, 60, 63, 70, 134–141
*stêthea/sterna* (chest), 19, 58
symposiast (banqueter)/symposium (banquet), 22–23, 65, 83–91, 93–97, 100, 107, 111–115, 117, 121, 130, 137, 153, 181–185, 190, 198–199

*terpein* (*terpsis*), 39–40, 43, 45, 47, 179
*thalamos* (nuptial chamber), 117–120, 143–145, 154, 160–161, 174, 184
*thelgein*, 44, 47
theogony, 179–180, 192–195
*thumos*, 19, 37, 43, 141, 184
tragedy, 5–6, 51, 129, 132, 135, 141–150, 183
violence, 15–16, 144–145, 149–150, 198. *See also* abduction
virginity, 126, 143

wedding. *See* marriage
wife (*akoitis, alokhos*), 4, 34, 43–44, 52–53, 60, 91, 111–112, 116–131, 143, 154–155, 179, 196

yoke. *See* domestication

## About the Author

Claude Calame is Professor of Greek Language and Literature at the University of Lausanne in Switzerland. He is the author of several works translated into English, including *Choruses of Young Women in Ancient Greece* and *The Craft of Poetic Speech in Ancient Greece*. The current book, *Poetics of Eros in Ancient Greece,* has been published in French and Italian editions.